The High-Tech Marketing Companion

The High-Tech Marketing Companion

Expert Advice on Marketing to Macintosh® and Other PC Users

Developed and edited by
Dee Kiamy

Addison-Wesley Publishing Company

Reading, Massachusetts • Menlo Park, California • New York
Don Mills, Ontario • Wokingham, England • Amsterdam
Bonn • Sydney • Singapore • Tokyo • Madrid • San Juan
Paris • Seoul • Milan • Mexico City • Taipei

Many of the designations used by manufacturers and sellers to distinguish their products are claimed as trademarks. Where those designations appear in this book, and Addison-Wesley was aware of a trademark claim, the designations have been printed in initial capital letters or all capital letters.

The authors and publishers have taken care in preparation of this book, but make no expressed or implied warranty of any kind and assume no responsibility for errors or omissions. No liability is assumed for incidental or consequential damages in connection with or arising out of the use of the information or programs contained herein.

Library of Congress Cataloging-in-Publication Data

Kiamy, Dee.
    The high-tech marketing companion : expert advice on marketing to
Macintosh and other PC users / by Dee Kiamy and the editors of Apple
directions.
        p.   cm.
    Includes index.
    ISBN 0-201-62666-7
    1. Computers--Marketing.   2. Computer software--Marketing.
3. Macintosh (Computer)   I. Apple directions.   II. Title.
HD9696.C62K46   1993
004.16'068'8--dc20   93-26759
                                                              CIP

Text design by Wilson Graphics & Design (Kenneth J. Wilson)
Set in 10.5-point Palatino by CIP, Coronado, California

1 2 3 4 5 6 7 8 9 -MA- 9796959493
First printing, September 1993

Addison-Wesley books are available for bulk purchases by corporations, institutions, and other organizations. For more information please contact the Corporate, Government and Special Sales Department at (617) 944-3700 x2915.

CONTENTS

ACKNOWLEDGMENTS

A tremendous number of people have made this book possible: the chapter authors, whose support and contributions have been phenomenal; the staff and management of *Apple Directions* and Apple's Developer Products Group (DPG), some of whom have moved on to other challenges—particularly David Krathwohl and Lisa Raleigh, who gave the marketing side of the publication its start; Paul Dreyfus (now the editor-in-chief of *Apple Directions)*, whose vision of making this a book and whose subsequent support led us down this path; Greg Joswiak, who has so steadfastly championed, supported, and guided our efforts; Dennis Matthews and the other DPG managers, who have so enthusiastically assisted us and supported our efforts; Martha Steffen, whose patience and hard work on our behalf made this book come together; and Gregg Williams, our technical editor, who at the same time has been one of the biggest critics and biggest supporters of the material in this book.

In their day-to-day work, many others at Apple (I wish I could name them all) have helped make this possible, including the *Apple Directions* editorial board, reviewers, and production team; the evangelists; and many others in ADG and the company at-large.

Special thanks to SB Master for her contribution to titling the book, and to Lisa Ferdinandsen and Gale Otterson for their assistance, patience, and good humor. I am infinitely grateful to the people who work with Open Door Communications who support me in every kind of way.

And finally, my heartfelt thanks to John Cook, to whom I owe *everything*.

PREFACE

AS an industry consultant, one of the roles I've had the pleasure of playing during the past few years is developing the business and marketing direction and content for Apple's flagship developer business publication, *Apple Directions*. (You may know it in its previous incarnation as *Apple Direct*.) The work in this book is excerpted from it. For those of you who have never read it, *Apple Directions* is a monthly newsletter published to communicate Apple Computer's strategic, business, and technical directions. Its goal is to help make computer product developers, software publishers, and in-house developers more successful.

Why does Apple think this kind of business information is important? To help explain, let me digress for a moment. Recently, comedian, actor, and talk-show host Arsenio Hall spoke about a comedy veteran who, near the beginning of Hall's career, had given him good advice: To succeed in show business he had to give the "business" end of the equation its due. So it goes in this industry. Some years ago, Apple recognized that in this trade of ours—which is littered with the husks of remarkable third-party products that didn't survive—it takes more than having an innovative product to succeed. In the development business, it's becoming increasingly clear that if your business is to be profitable, you must focus not solely on *development* but also on *business*.

So, in addition to technical support, Apple offers developers overall business assistance such as resources, industry connections, and how-to information. The goal is to provide business help to people whose main focus and first love is not business management but developing computer products. Out of that, *Apple Directions,* particularly its Business & Marketing section—and subsequently this book—was born.

If you're a smaller development company, you face special marketing challenges and therefore have unique needs. We've found a way to answer those needs: *Apple Directions'* Business & Marketing section focuses on practical, everyday marketing how-to. It offers in-depth, concrete, usable expertise that addresses the problems that smaller development companies face. (However, that's not to say that larger companies can't also benefit from it.) We recognize that this collection certainly doesn't address it *all*. But because *Apple Directions* publishes new material each month, we intend that over time this collection will expand as the publication continues to break new ground.

There's a special knack to high-tech marketing, and capitalizing on a diverse pool of know-how is what this book is all about. Our authors come from two camps. One contingent is composed of experts from a variety of marketing fields who make their living helping development companies confront marketing challenges. These people recognize that you may not have the resources of an Apple, or Microsoft, or IBM with which to make your mark. And in our publication they have, at times, given away their "trade secrets" to help our readers. To them I am most grateful for their contributions to this book, to *Apple Directions*, and to its worldwide audience.

The second group of authors are developers themselves. Several chapters in this book are mini-case studies that describe how these developers have met challenges, grappled with issues, or devised ways to beat the odds of being a smaller company operating in this ferociously competitive marketplace. I'm particularly fond of pieces written by such folks. There's truly no substitute for hearing it from the source, from people who have walked a mile or twenty in your Reeboks.

Some of these developer-authors are technically oriented people who also must wear a marketing hat—CEOs and other executives who have, at one time or another, had to do it *all* in the course of building their businesses and market presence. They often started conducting business with only the bare bones necessities—with no communications departments, no major PR or ad agencies, no channel marketing directors. Frankly, in the course of working with these developers, the *Apple Directions* staff has been surprised on more than one occasion by how candid their advice has been and by how much of their know-how and how many of their war stories they've been willing to share to help others along the way. To them I offer our admiration and thanks. And, as a marketing advocate through and through, my applause for and gratitude to those who recognize the need for and offer the venue in which to publish this kind of information.

Someone once said that luck happens when opportunity meets preparedness. So, on behalf of the editors and managers of *Apple Directions*, good luck, good reading, and *profitable* developing.

Dee Kiamy
President, Open Door Communications
Business and Marketing Editor, *Apple Directions*
June 1993

PART ONE

Introduction and Segue

If you market products to personal computer users and the sky is *not* the limit when it comes to mustering marketing resources, this book has been written just for you. This collection of practical how-to advice recognizes that in a market that moves at breakneck speed, smaller companies whose main focus is creating great products need a leg up on the marketing end of the development business.

Let's be candid for a moment: When push comes to shove, how effective your promotion and PR campaigns are and how good your packaging looks are just about as important as your product's underlying programming and technology. Don't get me wrong—having a solid product is an absolute *must*. But love it or hate it, the marketing side of your business is what brings your product face-to-face with customers.

Think of it this way: When you take even a brilliant piece of software or hardware out of development and drop it into the marketplace, it's voiceless. Marketing gives your product the voice to help it rise above the considerable noise (or should I say din?) in today's jam-packed market.

In your quest to rise above it all, you've undoubtedly read (or at least browsed) a variety of excellent high-tech marketing "think piece" books. You know—the ones that offer insight into how this market operates, describe trends and strategies, and help define what marketing is really about in this industry.

This book is the *how-to* companion to those volumes; it describes a variety of marketing techniques that can help you make the max of limited marketing resources: tried-and-true, try-this-then-do-that, or this-works-but-that-doesn't everyday life stuff.

The expertise in this book comes from some of the best and brightest folks, people culled from a variety of areas of the personal computing industry. Some of them are professionals who make a living helping developers do the marketing thing. Others are developers themselves, people who face the same challenges you do and have found out for themselves what works—and what doesn't. People who soar with eagles. And some that have, at one time or another, crashed and burned and risen from the flames to share the tale.

If it's your first time through a particular process such as creating a product package or doing direct mail, consider the material in this book as a starting point, a primer. If you've been there before, consider this a reality check: Have a look at what these people recommend and see how well it jives with your own experience. I'm betting you'll spot at least one new approach, one way to save time or money, or something that at least raises an eyebrow or makes you scream, "They say I ought to do what!?"

If the advice in this book can help prevent you from committing even one cardinal marketing sin, if it saves you money or reduces the amount of time you spend finding the right approach to a marketing problem, if it inspires even one new idea or helps you circumvent at least one major "uh-oh," then I'll consider my job done and this book (I hope) well worth your bookstore dollars.

HOW TO GET THE MAX FROM THIS BOOK

How might people read this book, I've wondered. Would they read it sequentially from part to part, cover to cover? Or would they just "graze" through, stopping at whatever piques their interest? One colleague often kids me, "When I want you to have an opinion I'll give you one." So if you don't mind hearing an opinion, here's my suggestion: Look over the table of contents, pick two or three topics that are today's hot buttons, and start there.

Has packaging been on your mind? Start with Chapter 14, "The Ten Commandments of Product Packaging: How to Create Packages That Sell." Just starting to put together an opinion leaders campaign or not getting the number and kind of reviews you want? Read Chapters 10 and 11, "Influencing Opinion Leaders: How to Get High Impact for Low Investment," and "Getting the Maximum from Product Reviews: A Practical Guide for Creating a Reviews Campaign." Having trouble choosing a target market? Chapter 4, "Target Markets—Easy to Pick, Hard to Stick: How to Choose and Stick with the Best Target Market," will tell you how. Doing upgrade campaigns? Chapter 29, "The Upgrade Black Hole: Why Some Upgrade Campaigns Get Stalled," may be the starting place for you.

Each chapter is a self-contained, stand-alone snapshot of a particular subject. (In case you decide to skip around, within each chapter I've cross-referenced any other pertinent chapters that may interest you or give you more information about a given topic.) On the other hand, since marketing is not an event but a series of intertwined processes, the book as a whole paints a much larger, more integrated picture. (Each part of the book also features an introduction that highlights the chapters within it.)

For those who prefer taking a lighter approach: Have you ever tried using the elevator test to position your product? (Chapter 2.) Do you understand why sewing needles compete with the duct tape market, and how refrigerator magnets could compete with software? (I'm serious. Chapter 8.) Have you had to deal with unfair reviews or editors who seem to be out to get you? (Chapter 11.) What roles do rugby and relay races play in global product launches? (Chapter 35.) How do you get computer users to work for you—almost for free? (Chapter 32.) Do you know how to harness the secret power of a national distributor's pyramid? (OK, I live in California. Chapter 19.) How far apart are a pat on the back and a kick in the butt? (Chapter 12.) Who says marketing isn't all fun?

SEGUE

With that said, I'd like to segue into the heart of the book. For those of you who decided to start at the beginning of the book and work your way back, here's Chapter 1, "Ten Common Product Launch Mistakes;" it's about a topic that hits us all where it counts: product launches.

Whether you've done one or ten, they're never exactly the same. They are liberating (how many of you have finally taken that well-deserved vacation after the launch is over?), but they also can be frustrating. Hindsight is 20/20: Try as we may, after a launch we always think of something we could have, should have, or shouldn't have done. So for all of us, novices and veterans alike, here's a checklist of the ten most common product launch mistakes and how to avoid them.

CHAPTER ONE

Ten Common Product Launch Mistakes

By Leigh Marriner, Marriner Associates

Leigh Marriner is the managing partner of Marriner Associates, a firm located in San Rafael, California, that develops competitive strategies and marketing programs for personal computer software companies.

SOMETIMES, especially in small software companies that are resource-strapped, you're launching your first or second product at a time when most people in the company are almost too busy just getting the product out the door to think about marketing. You're pushed for time, your resources are strained to the max, and THE DEADLINE makes all else seem unimportant. So it's no surprise that we've all made some of the most common launch mistakes—and sometimes more than once.

There's a lot of time and money riding on the launch of your product and a lot to be gained by doing it the best way possible. Here's a checklist of the ten most common product launch mistakes and how to avoid them.

#1: SHIPPING A SECOND-RATE PRODUCT

The best marketing campaign can't make up for a lackluster product. Product quality is still the key to success in this industry, although many good products die for lack of adequate marketing support. Launching a weak product is usually a waste of money. This kind of product tends to struggle along; a small group of committed users continues to buy it, but the product never gets a mass audience. The developer never makes a profit, because the cost of keeping the product alive outweighs the revenue generated.

To avoid this, once you're nearing the end of product development, you need to ask yourself some very tough questions and be (sometimes painfully) candid in your answers: Is the product really worth publishing? Are customers willing to pay for this product?

The investment of several man-years in developing the product isn't enough to justify bringing it to market. A product that started out as a brilliant idea may have been implemented poorly. Or the competitive situation may have changed since development started. To make the product marketable, you may have to invest several times your development costs in marketing, sales, tech support, and manufacturing. Don't let the already-spent development dollars keep you from being prepared to consider the option of abandoning the product. Deciding to abandon your "dream" product is certainly one of the most difficult choices you'll ever have to make, but weighed against the possible alternative of bombing in the marketplace, it may be the wiser course of action.

Too often, companies are blind to their product's potential—or lack of it— by the time it gets to the end of the development cycle. If you have questions about whether the product is good enough to ship, try letting 10 to 20 target customers use it and then listen to what they have to say. Gauge their enthusiasm. Do they understand why it's so good? Is the product advantage important to them? If they don't rate it an 8 or higher on a 10-point scale, you're in trouble.

If you do launch the product, pay attention to early reactions from the press, industry influencers, bulletin board users, and so forth. If there isn't a strong positive reaction, then you may want to reconsider making any further marketing investment unless you also make substantial product changes.

#2: SHIPPING A MARGINALLY BETTER PRODUCT (COROLLARY TO MISTAKE #1)

Shipping a me-too product in an established category without a strategy for overtaking the category leader doesn't work. Being 50 percent better than the category leader isn't enough. Unless the product is at least 100 percent better, the product differences alone aren't enough to make the necessary impact on the market. (And it's rare to see products that really do leapfrog the leader.) Almost all the profit in a product category is made by the Number 1 and Number 2 players. Being Number 3 or 4 may generate revenue but not much profit. Don't let the size of a category fool you into thinking there's easy money to be made. It's better to be top dog in a smaller market segment than one of the pack in a large one.

To successfully launch a product in an established category, you need to define a reasonably sized and growing segment in which your product can become the leader. Identify the circumstances in which your product offers users real advantages. Pick a segment in which you know how to reach the customer and in which you can target your limited marketing resources. Segments can be defined by hardware platform, specific vertical markets (such as magazine publishers), demographic group (such as K–5 children), channel, and so forth.

#3: IGNORING FEEDBACK FROM USERS

Alpha and beta tests are critical for finding bugs and also for gauging how well the product will be received by users. Too often, beta tests aren't done at all or aren't done until it's too late to act on the feedback. Developers often feel that there isn't enough time in the development cycle to allow three to four months for a beta test. Even if your company has an excellent internal testing department, real-world beta tests are invaluable for finding unexpected anomalies when the product is used with various hardware configurations. If you fail to get this kind of feedback or don't give it its due, it can result in the kind of mistake from which a smaller company can't easily recover.

Measuring user acceptance at the beta stage often is even more important than testing for bugs. For example, I was involved in launching a product that helped users collate group writing projects. If we had really listened to the feedback, we might have realized sooner that the people who stood to benefit the most from the product were low-level collators—and they weren't usually in a position to recommend the purchase. In contrast, by listening to new users talk about their experiences in getting started with a new adventure game, we learned that it took too long to build a new playing character. So we decided to ship the product with premade characters. This is truly the point at which to ask the sometimes politically difficult questions about whether a product is viable and ready to ship.

#4: WAITING TOO LONG TO PLAN THE MARKETING PROGRAM

How often have you finished a product, heaved a sigh of relief, and then said, "Now we have to hire a marketing expert and launch the product"? A marketing plan should be completed and ready to implement at least four to six months before the ship date.

Doing so will enable you to save money in many ways. Money won't be wasted on rush charges due to the innumerable last-minute changes caused by starting late. You'll have time to undertake pieces you can do yourself, such as writing first drafts of box copy or press releases, without having to pay someone else to do it to meet an almost impossible deadline. Most importantly, developing a marketing plan far in advance lets you have an overall view of the objectives for the product and how you are going to accomplish them with your scarce resources— before you start spending money.

Otherwise, commitments for longer lead-time items such as ads, direct-mail campaigns, and reseller promotions will be made before you know whether they are critical to your launch. Too often you may decide that you must create a presence at Comdex or Macworld, spend $15,000 before all is said and done, and then realize that the trade show was only a third-level priority—and that the money spent is badly needed elsewhere.

There is no cookie-cutter approach to deciding what the elements of a marketing plan should be. The key is to ask the following kinds of questions to determine what marketing approaches will work best for your product, and then build the answers and resulting required actions into a plan.

- Is this an emerging market in which it is hard to identify scattered prospects, which necessitates your investing in lead generation? Or is this a mature market in which making the purchase process easy is most important?

- Exactly who are the customers?

- Where can you reach the customers?

- Where do customers get information? Who are the influencers?

- How can you overcome customers' reservations to get them interested?

- Is a trial-use or demonstration program necessary?

- What is the customers' purchase process? Who has to approve the purchase?

- How can you make the purchase easy?

- How much sales support is required?

Answering these questions and others like them will keep you from undertaking programs without thinking through the objectives and challenges for your specific situation.

#5: FAILING TO DRAFT A PRODUCT-DIRECTION SHEET

Before you start producing materials and writing copy, it helps to develop a direction sheet to guide the marketing staff and creative agencies regarding what should be said about the product. This guide should specify the most important advantages and benefits of the product so that all staff, consultants, and agencies are working from the same script.

Package copy, press releases, sales promotion items, advertising, direct mail copy, and all other customer communications should be based on this document. At the very least, the direction sheet should include the following:

- a one- or two-sentence description that precisely and concisely states what the product does and who the target audience is

- the one unique selling point that makes this product different and better

- secondary consumer messages

- dealer messages

- key features and benefits

- typical applications the product is used for or examples of game play

- price

- competitors.

Drafting a direction sheet early in the launch process has several advantages. It forces you to think through what is really important about your product. It also helps guarantee that all the marketing materials will work together and that you don't send mixed messages to customers. (For example, it helps ensure that you won't have different tag lines on the box and the product's sell sheet.) Customers need repeated exposure to the same message to be motivated to buy, and all materials should work together to convey a consistent message.

Having a direction sheet also prevents the art department from driving the creative process. The marketing and communications aspects should be paramount. For example, we've all seen pretty packages that would make nice posters, but you can't read the product name on them, or the tag line isn't descriptive. Using a direction sheet ensures that everyone is aware of the communications objectives.

Also, having the product's direction on paper means that you won't waste time rethinking the features and benefits of your product each time a new communications piece has to be written. Your consultants and agencies will work more efficiently, which will save you money.

#6: FAILING TO FOCUS ON A SINGLE DISTINCTION FROM THE COMPETITION

Every software product has competition, even if it's just the nonelectronic way of doing something. Most customers are going to absorb only one major point about your product. There has to be one crucial factor that compels them to take the time to try it rather than continue doing things as before.

Customers are likely to ignore a complicated message. A laundry list of features doesn't pack the same punch as information about one easily understandable advantage. Ideally, you build a product that you can describe in one sentence so that the intended user will respond. Building a product that delivers a specific benefit is the most cost-effective way to communicate with customers. Smaller developers often don't have enough marketing dollars to effectively convey a more complicated message.

#7: PLANNING ADS TO BEGIN ON THE PRODUCT'S SHIP DATE

As we all know, most products aren't ready to ship on their original ship dates. Almost always there are last minute delays: The manual needs to be rewritten, the pre-holiday rush makes the printing company take longer than planned, the last bugs take longer to fix than anyone expected, and so on and so forth. Since advertising and many other marketing programs must be planned four or more months in advance (for adequate production and space reservation time), it is often difficult to decide exactly when to start running them. There is usually pressure to have the ad campaign premiere as soon as possible so that demand for the product will begin to build.

However, a good rule of thumb is to never plan to run an ad until at least one month after the stipulated product ship date. If your ad runs before the product is available, you haven't gotten the most out of your money. It takes one to three weeks for initial stock to make it into the channel. The customer who reads the ad but can't find the product anywhere will have forgotten about it by the time the product ships. This rule of thumb is especially true for small launch budgets, where "teaser" or "preview" ads aren't feasible.

#8: RELYING ON A BIG AD CAMPAIGN TO MOVE THE PRODUCT

Relying on magazine ads alone is a lazy approach to marketing. To many people, marketing equals advertising. However, a business product usually requires a minimum advertising expenditure of $100,000 before the ads start to build significant product awareness. This is just too expensive for small developers (unless you create a direct-response ad that pays for itself).

Editor's note: For more information about these kinds of ads, see Chapter 16, "Selling Off the Page: Guidelines for Creating Successful Direct Response Ads."

There are more prudent and valuable options. You may find it more worthwhile to invest in better packaging or to put your CEO on the road to talk to the press, influencers, user groups, industry consultants, and so forth.

#9: BEING STINGY WITH EVALUATION COPIES

Building word of mouth and influencing the inner circle are the most important factors in the success of new products. Fully functional evaluation copies are one of the least expensive advertising vehicles. Give them to the press, dealers, store salespeople, industry gurus, user groups—anyone who talks to others about software products. Giving dealer sales representatives a free copy of your product can be an especially powerful method of influencing them to recommend it. There are only two ways to get salespeople's attention: Have customers ask for the product or have the salespeople be users themselves.

In a survey we did for an entertainment publisher, we sent to 500 stores copies of a sports game to the salesperson specializing in games. Four months later, we measured the effects and found that 90 percent of those who had received a copy had played it, versus only 60 percent for the leading game in that category. And most of them had talked to other sales staff members about the game and felt that it helped them answer customer questions.

#10: EXPECTING DEALERS TO PUSH THE PRODUCT

This mistake should be old hat by now, but I still talk to developers who think that if they can just get their product onto a dealer's shelf their worries are over. In most reseller chains, a product has 6 to 12 weeks to prove itself and move the required number of copies per store. If it doesn't, it's off the shelf permanently. No marketing campaign can build sufficient demand in this time period if it isn't already in place and working when the product hits dealers' shelves.

Dealers put the product onto the shelf, but they expect you to stimulate the consumer demand to move it out the door. Dealers carry thousands of products, and in most cases the salesperson tries to sell whatever is easiest—either what the customer asks for or what is already moving well. Resellers do provide several (often expensive) marketing programs and are willing to work with you to create demand. But many small developers cannot afford to spend $60,000 to $80,000 working with one chain on a program that will last for less than a month.

Much of the product launch process is just common sense, yet at one time or another, veterans and novices alike make the mistakes discussed here. The next time you see a new product coming down the pike, resensitize yourself to the potential dilemmas; take a few minutes to rethink these all-too-common mistakes—even if you've done many launches. Odds are that it will be a few minutes well invested.

Happy launching.

PART TWO

Positioning and Market Targeting

Ready, fire...aim! Please raise your hand if you've never been caught in this trap. No? Come on, admit it, we've all been there sometime; you're in good company. When we're trying to get a product out the door, sometimes we're more occupied with getting to the door than making sure the door opens in the right direction.

It's tough, virtually impossible, to hit a bull's-eye when you haven't clearly focused in on it—or the target just keeps moving. It eats your time, wastes your money, and consumes valuable cycles by forcing you to reset your sights time and again. Positioning is the process of developing your focus, a ritual in which you define your bull's-eye and how you'll hit it. These chapters—particularly Chapter 2, "Positioning Your Product Using the 'Elevator Test': How to Nail It in 14 Floors—or Less," and Chapter 4, "Target Markets—Easy to Pick, Hard to Stick: How to Choose and Stick with the Best Target Market"—take a most unusual (and very practical and effective) approach to product positioning and zeroing in on your target market.

How many renditions of the traditional product life-cycle curve have you seen in marketing books, product plans, and speaker presentation slides at conferences? Chapter 3, "Breaking Into the Mainstream: How to Move from Early Success to

Mainstream Market Leadership," contains yet another one, but be prepared—it's much different than any you've encountered before. It also tells you how to climb out of the sales slump many companies experience after all the technology enthusiasts have bought a product—and how to begin selling into the mainstream.

So, this brings us to the office of a prominent positioning guru, feet propped up on his desk, eyes glazed with that faraway look he gets when pondering something of truly immense proportions....

CHAPTER TWO

Positioning Your Product Using the "Elevator Test"

HOW TO NAIL IT IN 14 FLOORS—OR LESS

By Geoff Moore, Geoffrey Moore Consulting

Geoffrey A. Moore, a former partner at Regis McKenna, Inc., is the president of Geoffrey Moore Consulting, a firm based in Palo Alto, California, that provides consulting and education services to high-technology companies. He also is the author of Crossing the Chasm: Marketing and Selling Technology Products to Mainstream Customers.

I got the call at 3:30 P.M. on a Friday. It was a slow day at work. My feet were up on my desk. I was thinking. Then the phone rang.

"Mr. Moore, you don't know me, but I attended the Software Publishers Association conference at Orlando where you spoke on positioning, and I'd like to ask you some follow-up questions, if you don't mind."

After exchanging a few pleasantries, I learned that my caller was a Cambridge-based software developer of PC as well as Macintosh products, with an "information product"—his words—that he was ready to release. Now that the product was complete, he was interested in looking at marketing issues.

"No time like the present," I quipped. "What can I do for you?"

"Well, first of all, everyone tells me that the key to success with this product is to position it correctly, but I'm not exactly sure what all that entails." I told him to put his feet up and spent the next few minutes explaining the importance of positioning.

THE IMPORTANCE OF POSITIONING

1. Positioning is both a noun (as in the position/space something occupies in people's heads) and a verb (something you do to influence the position you get in people's heads).

2. The most important thing to know about positioning as a noun is that the space you get in other people's heads is very, very small—typically no more than a phrase or two.

3. The most important thing to know about positioning as a verb is that if you attempt to pack the positioning space in people's heads with more information

than they can hold, the space overflows, your "entry permit" is canceled, and your entire message is rejected as noise.

"But that's impossible!" spluttered my caller. "With a new type of product like ours, you can't possibly explain everything in a phrase or two."

"True, but since your customers don't want to know everything, so what?"

"So how do I know what to tell them?"

I explained that this was what consultants charged money for, and he explained that he was a bit short of funds at the moment, having just been through a painful, expensive, and unrequited acquisition attempt—too painful to discuss. I could relate to that; I had just priced a new car myself. Anyway, he asked if I could elaborate a little on how one went about solving this type of problem.

THE ELEVATOR TEST

"Have you ever heard of the elevator test?" I asked. He had not. I explained that the elevator test worked as follows: You and another person get on an elevator. As you press the button for, say, the fourteenth floor, the other person asks, "So, what exactly is this new product of yours all about?" If you have answered this question to the other person's satisfaction before the doors open, you have passed the elevator test.

This test is one that venture capitalists like to apply to new companies as well as new products—before they fund them. They know that the success of any new venture depends in part on a successful word-of-mouth communication campaign. They figure that if the developer can't explain things in a few words, then no one else is likely to be able to either and any kind of consistent word-of-mouth communication will therefore be doomed to failure. So it is *crucial* to pass the elevator test.

"Wait a minute!" interrupted my caller. "In the first place, my building doesn't have 14 floors—so I can't even practice this test. Besides, you haven't helped me at all. You've just restated my problem."

Drat. This guy was too savvy for me. I was beginning to suspect that he had been a consultant himself in some prior life. "OK, OK, I'll give you some of the basics. But this is my lifeblood I'm giving away."

HOW TO PASS THE ELEVATOR TEST

Basically, I asked him to draw a simple x,y graph, and then label the x-axis Key Benefit and the y-axis Key Differentiation. I drew the graph (see Figure 2-1) while we talked, hoping that he was doing something similar at the other end of the phone.

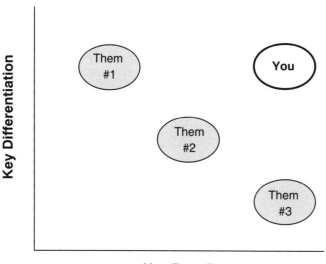

Key Benefit

FIGURE 2-1   Positioning space, defined

The simplest way to think about the positioning space you get in people's heads, I explained, is to break it up into two components: the Why buy? component (the *x*-axis, Key Benefit) and the Why me? component (the *y*-axis, Key Differentiation). You get only one "sound byte" for each axis.

"But there are seven or eight great reasons to buy this product!" exploded my caller.

"Great," I replied, "but for any one type of audience, pick one. Throw the other seven away. Otherwise all you'll generate is noise."

"But for any one benefit, there are all kinds of competition," he moaned.

"That's what the *y*-axis is for. You get one shot at differentiating yourself from all that competition. Again, why one?"

"Because people won't listen to more than one," he intoned, his voice pitched halfway between evident pleasure in anticipating my point and the ensuing depression of realizing its implications. "I get it. I get it. But give me an example."

I thought for a minute back to a project we'd done to help a developer introduce a new monitor. The product, I explained, is a video-display monitor that can pivot between landscape orientation (11" × 8½") and portrait orientation (8½" × 11"). The idea is that for spreadsheets and presentations, landscape is better, whereas for letters and documents, portrait is preferable. So why not just switch whenever you want?

"How does it work?" he wanted to know.

"Never mind how it works," I replied. "The question is, how do you position it?"

"Oh, yeah. OK. How did they position it?" I talked him through the diagram in Figure 2-2.

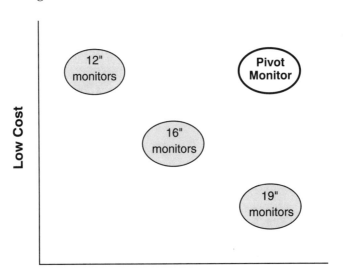

Full-Page Display

FIGURE 2-2   **The pivoting monitor example**

There are actually quite a few reasons a person might want a such a monitor: It looks cool, it saves desk space, it lets you switch back and forth in real time; but the developer decided that for its prime target customer—an administrative support person—the main attraction was getting a page-at-a-glance image for documents (portrait) as well as presentations (landscape). They called this benefit Full-Page Display. Now, it turns out that with displays that do not pivot—landscape-only displays—you must have at least a 19-inch monitor before you can see a full 8½ × 11-inch vertical page. With a pivoting monitor, you can get the effect with a 15-inch display. That gives this new monitor a major cost advantage. Hence, low cost was chosen as the key differentiation.

"But what about the pivot itself?" he asked. "Surely that is the key differentiator."

Well, yes and no, I answered. Yes, pivoting is a unique and memorable differentiating feature. But no, it isn't the key differentiator, if what we mean by that term is the basis on which customers will prefer your product over its competition.

Customers are rarely comfortable allowing a "unique" feature to be the basis for determining a competitive choice. Hence, the early problems in positioning fault-tolerant computing and the problems in positioning and finding a niche for the current pen-based computers. In this context, the pivot—alone, only as a pivot—is no more than a gimmick. But the pivot as the key to a low-cost implementation of a full-page display is the basis for a competitive preference.

"Well, that's all well and good. That company has something tangible to sell. But we've got a software product that is part data management, part data selection, part data display—plus we supply the data to go with it, along with our commitment to update it on an ongoing basis. We'll never get it down to anything this simple," said my caller.

"Look, this is all in my book, Chapter 6, pages 155 and following—so if I tell you all this, will you promise to go out and buy it?" He said he would, and I made him memorize the ISBN number, which my mom has had stenciled on the inside of all my underwear.

CREATING A POSITIONING STATEMENT

OK, here is a method for capturing your positioning strategy in a simple, two-sentence formula. The formula is as follows:

For	<target customer>
Who	<compelling reason to buy>
Our product is a	<product category>
That	<key benefit>.
Unlike	<main competitor>
Our product	<key differentiation>.

"Whoa, slow down. What's this all about?" he asked.

Positioning, I explained, is based on winning the battle for mind-share in any given market segment. A market segment is in part defined by specifying a target customer and a compelling reason to buy. Change the target customer or the reason to buy, and you change the segment you are attacking.

"Why compelling reason to buy?"

I explained that in a high-tech market, if the reason to buy is not compelling then it is all too likely that potential customers will not buy at all.

"So in the case of the pivoting monitor," he said, "the target customer was an administrative assistant. But what was the compelling reason to buy?"

I replied that the target customer was actually the administrative assistant's boss, the one who would have to approve the product's purchase. And the compelling reason to buy was to improve productivity on a task that made up the bulk of their relationship with each other.

The statement, in other words, should begin like this: *For* executives with administrative assistants *who* need to generate documents and presentations frequently and with rapid turnaround, *our product is* a video-display monitor *that* provides a full-page display regardless of whether the page orientation is landscape or portrait. *Unlike* any other VDT that provides this capability, *our product* costs thousands of dollars less.

"So what is this—the advertising copy?" my caller asked.

Not at all, I replied. This is the positioning statement. As such, it governs all positioning activities related to the product. It has an effect not only on advertising but also public relations, sales presentations, brochures, demos, and any other form of marketing communication. That is, the statement sets the criteria for accepting or rejecting ad copy, press releases, and the like. If the copy is not "on strategy," as defined by this two-sentence statement, then no matter how catchy it is, it is not acceptable and will be less likely to sell the product.

"But most importantly," my caller interjected in a voice bright with enthusiasm, "this will let me pass my elevator test."

"Right," I said.

"Now, if I can just keep an executive staff long enough to come up with a good statement...."

And with that reply, my caller hung up.

CHAPTER THREE

Breaking into the Mainstream

HOW TO MOVE FROM EARLY SUCCESS TO MAINSTREAM MARKET LEADERSHIP

By Geoff Moore, Geoffrey Moore Consulting

Geoffrey A. Moore, a former partner at Regis McKenna, Inc., is the president of Geoffrey Moore Consulting, a firm based in Palo Alto, California, that provides consulting and education services to high-technology companies. He also is the author of *Crossing the Chasm: Marketing and Selling Technology Products to Mainstream Customers.*

IT was a Wednesday afternoon, and I was hard at work. My feet were up on my desk, a cup of coffee resting comfortably on my stomach, my eyes focused somewhere between my desk and the door. I was just about to have a flash of marketing insight—you get to where you can feel one coming, sort of like a migraine, only different—when the phone rang.

"Hello, Geoff?"

Drat. It was him again. The same guy who'd called up a couple of months ago to find out how to position his product with the elevator test. That's what you get, I thought, for answering your own phone.

"Say, Geoff, I understand you got a new book out, something called *Crossing the Chasm*," he said, pronouncing the *ch* as in *ch*url instead of as in *ch*arisma. "I think maybe we are in the chasm, and I can't wait around to read the book. Just give me a few pointers—you know, like last time."

From past experience, I knew I wasn't going to shake this guy, so I reluctantly put my feet back on the floor.

DEFINING THE CHASM

The basic idea, I explained, is that high-tech markets do not develop in a continuous fashion. Specifically, when you factor in the time element, they do not follow the bell-shaped curve predicted by the traditional technology adoption life cycle curve (see Figure 3-1).

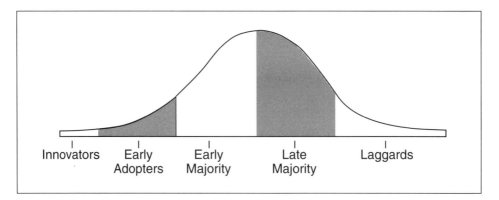

FIGURE 3-1   Traditional adoption curve

Instead, they develop in the following phases (see Figure 3-2):

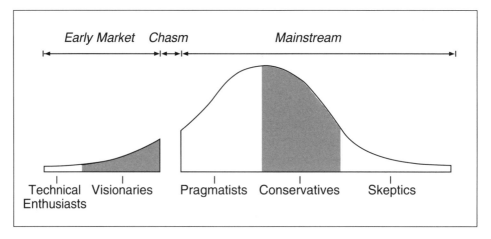

FIGURE 3-2   Revised technology adoption curve

Phase 1: The Early Market

The bulk of customers in this phase are technology enthusiasts and visionaries, the two customer types that populate the very front end of the technology adoption life cycle. The former get involved with high-tech products early on simply because they love technology and like to play with the latest and greatest toys. The latter, the visionaries, get involved early because they want to revolutionize some aspect of their business to gain a dramatic competitive advantage. Both these groups, in other words, see an advantage to being the first to adopt a new product.

Phase 2: The Chasm

This is a "nonmarket" phase, during which there are really no natural customers for your high-tech product. It is as if the front part of the life cycle has broken off from the rest of the curve; this phase represents the gulf separating the two.

During this time, the product has by now been on the market long enough for technology enthusiasts and visionaries to have heard about it and, if they are interested, to have bought it. But the product is not yet established as a "safe" buy; it has not, in other words, secured a market leadership position in any particular segment of the market. From the point of view of a pragmatist or a conservative, it is simply too soon to take a chance on the purchase. As a result, during the chasm phase, sales dip precipitously—often just at the point where you have promised your investors a surge in revenue.

Phase 3: The Mainstream Market

This is the phase of market development in which all high-tech wealth is generated. It is represented by the bell part of the life cycle curve. The primary customers now driving sales are the pragmatists. Later on, if the company stays in the market and continues to support its product, it will sell more and more to conservatives.

Pragmatists use technology products to improve productivity in a nondisruptive way. They prefer to go with the leading product, because it is one they'll be able to live with for a while and because market-leading products tend to attract third-party support, thereby augmenting the value of the product at no cost to the customer. Winning acceptance among pragmatists is what causes the dramatic acceleration in revenues that characterizes the most successful high-tech products.

The conservatives who follow in the adoption cycle are looking to get by with the safest, cheapest technology they can find. Fundamentally, they are afraid of technology purchases—afraid they will choose the wrong thing, afraid they won't be able to make it work right, afraid they will break it or just make themselves look stupid trying to use it; so they will choose only a fully proven, absolutely bulletproof solution—and even then will worry about it. Finally, because they delay their purchases until the back end of the product's life cycle, conservatives also expect—and get—low prices.

During the mainstream phase, the product has been accepted as an established part of the high-tech landscape and usually is the leader in at least one market segment. (Products that are not leaders—that are simply third, fourth, or fifth in the market—typically get "shaken out" over time; they are eventually acquired by the market leader or go out of business.)

ARE YOU IN THE CHASM?

"So how can I tell if we are in the chasm?" my caller asked. I asked him to tell me about his product.

"How about if I give you my elevator test positioning statement?" he asked. *[Editor's note: For more information about what the "elevator test" is and how to use it, see Chapter 2, "Positioning Your Product Using the 'Elevator Test': How to Nail It in 14 Floors—or Less."]* The guy knew how to go after my soft spot.

"Here goes: *For* market researchers and marketing executives *who* use census data to target prospective customers, *Infomagic* is a CD-ROM database and data-retrieval tool for the Macintosh that puts this information at your fingertips. *Unlike* on-line census information databases, *Infomagic* is usable by anyone in the marketing organization and does not generate expensive phone-access charges." (For budding entrepreneurs in the information business, Infomagic is not the real product name; if it passes the trademark test, it's yours.) "How was that?" he asked.

Pretty good, I had to admit.

"So am I in the chasm?"

Well, I asked, how are sales? Not as good as he was hoping. Why not? "Well," he explained, "at first they took off like a rocket. We even had back orders for a while. But lately they are going nowhere."

How come? All kinds of reasons, he complained. "First of all, not that many people have CD-ROM drives for their Macintosh computers yet. And second, a lot of people think that market analysis is just for specialists. Furthermore, the distribution channel doesn't want to carry the product because it is too specialized. But when we give it to VARs, they try to make the distribution too complicated. For a while we were successful with a money-back free trial, but now even the response to that offer has dried up," he said.

"It definitely sounds as if you are in the chasm," I said. "That free-trial offer is a great tactic when your product is in the early market phase, but mainstream pragmatists aren't worried as much about the cost of purchase as the cost of ownership. They simply don't like to be the first people to experiment with new things."

"Help me out here," he said. "Who *isn't* in the chasm?"

Who's In, Who's Out

As with everything else, I told him, it is often a matter of opinion, but let me give you some of my picks for 1992.

Early Market:

- any QuickTime product

- any pen-based product

- any kind of collaborative application

Chasm:

- any user programming product

- any kind of scheduling or calendaring groupware

- any CD-ROM–based product

Mainstream (just arrived):

- fax-based products

- remote E-mail products

- any product especially suited to Macintosh PowerBooks

Editor's note: This chapter was written in 1992. Here are Geoff's picks for 1993: Early Market: any QuickTime product, pen-based product, and wireless computing (communications) product. Chasm: any user programming product, scheduling or calendaring groupware; and natural language. Mainstream: CD-ROM–based products, fax-based products, and remote E-mail products.

"You just make this stuff up or what? What's the idea here?" he asked.

Articulate chap, I thought. Actually, I explained, the key difference that determines whether a product has made it into the mainstream is the existence of the "whole product."

THE "WHOLE PRODUCT" CONCEPT

I continued my explanation: The whole product is the complete solution, the entire set of products and services needed by users to achieve the value proposition promised by the product you are selling. Pragmatists evaluate products based on whether the whole product is a proven solution and one that is readily available. Until it is, they won't buy.

In the case of new entrants to the mainstream—fax, remote E-mail, PowerBook software—all have been enabled by the emergence of the PowerBook as a suitable Macintosh portable. This was the last piece of the solution that was necessary, since other PC laptops had already established the need for, and had driven the adoption of, such things as support for data and fax modems and the installation of remotely accessible E-mail packages.

The reason why QuickTime and pen-based products are still in the early market phase is that the whole product is nowhere near ready for "prime time." Only people who have either the skill (technology enthusiasts) or the drive (visionaries) to make these products work—no matter what—will be customers in the near term. However, because these products represent the latest and greatest technology, they will attract some early adopters.

The whole product is not just made of hardware and software. It can also incorporate something as abstract as "accepted behavior." The reason why collaborative applications, for example, are still early-market products has little to do with hardware or software. Everything you need to implement it is available off-the-shelf—what is missing is the necessary paradigm shift.

"The what?"

OK. A change in behavior. People aren't used to collaborating via computers. It's not that it can't be done but more that it "isn't done." As a result, perfectly good solutions aren't really solutions at all because they don't reflect the way people actually work together. Until some significant evangelism creates this change in behavior (that is, in the way people collaborate) and users can celebrate the competitive gains achieved by it, these products will stay in the early market position.

"But what about the chasm itself?"

Products fall into the chasm when they lose the sizzle of being a brand-new technology but still lack either the whole-product infrastructure or the paradigm shift needed for customers to readily achieve desired benefits. In 1992, CD-ROM titles fit into this category simply because CD-ROM drives were not yet ubiquitous. It's a little bit like the old VCR versus VCR-titles situation: There wasn't enough of either one to generate adequate investment in the other.

User programming suffers from a paradigm problem—in my opinion, one that may become permanent. The problem is not only that languages are hard to learn but also that most end users lack the systems-analysis skills to design what they want, regardless of how easy it might become to actually program it. To climb out of the chasm, group calendaring will also have to overcome a paradigm problem, this one resting on the inability to get any group of people with whose schedules you want to coordinate to consistently obey the protocol of keeping their calendars on line and up-to-date.

HOW TO CROSS THE CHASM

"All right. I think we're in the chasm. Not only do we rely on CD-ROM drives, but we also seem to be introducing a new paradigm. So what do we do now?" my caller queried.

Crossing the chasm, I replied, is like invading Normandy. (I figured he probably didn't know much about World War II but must have at least played Axis and Allies.) Your ultimate goal is to liberate all of Europe, but your immediate goal is just to gain a beachhead on the continent. So you direct all your forces solely to that end.

"I've never been to Normandy." My caller was nothing if not literal.

The key to getting out of the chasm, I began again, is to target one specific segment in the mainstream and focus all your efforts on accelerating the formation of a whole product and affecting a paradigm shift just for that one segment. The idea is to achieve a visible market-leadership position within that segment—proven acceptance by at least one group of pragmatists—and then use that beachhead as a basis for moving into related "adjacent" segments of pragmatist customers.

"Wait a minute, wait a minute. Our product is truly horizontal. It works across many different vertical segments. Why should we narrow it to just one?"

The problem, I explained, is that although all the segments may share common needs, each also has its own unique ones. In the case of Infomagic, this might be special data sets, or special metrics for different industries, or some industry-specific database that most customers merge with their other data, or simply a vocabulary unique to that industry. Accelerating the whole product typically involves doing some custom work to ensure that these pieces all fit together correctly. Most developers simply do not have enough resources to accelerate the formation of multiple whole products at the same time, so they should choose just one.

"Well, it's true that a lot of the fast-food people wanted us to interface to a Geographic Information System mapping program to help with their site-location planning, and the recording industry was looking for additional data about dependents under the age of 18, and the snack-food people needed to correlate data with their scanner-output records. I see what you mean. But how do I pick which segment to focus on?"

SO MANY SEGMENTS, SO LITTLE TIME

This is indeed, I explained, a tough problem. If you don't pick a segment quickly, you can easily become permanently stuck in the chasm. But since all segments at this point in the product's life cycle look pretty much alike and since there are so many of them, how to proceed is often confusing. The best approach is to begin defining possible target segments through a process called application-scenario generation—each scenario is built around a before/after-your-product-was-adopted "day in the life" for a potential target customer. These scenarios are then ranked against each other, with two key criteria.

- How compelling is this customer's reason to buy your product?

- How feasible is it for you to ensure the availability of the whole product needed to fulfill this target customer's compelling reason to buy?

The rating and ranking process is conducted in-house, leveraging whatever expertise you have readily available from your own employees or from informal advisers to your company.

Editor's note: There's a complete discussion about how to create application scenarios in Chapter 4, "Target Markets—Easy to Pick, Hard to Stick: How to Choose and Stick with the Best Target Market."

"So, what I have now is a bunch of made-up stories about what might be the possible applications of my product?"

Basically, yes, I said, reminding myself once again that marketing is, in essence, just another literary form. Each of these "stories" functions as a kind of placeholder for a possible target market. Segments that score highly, based on the previous two criteria, warrant further attention and should be assessed with a variety of additional criteria, including the following.

- Where we need the help of a partner or ally to provide some piece of the whole product, do we already have a relationship with this company or must we start building one from scratch?

- Are target customers likely to want to buy from our existing distribution channels?

- Is our current pricing consistent with the value proposition that motivates these particular customers and with their estimated purchasing power?

- Are customers already well served by a competitor, or are their needs largely unmet?

Again, prioritize the scenarios, based on what you believe you already know about the market.

Finally, ask one last question: If we win over these target customers—if we dominate the market segment that they, as a group, constitute—will that provide an entrée to additional market segments (the way, for example, that winning over graphic artists to desktop publishing eventually provided an entrée into sales and marketing departments)?

The one or two scenarios that fare best in this entire rating and ranking process are the ones you should nominate as target segments.

"Look, I'm happy that I'm not spending a lot of money on you high-priced consultants, but don't I run the risk of bathing in my own bathwater?"

Now there's an appetizing image, I thought. "Yes, you do, so at this point you'll want to bring to bear whatever market-research resources you can to get an external perspective on the problem," I replied. At a minimum, I explained, you need to phone a representative sample of people who meet the criteria for your target customers and simply interview them to see if you've understood their needs and issues. Typically, you also call other third parties who have market knowledge—distributors, consultants, industry analysts, hardware evangelists, other software developers, and the like. The goal of these conversations is to validate or correct your marketing assumptions so that at the end of the process, you have a confirmed strategy.

BUILD THE BRIDGE

"What I have at this point, I guess, is a top-priority target market segment. But what do I do now?"

I looked at my watch. How much longer was I supposed to humor this guy? I covered the mouthpiece, made some rumbling noises, and let him know that I had just been called into an important meeting. So real quickly, I said, what you have to do now is communicate your whole-product strategy to the key players in your target market—the customers, of course, but also every other constituency that will play a role in either delivering the whole product or establishing your reputation as the leader of this particular market-development effort. The communication is a two-way dialogue because every player in your scenario has to win something from the endeavor—and you need to confirm both that you understand what constitutes that win and that the others see how your effort supports it.

This win/win approach to all the constituencies is what allows the market segment to develop at an accelerated pace, catapulting your product to early acceptance and your company to the status of perceived market leader. I was doing my best to end on a high and glorious note: "Once you've won one segment, it becomes a lot easier to leverage your reputation into adjacent markets, transforming what begins as a highly focused marketing effort into what eventually becomes broad-sector leadership."

"OK," he said. "Say, this has been good advice."

"You think I should write a book?"

"Oh, yeah. Sure. Send me a copy."

And with that he hung up.

CHAPTER FOUR

Target Markets—Easy to Pick, Hard to Stick

HOW TO CHOOSE AND STICK WITH THE BEST TARGET MARKET

By Geoff Moore, Geoffrey Moore Consulting

Geoffrey A. Moore, a former partner at Regis McKenna, Inc., is the president of Geoffrey Moore Consulting, a firm based in Palo Alto, California, that provides consulting and education services to high-technology companies. He also is the author of *Crossing the Chasm: Marketing and Selling Technology Products to Mainstream Customers.*

*B*RRRING. "Good afternoon," I said to my caller. "May I help you?"

"Geoff. It's me, Jim, your old buddy."

Drat. Good old Jim, always good for a lot of questions, but never a nickel in payment. "Hey, Jim, what can I do for you?" I asked, mentally cursing myself for giving him such an easy opening.

"Well, now that you mention it, I do have a problem. And actually, since it grew out of reading your book, you sort of owe me on this one. Here it is: Remember when we last talked and we agreed that my product was in the chasm?" (The *chasm* refers to the gap in a product's life cycle between early success, spurred by sales to technology enthusiasts and visionaries, and the later mainstream market success that comes from making sales to mainstream pragmatists and conservatives.)

Editor's note: In case you haven't already read it, Chapter 3, "Breaking into the Mainstream: How to Move from Early Success to Mainstream Market Leadership," gives an interesting and detailed description of what constitutes the chasm.

"Yes, I think so," I responded, racking my brain to remember which product he was talking about. "The CD-ROM information base, wasn't it?" It was coming back to me. Jim had acquired the rights to a lot of 1990 census information and had packaged it for use in market analysis applications.

"Yeah, well, remember how you said the key to crossing the chasm was to pick a single target market and focus on getting a leading share within it?"

"Sure," I replied, reminding him of the D-Day analogy in which the Allies focused all their armies on taking Normandy Beach, even though their long-term goal was to liberate all of Europe.

"Yeah, well, it doesn't work."

"What doesn't work, Jim?"

"This segmentation stuff. We picked a segment, but it didn't work."

"What did you pick?" I asked, seeking to determine the precise number of paper clips it takes to build a two-foot chain.

"We picked information workers who want customer data for market analysis."

WHAT CONSTITUTES A SEGMENT

"Hold on," I said. (Now he had my attention.) "Remember, there are two key things that define any high-tech market segment. First, everyone in the segment must have a common use for the information. This ensures that as additional functionality is added (during further development or through partnerships or "bundles" with companion products and services), these additions all remain focused on—and offer more value to—a given set of customers. On this score, it sounds like you do have a segment.

"But the second criterion is that the group you've defined must constitute a single word-of-mouth community. The people in that segment must reference each other (that is, consult with each other) when making a buying decision about a high-tech product. This ensures that early customers spread the word to mainstream users more quickly, helping to create the perception that you are the market leader. If all the early customers are in one segment, you'll very quickly develop the reputation of being the up-and-coming solution that fills this segment's needs. But if each early customer is in a different word-of-mouth community, then each is a lone voice in the wilderness, and no perception of market leadership can be created.

"The problem, Jim, is that 'information workers' isn't a community in the sense of being a group of people who would consult with each other about high-tech purchase decisions. So let's take a step back and see what word-of-mouth communities you have touched. Who was actually using your product to analyze customer data?"

"Well, let me see," Jim replied. "There was the product marketing department at a major consumer products company and the research department at an ad agency; a political party is a big user, and also a hospital looking at the demographics of its customer base."

"That's at least three, maybe four different word-of-mouth communities," I replied. (Consumer products people talk with ad agencies a lot, so they might be considered parts of a single segment.) "You have to pick a *single* segment to focus on—for example, marketing managers at hospitals or in consumer products companies."

"That's ridiculous!" he exploded. "If I did that, I'd have no sales at all. I have to make at least $1 million from this product during this fiscal year or I'm in big trouble."

"How much have you made so far?"

"Well, our sales are just getting ramped up....Uh, we've sold several hundred copies."

"At what price?"

"It lists for $2,450."

"But perhaps you've offered discounts to early customers?"

"Well, we're trying to seed the market."

"So...?"

"We're almost to $100,000 in sales."

And this was the fifth month of the quarter. "OK, Jim. Sit back and try not to interrupt for a minute, although you aren't going to like what you hear."

WHY ONE IS ENOUGH

"Let's revisit some basic principles," I said. "The whole point of marketing is to achieve the benefits of market leadership—premium pricing, higher profit margins, lower cost of sales, strong word-of-mouth recommendations, and the like. The only way to get those is to be perceived as the market leader; and the only way to become that, when your company is small, is to focus on a single market segment. It's a big fish/small pond game. If you don't manage the size of the pond, you'll end up being just another minnow in the ocean with a very short life expectancy."

"But I need the revenues!" he howled.

"Don't we all. But you have to *earn* them. I've seen your product and it's very good—that's the first step toward earning your right to the customer's money. But you also must establish a market leadership perception for the product. Without that, only the early adopters will be willing to risk buying it. Everyone else will see it as a fad and will steer clear. But if you can get at least one group of customers to adopt it more broadly, then you have a beachhead from which to attack the mainstream marketplace. Focusing is a shortcut to establishing the beachhead; from there you can expand onto the continent—into the mainstream—carrying the leadership mantle with you."

"OK, OK," he said. "Just suppose I go along with you on this. How do I do it? Say I just pick consumer product marketing managers, for example. Now what?"

"Careful," I warned. "There's a problem with 'just picking' a target market segment: For the focus to work, it must be sustained for at least a year."

"Why a year?" Jim asked, typically *sotto voce*.

"It typically takes 90 days to develop a marketing communications roll-out that solicits initial sales for any target segment. Another 90 days passes before you can measure any impact the program has. But to get a critical mass that begins to convey that you're a market leader, it usually takes another six months," I explained. (What I didn't say, because I suspected Jim wouldn't be thrilled to hear it, is that this applies only if you target a reasonably modest-sized segment.)

Why Stick?

"So to get any results," I continued, "everyone in your company has to buy into the choice of target segment and stick with it. Most targeting efforts fail because the developer keeps switching from target to target—I call it the 'target du jour approach'—and achieves no focus at all. And part of the reason for not sticking to any given target is that the developer's selection process was insufficiently rigorous to choose a segment that it could make a long-term commitment to."

"Well, in *my* company whatever I say goes, of course. So that shouldn't be a problem," Jim said.

Right, I thought. "Yes, it should be a problem," I argued, "because a) you may end up second-guessing yourself, and b) to truly be successful, a company requires internal consensus when it comes to the critical factors."

HOW TO SELECT A TARGET

I continued: "The point is that you need a reliable mechanism or process that allows you and your key managers—your 'strategy development group'—to survey a broad range of opportunities and come to a rational decision about which beachhead target segment to focus on. The process must generate a focal point that your entire team will commit to for at least a year. The method I recommend is to generate *target application scenarios.*"

I explained the concept to him: The reason we use such scenarios is to help overcome the basic problem in all market segmentation work. The boundaries of any segment are inherently fuzzy, and if you focus on defining a segment by its boundary line—who's in or out—you'll end up in a perpetual debate. So instead you should define segments by their center point. The center point of any segment consists of an ideal customer using the product in an *application* (not in the computer program sense, but in the "how a product is used" sense) that produces the maximum benefit. Describing that customer and application is the function of an application scenario.

The scenario is a before/after story. That is, first you describe the target user and "a day in the life *before*" he or she gets your new product, focusing on some excruciatingly frustrating moment when, because that person doesn't have your product, things turns out very badly. Then you describe "a day in the life *after*," replaying that same moment as if the user has your product—so that things turn out very well. The resulting document, which should be no more than one page long, is the target application scenario.

Each scenario should represent a possible target market segment. The idea is for your strategy development group to generate as many scenarios as you can (40 is typical, 70 is more than enough, 20 is probably too few) until you collectively feel you've exhausted all the imaginable possibilities. Then you evaluate each one and finally select the single best target. Each scenario stands for a possible target market segment, and you rate its attractiveness in terms of the following criteria using a 1 to 5 rating, with 5 being best.

- *Compelling reason to buy.* The question here is how strong this potential customer's motive is for adopting your product. If it is nice to use your product but not critical, then rate it low (maybe 2). But if the product solves a crucial, persistent problem that directly prevents users from accomplishing their primary functions or goals, then the scenario gets a high rating, typically 4 or 5.

- *Whole product feasibility.* The whole product is your product plus all other products and services that target customers need for fulfilling the compelling reason to buy. The question is, how realistic will it be for the user to get the complete solution set required to achieve his or her compelling reason to buy? If, with the addition of your product, it can be done "off the shelf" using existing products in a plug-and-play way, then it is highly feasible and gets a 5. But if it requires special programming or an unusual set of companion products, then it gets a low rating.

- *Partners and allies.* Most whole products result from the cooperation of other developers or vendors to provide necessary services and support, as well as the application-specific hardware and software interfaces needed to connect your new product into the customer's installed systems. How well known are you to these vendors, and vice versa? If you are using proven relationships to make the scenario work, then give yourself a high rating. If your scenario requires developing relationships with a new group of vendors, give yourself a low one.

- *Whole product pricing.* Pricing is critical to market development; however, for the purposes of the scenario, the key is not the price of your product alone, but the price of the whole product solution. If the whole product can be delivered at a market-making price point, then give the scenario a high rating; otherwise, give it a low one.

- *Whole product distribution.* Distribution (or where customers buy the product) is also crucial to making a market take off; but again, it is not only how *your* product is distributed but also where the customer would buy the whole product that is important. If there is a natural, one-stop place for the customer to purchase the whole product and you already have established a relationship with that channel, then the scenario gets a high rating; otherwise, rate it low.

- *Competition.* The question here isn't "Is there an existing product that has similar features and benefits to yours?" Rather, it's "Is there a developer who has already won your customer's heart with respect to the target application?" That is, you shouldn't worry about whether there are other suitors with your qualifications wooing your customers. Instead, worry about whether the target of your affections is already married. If the user is already well served, give the scenario a low rating. If not, give it a high mark.

- *Positioning.* Is your company's current image consistent with the role you must assume in serving the target customer as specified in the scenario? For example, if you're like me, Newton from Apple feels good. But how would you feel if Apple introduced a mainframe? If what you're proposing is the sort of thing you have succeeded with in the past, give it a high rating. If you are entering a new domain, give it a low one.

- *Leverage.* Is this market segment a dead end or can you leverage it to win additional segments? Suppose you became the market leader in a market segment: Can you leverage this lead into other segments, say, the way Apple leveraged success with corporate graphics departments (desktop publishing) into success with designers in advertising and prepress companies—as well as into success with other sales and marketing professionals? If so, the scenario gets a high rating for leverage. But if the market segment appears to be a dead end, then give it a low rating.

"That's the rating system," I concluded.

"Great," Jim said. "So, let me get this straight. We write up the scenarios and rate them. Then what?"

GET OUTSIDE VALIDATION

"Well, after you have rated all the scenarios, throw away all but the top few. Your final target should be taken only from the top two to five scenarios. But before you make the final choice, you must do some market research," I said.

"Market research—as in pay money for?"

That's my Jim. " 'Fraid so. See, up to this point all you've used is your own intuition and experience. That's fine for cutting your search down to the final few. But before you make the final call, you really ought to get some outside input as well."

"Such as?"

"Typically, you should interview five to ten users for each scenario that's still in the running. To help ensure that you get the right input, write a two- to three-page market development strategy statement for each scenario; it should consist of a profile of the target market, including paragraphs that address each one of the eight criteria in the target application scenario. Give this to your interviewer and ask that person to test its validity through phone conversations or focus groups with people who fit your target user profile.

"You also should talk to three to five potential partners and allies who are already serving the target customer, just to see if your strategy makes sense to them. This is particularly important if you would be highly dependent on any particular partner to make the whole product successful. Once you get the input from each of the two to five 'final candidates,' you're essentially done with the preparation phase; then you make your choice. The good news is that having reviewed your options this thoroughly, you are well positioned to make the choice stick. The bad news is that the choice to focus is never comfortable."

"Why's that?" he inquired.

FOCUS WORKS

I explained that no matter how much you buy into the concept of market focusing, you'll always worry that by doing so you are somehow giving up a sale that you otherwise might have gotten. It's true: You are. But console yourself with the thought that a sale within your target segment not only yields revenue but also contributes to market leadership perception—and that's where the real return on investment lies. Only market leaders can charge the premium margins that make them profitable in the long run.

"I don't know, Geoff. The whole process seems too complicated to me."

"Yeah, I sympathize. But the alternatives are worse. If you don't do this kind of thorough review, you won't have a strong basis for sticking to your selection. The next time the going gets rough or a hot new opportunity pokes its head up, you'll more easily give up your focus and begin to pursue a new target. In the end, you'll never focus at all.

"The key thing to remember is that people fail at focusing not because they pick the wrong target—the truth is, any reasonable target will work and even a suboptimal target is better than none at all—but rather because they keep jumping from target to target, never sticking around long enough to develop a real market-leading position."

"All you are saying is, 'Focus works.'"

"Yeah."

"Focus works."

"Yeah, you got it, Jim....Bye."

PART THREE

Using Market Research

Questionnaires, surveys, focus groups, ream after ream of "raw" data: Of and by itself, market research data is useless. But used correctly, it's priceless. These chapters give you a starting point for approaching market research: an overview of what you can accomplish with it, how to use it, and suggestions about how to do it inexpensively. Chapter 5, "A Market Research Primer," and Chapter 6, "Tips on Writing an Effective Market Research Survey," are therefore focused on some of the nuts and bolts aspects of market research.

But beyond that, this part of the book offers some interesting viewpoints on how you can put raw data into perspective and into use. That's why it also includes Chapter 7, "The Practice of Customer Focus: The Importance of Driving Business Decisions with Customer and Market Data," which discusses the day-to-day exercise of customer focus. It's a case study about how one company maintains its strong customer focus by making intelligence gathering a *daily* activity that permeates all levels of the company. Among other things, company employees follow their customers home. (How can they do *that*? It's all in this chapter.)

And by the way, as alluded to earlier, this is the part of the book in which you'll find the secret of how sewing needles compete with duct tape and how refrigerator magnets may compete with software. It's all revealed in Chapter 8, "Understanding the Competition: How to Distinguish Who You're Really Up Against."

CHAPTER FIVE

A Market Research Primer

By Dan Rubin and Pat Bentley, Apple Computer, Inc.

Dan Rubin and Pat Bentley are senior analysts in Apple Computer's customer research group.

A S our industry has matured, it has become more complex, competitive, global, expensive to compete in, and—in a word—risky. Because most companies don't have the resources to float them through an unsuccessful product launch, reducing the risks is critical. Although inspiration, technical aplomb, and capital are certainly ingredients of success, one of the best ways to reduce risk is to make better-informed decisions by using market research. Even a little goes a long way, and well-done research separates the half-baked ideas from those that will succeed.

In this chapter, we'll discuss research basics: the two kinds, how they differ, when each is useful, what sources are available, and when and how to hire professional researchers. Chapter 6, "Tips on Writing an Effective Market Research Survey," will discuss how to write a good survey questionnaire and focus group discussion guide.

Market research is not as difficult or cumbersome as it may seem. In simple terms, it's the process of finding out what customers want and need and how they want to get it. More broadly, it includes scoping out the competition, sizing up the market, identifying industry trends, and so forth. There are two kinds of research: primary and secondary. Primary research entails generating your own information through direct observation and measurement. It yields more precise data than does secondary research, which is the art of finding germane information in already published sources. Generally speaking, it's worth the effort to begin every research project by doing as much secondary research as you can; this will help you define what questions you need answered and determine precisely what, if anything, you need to explore through primary research.

However, before you begin any market research effort, it is important to be very clear about what you are trying to find out. If you try to find out everything you can, you'll expend a lot of effort, collect a lot of paper, and probably end up confused. Instead, start by articulating the decisions you need to make; then identify and prioritize the information needed to help you make them.

WHEN SECONDARY RESEARCH IS USEFUL

Secondary research is useful in several key areas of the personal computing industry. One is identifying a market opportunity—that is, the size of a market and how to segment it. Although information from secondary sources may not always directly relate to your exact product category, it can still be very helpful. For example, if you wish to develop a Macintosh accounting package for small legal firms, you probably won't find data specifically about the market for Macintosh accounting software for small legal firms. However, you may find information about the computing or accounting environments in small legal firms. That should provide you with valuable insight into the potential market opportunity. At this point, it's usually best to concentrate on identifying the general scope of a market opportunity and not worry much about how precise the data is; use it to help make your best estimates.

Secondary research is also useful in investigating customer buying behavior and product use patterns, such as how many users are connected to a local area network, how many people use spreadsheets, how many access data from mainframes, and so forth. The recent trend in research has been to focus on what users want and need rather than on just how many of what products companies are selling.

This kind of research is also excellent for tracking industry trends: pricing, number of manufacturers, sales volume, product characteristics, and competitive information. Usually, there's no need to go beyond secondary research to get that kind of data. It exists, and much of it is very useful.

SOURCES OF INFORMATION

In the computer industry, there are hundreds of trade publications and specialized newsletters, lots of syndicated research firms and financial analysts—the list goes on and on. Because the information is so abundant, there's a tendency to automatically assume that what you need is out there, somewhere. Sometimes that's true, but be prepared for some disappointment; more often than not, what you uncover will fall short of what you really need in some important way.

Two very common problems are outdated information and inconsistent terminology. If data is two or three years old, you should question whether it's still meaningful in an industry that changes very quickly. The computer industry also suffers from inconsistency in defining its zillions of terms. For example, what is an "intelligent terminal"? A "workstation"? Authors don't usually indicate how they define product categories. Sometimes the differences between their definition and yours is wide enough to make a significant impact on your conclusions. So be sure to ask yourself whether the author is truly talking about the same thing you're seeking information about.

There are excellent sales statistics for many industries because manufacturers make the information available (usually through an industry association). In some cases, a rigorous third-party auditing process facilitates some kind of marketplace measurement. Unfortunately, personal computing is not one of these industries. There is no single source that can offer all the statistics you might need.

However, there are some helpful sources. The Software Publishers Association can provide some information. Also, by scrutinizing hardware data you may be able to make some assumptions about corresponding software opportunities. But the data that is available about hardware are, by and large, purely estimates—and some of it is very inaccurate. Nondisclosure has traditionally been the unwritten rule in the hardware industry, and many manufacturers have attempted to decoy analysts into thinking that they've sold more product than they have. In the hardware business, there are few truths when it comes to market numbers.

Other Sources

Another source is government data, which can be found in public or business libraries. (If not, libraries usually have a directory of where the data is available.) When applicable, it can be very useful, inexpensive, and easy to get. Government sources are especially good for demographic information—census-type data such as how many people work in a given profession or industry, how many companies there are in an industry, how big they are, and so forth. The information is usually old—at least two and sometimes four or five years old. But that's usually OK, because in the world of demographics, few things change very quickly. You should also be careful not to assume that the information is accurate just because it's published by the government and it looks "official." Remember, data collection methods vary widely and aren't always sound.

Trade publications contain a lot of information. To get it, you don't have to labor through thousands of magazines. Most of it is stored in databases that are available through on-line services such as Dialog. If such services aren't available within your company, you can access them through third parties such as information brokers or syndicated research services. When you search a database, you should use the guidance of an experienced, knowledgeable professional; otherwise you may be overwhelmed with citations (many of them obscure) that will doom you to trying to find a needle in a haystack.

Editor's note: Chapter 8, "Understanding the Competition," includes a listing of some additional resources.

Professional and trade associations can be especially good sources if you're developing software for a specialized area. Some of them sponsor or conduct in-house surveys about the state of computing among their members, and they may make this information available to you. You may also be able to attend their annual meetings, which is a useful way to connect with people in professions you want to target.

Connecting with Sources

When starting your search, try to find a business-specialty library. Such places have reference librarians trained in finding and using sources and indexes for business and government information. For example, in the United States you can identify trade associations through the *Encyclopedia of Associations,* which most libraries carry. There's usually a business branch of the public library in major cities. Sometimes you can also get access to the business library of a local graduate business school.

DO IT YOURSELF?

Whether to do secondary research yourself or hire someone should depend on your resources and deadlines. If you prefer to get assistance, look in the *Yellow Pages* or business directory of your telephone book, where you can find independent information brokers, people with library training that are not affiliated with a public or corporate library. This is a growing segment of the information industry, and its quality of services is becoming very good. These people work for a fee and can do on-line literature searches, find citations and the articles you want, deal with copyright fees, and so forth. Such firms can also help you find specialized market research reports, which abound in high-technology areas. These reports cost anywhere from a few hundred to several thousands dollars. They usually cover a specific topic in depth but they vary widely in quality. Caveat emptor.

Another approach is to work with a syndicated research company such as Dataquest, InfoCorp, IDC, or one of many others. However, it can cost $10,000 to $20,000 a year to subscribe to a single service of such a company. (You usually purchase a one-year subscription to one or more of the many services offered by a firm, such as its software service, PC-hardware service, and so forth.) In the best case, this kind of company can serve, in a limited capacity, as your market research department. You receive the (very) part-time services of a researcher or industry analyst who can leverage a good library and other resources.

If you decide to employ one of these firms, first investigate it thoroughly. Make sure that the people you'll be working with have some knowledge about your business and that you have confidence in them. That way, you'll be working with professionals who have enough experience to evaluate your marketing assumptions and collect information, who can talk to competitors, customers, distributors, and so forth.

You're not likely to get a lot of very specific data from these firms, because the staff that supports each of them is usually small (four to six people) and must serve many clients. The bottom line: Be a really smart shopper; carefully evaluate whether the firm can truly add value—and if you can afford it.

PRIMARY RESEARCH

After you've done as much secondary research as you can, the next step is to consider primary research—developing your own information by querying current or potential customers about specific issues. There are many methods to choose from, but they break down into two basic types: qualitative and quantitative research. The key differences between them are the number of interviews conducted and the type of analysis applied to the results.

Usually, in a qualitative study no more than 10 to 40 people are interviewed in depth about perceptions, judgments, feelings, attitudes, and reactions. The interviews tend to be free-flowing and open-ended. The analysis of the interviews is mainly synthesis followed by judgment—you listen, but you don't keep score. Qualitative techniques include such things as focus groups, mini focus groups, and others.

On the other hand, with a quantitative approach, the number of people interviewed is usually 100 or more and the analysis is numbers-oriented: How many people use a hard disk? What percent prefer this as opposed to that? How many users are female? How many have a color monitor? Which of our three concepts is preferred? The questions asked are quite structured and are mostly multiple-choice or other kinds of closed-end questions. Quantitative techniques include such methods as mail or phone surveys (or a combination of the two).

When to Use Primary Research

Primary research can be used at almost any time to address issues that customer/ user input can conceivably affect. Research can be tied to a product's life cycle. Generally speaking, early in a product's life you work with less well defined concepts, which lend themselves to qualitative research. As you become more specific about the product and marketing strategy, you use quantitative methods (sometimes combined with qualitative ones) to hone in on specifics and fine-tune the product.

Early in a product's life cycle (what we call the need-identification stage), you need to identify market or product gaps you can fill. Here, research can be used to investigate how customers currently use related products and to illuminate their perceptions about these products' strengths and weaknesses. A qualitative approach—either focus groups or one-on-one interviews—is often most helpful here.

At the next stage (product definition), you'll want to test some concepts that meet the needs you identified earlier. Again, qualitative evaluation will probably give you the best information. Present your concepts to a good cross-section of potential customers, and use their reactions to help gauge which ones to pursue.

Research done during product definition often affects the next stage in the product life cycle—product-concept refinement. Here, you make price/feature and feature/feature trade-offs that you hope will make the product as appealing as possible—and cost-effective. Often, a quantitative survey that confirms or clarifies findings from the previous stage is useful at this point. This survey can also be used to help segment the target market (which customer groups liked the product the most), test promotional messages (which description is most appropriate, believable, or appealing), and test price perceptions (at what point this product is too expensive).

At this point, most software developers and some hardware manufacturers put their products through beta testing. This is a terrific opportunity to use one-on-one telephone interviews of users to thoroughly assess their reactions: what they like and don't like about the product, how well it meets their needs, what products or changes they'd like to see, and so forth.

One area that is often overlooked as you approach the product introduction is advertising research. Advertising is expensive, and you can save a lot of money by testing it before you run it. This research doesn't have to be expensive or time-consuming. It can be as simple as showing a rough, early version of the ad to carefully chosen potential customers and asking some simple questions: What does the ad say to you? What does the headline say? How relevant is the ad's message to you?

Once a product is on the shelves, doing primary research can be as valuable as traditional sales tracking. Continue to research your customers: What are their opinions about your product and about the competition?

Limitations of Primary Research

Primary research used alone has significant limitations; what you do with the results must be compatible with your resources. It won't answer all of your questions. The quality of the information you get is limited by the quality of the questions you ask and the experience and proficiency of the people interpreting the answers. The key to getting the best possible data is to understand beforehand what actions you'll take or decisions you'll make based on the results. Only then should you formulate the questions you must ask to get that information. Often, the best questions are not direct. The art of research questionnaire development involves asking a series of questions whose answers, taken together, will paint a meaningful picture.

Research about Pricing

The basic problem with price research is that simulating reality adequately enough to make realistic price/volume projections is difficult. We suggest limiting pricing research to developing general perceptions about price—that is, determining where along the scale buyers perceive your product as being a good value versus being expensive or cheap.

USE EXPERIENCED PROFESSIONALS

It's always a good idea to use professional help when undertaking a research project. It can save you a lot of time, trouble, and money in all aspects of the research project: setting up the project, defining criteria for who will be researched, screening and recruiting respondents, authoring a questionnaire (or "discussion guide" if it's a qualitative approach), interviewing objectively, processing the data, helping interpret results, and preparing a summary report or presentation. Keep in mind, however, that a research professional helps mostly with the process and the mechanics—you need to be involved in every step to ensure that the questions you want asked are being asked, that the terminology is correct, and even that the interviewers are pronouncing the words correctly.

Remember that anyone can hang out a shingle; however, some researchers are better than others, some are specialized, some are generalists, some firms are large, and some are small one- or two-person offices. Finding one that matches your needs and budget can be a lot like finding a doctor or lawyer: Personal referrals can work well, but you may want to get more than one person's opinion. Other sources for names are the *Yellow Pages* (in the United

States), the American Marketing Association, the *Market Research Green Book,* and *Quirk's Marketing Research Review* (available in some business libraries).

Finding a consultant for qualitative research is a little trickier than finding one for a quantitative project. The in-depth, exploratory nature of qualitative research requires an interviewer with some level of expertise or background in the area you're addressing. And in either type of study, if you need feedback on a really technical subject, you may have to educate the consultant before the interviews can be conducted. Obviously, you'd like to be spared that effort, but sometimes highly qualified research professionals just aren't up on the latest computer technologies.

Read on. The next chapter provides a practical guide to writing a good survey questionnaire.

CHAPTER SIX

Tips on Writing an Effective Market Research Survey

By Pat Bentley, Apple Computer, Inc.

Pat Bentley is a senior analyst in Apple Computer's customer research group.

GARBAGE in means garbage out. Yes, it's a cliché, but it's the best reason I can think of to take the time and effort needed to write a *good* questionnaire for your next market research survey. Aside from the interpretation of the results, the questionnaire itself (whether it is to be filled out by a respondent or used by an interviewer to ask questions) is probably the single most important determinant of how useful the survey results will be.

Whether you write it yourself or must evaluate or direct the work of a colleague or outside consultant, knowing the basics of what constitutes a good questionnaire can help make the difference between a study that will collect dust on a shelf and one that will illuminate the road ahead and galvanize your plans. Here are a few tips that can help make the difference.

BEFORE WRITING THE QUESTIONNAIRE

Before you begin, you should ask yourself some planning-oriented questions. What are your objectives? Exactly why are you doing the survey? What decisions will you make, based on what you learn? The answers to these questions will be the driving force behind the questionnaire. Knowing precisely what you want to accomplish will help you structure the questionnaire and give you clues about how to tabulate and digest the information. If you're too vague, you'll probably end up with survey data that won't be focused enough to act on. For example, it may be too general to say, "I want to find out what customers think about my product." A better, more explicit objective may be to find out exactly what product changes would be best received by or most useful to customers, so that you can increase sales by improving customer satisfaction (or whatever). Or it can be to find out what aspects of the product most strongly influence buying decisions—which can lead to changes in your advertising messages.

Also, the more focused your objectives the better, because a questionnaire can hold a respondent's attention for only about 15 to 30 minutes, depending on the topic, the nature of the survey and product, and the quality of the questionnaire. Researchers in the computer industry are fortunate in that people seem to enjoy talking about our products; thus, they are often more tolerant of longer questionnaires about computer products than of those about some other products. However, at some point even computer enthusiasts tire and lose interest. Subsequently, the quality of their answers drops rapidly.

Furthermore, you should determine what kinds of customers you will question and how you'll group them in your cross-tabulations. Make sure to ask questions that will identify respondents by their respective market segments or usage groups, and structure the questionnaire and tabulation instructions accordingly. That way, your results will more clearly show the different needs of these groups. For example, if you plan to use the information to make product improvements, you may find that accountants want extended math capabilities whereas users doing marketing jobs want better text processing. If you can't segment the various types of users, your research will show only that some users want this and some want that. The "who" and "why" will remain a mystery.

All these things—objectives, plans for using the information, whom to survey—should be committed to paper. Everyone involved in the project, especially those who will write the questionnaire, conduct the survey, and interpret the results, should fully understand them.

STRUCTURING THE QUESTIONNAIRE

The order in which you ask questions can be almost as important as the questions themselves. Although questionnaires run the gamut—depending on objectives, timing, and budget—a good one usually flows like this.

1. An introductory script or cover letter that identifies the interviewer and topic

2. Questions to qualify respondents

3. General questions about the main issue/topic

4. Specific questions about the main issue/topic

5. Questions about secondary issues

6. Questions to determine respondent demographics or characteristics

- *Introduce yourself.* This should be very brief and to the point. The script for a phone survey might say, "Good afternoon. This is Fred Smith of Alpha Omega Software. My company is surveying users of our XYZ product. Our registration records show that you recently purchased this product. Do you have a few minutes to answer some questions?" If so, go immediately to the first question. If not, ask if there is a more convenient time to call back. If you're doing a mail survey, the cover letter or beginning/introduction to the survey should be similarly brief; be sure to include a statement of your gratitude for the respondent's taking the time to fill it out and send it back.

- *Qualify the respondent.* Do this early in the survey to make sure you're talking to the right people. Ask very specific questions that will help you determine that these people have the appropriate background to give you credible answers. For example: "Do you own product XYZ? How often do you use it: every day, a few times a week, a few times a month, or less often? Do you use it in business, for personal enjoyment, or for some other reason?" If the respondents don't qualify (that is, meet your criteria), tell them you're finished and thank them for their time.

  If you're doing a mail survey, the qualification should take place either before you mail the survey or in the cover letter. In the letter, you might say, "Your name is on our list of registered owners of XYZ product. If you aren't the person who uses it most, please give this questionnaire to the person in your department who does use it most."

- *Move from the general to the specific.* Once you know you've contacted the right person, you can begin to broach the survey topic. Start with basic background questions about your issue or subject that begin to bring it into focus for the respondent. Then get more specific. Some general questions might be, "How long have you used product XYZ? Which version are you using? Have you used a previous version? Have you used a competing product? What is your main purpose in using XYZ?"

  With the general questions answered, you can then ask more specific, probing ones. "What do you especially like about XYZ? What else?" If you are fishing for something particular in a phone interview and the respondent doesn't mention it, you can ask about it specifically: "How would you rate XYZ on its ability to handle multiple data sets? What do you dislike about product XYZ?" You might also want to encourage the respondent to be frank with you and indicate that an honest response won't offend you.

  These "likes and dislikes" questions are usually open-ended; they have no set of precoded responses for the interviewer to check off. However, if you can conjecture about likely answers, you can save a lot of interviewing (and data processing) time by writing the probable answers into the questionnaire. But be sure to leave plenty of space for responses in the "other—please specify" category.

- *Explore secondary issues.* At this point, if you have space or time, you may want to probe more deeply to elicit responses about your primary issues or to ask about secondary ones. Secondary issues are usually those that ended up taking a backseat when you finally came up with the study's objectives. For example, you may have decided that the study would primarily address product changes; pricing and packaging were also important, but less so for this study.

- *Record demographics, personal characteristics.* You can conclude the survey with questions that people are more comfortable and familiar with, such as those about demographics or personal characteristics. For example: "Do you own a home or rent? Do you have children? If so, how many and what ages? What is your job title, industry, and the size of your company? What is your age, education level, income?" Be aware that questions about income can put off many people. You may opt not to ask about it, or you can ask for an income range, as in "Is your income $10,000 to $20,000? $20,000 to $30,000?" and so forth.

To close, you may want to ask if the respondent wishes to say anything more about the XYZ product or the company that makes it. And always end the survey, whether by phone or mail, with a polite "Thank you very much for your time."

CHOOSING THE RIGHT STYLE OF QUESTION

There are several styles of questions to choose from. Whichever you use should be dictated by your needs. If you want to know "why" or "what," you should ask open-ended questions that allow for unstructured answers. If you want to know "how many," ask closed-end questions that restrict the respondent to a list of possible answers.

Surveys with mostly closed-end questions are much faster for a respondent to complete and are much less expensive; they reduce interviewing time and data-processing efforts. The more closed-end questions you ask and the more specific they are, the quicker and cheaper the survey process. However, you should always allow time/space for an "other" category. Many people will have answers outside of those you've provided, so if you give them an opportunity to specify "other," it makes them feel better about the survey— and you get better information as well.

When and How to Use Scales

Most questions require more than a simple yes or no response. When you want respondents to rate or compare things or answer how much, how often, and so forth, a good way to structure those answers is to use a scale or ranking. Devise one, and ask the respondents to choose the option that suits them. For example, if you ask how often someone uses a product, potential rankings might include never, not very much, sometimes, a lot, once a day, twice a day, twice a week, rarely, often, three hours a day, three hours a week, and so forth. To get usable and understandable data, devise a scale that is realistic, that means something to a marketing manager, and that doesn't allow ambiguous answers.

If you want to rate and compare things, a 1-to-10 scale can be useful. Usually, a ranking of 1 means poor and 10 means excellent. This makes it easy to compare average scores. Be careful, though. Be sure to look at how the answers are distributed over the scale; you may get an average of 5, but if you don't examine the distribution, you won't know that half the people rated the item a 1 and half gave it a 10.

"WHO SPONSORED THIS STUDY?"

Whether to identify the survey's sponsor is a real judgment call. It's usually better to leave the sponsor's name out of the process. That way, any biases people have toward the sponsor will not be reflected in the results. However, if you are investigating a specific product or trying to gauge the perception of a company's image, it may be best to reveal the sponsor. That's OK, as long as you screen respondents to make sure they aren't working for a competitor or a competitor's advertising or PR agency.

Often you can ask several questions up front before having to reveal the sponsor. However, sometimes it's helpful to reveal the sponsor at the start so that the respondent perceives that the survey is legitimate (this is often the case with business people or in very product-specific surveys). Sometimes it is possible to complete a questionnaire without revealing the sponsor. In such cases, if you haven't given out any confidential product information during the survey, you may want to give the company a little PR boost and close by telling the respondent that "This was sponsored by the XYZ company; they appreciate your time and thoughtfulness. Do you have anything else you'd like to say to them before we conclude?"

PILOT TEST THE QUESTIONNAIRE

Before you do the survey on a large scale, it's always a good idea to test a questionnaire to make sure that the questions flow well and that respondents clearly understand what you are asking. A good pilot involves going through all the actual steps—using a much smaller sample—that you would take if you were doing the full-blown survey. Then you can check with the interviewers and respondents to see if there was any confusion or to identify places in which the flow was rough. With phone surveys, it's a good idea to listen in on at least a couple of interviews. A shortcut pilot mail survey involves administering it to some people in your office or their spouses and getting their feedback.

So ask the right people the right questions and you will get the right kinds of answers—those you can act on. By avoiding the "garbage out" syndrome, you'll save time and money and will be more likely to start your decision-making process on the right foot.

CHAPTER SEVEN

The Practice of Customer Focus

THE IMPORTANCE OF DRIVING BUSINESS DECISIONS WITH CUSTOMER AND MARKET DATA

By Linda Itskovitz, Intuit

Linda Itskovitz is a Quicken product manager for Intuit, a personal finance-management software company based in Menlo Park, California.

"IF you think your customers are bothersome, just try doing without them for 30 days." I'm not sure who said it or if those were the exact words, but that's what stuck with me. Without customers, we're nothing. That's easy to say, but the difficult part is to put your money where your mouth is.

To be truly customer-focused, you must believe that the most important element in being successful is doing right by the customer. You can never be satisfied with doing 99 percent of the job; instead, you have to give the customer 110 percent. That means spending the time, money, and other resources to find out what "doing right by the customer" means *to your customers* and then putting it into practice.

Generally speaking, it means (a) learning who your customers are, (b) learning what they need and like and why they buy, (c) understanding what satisfies them, (d) testing your premises, and (e) applying the results to your products and services. Although these steps may seem obvious, it does take a certain mind-set, focus, and infrastructure to put those principles into practice. In addition to having a product customers need and like, there are four other things that help keep us customer-focused.

- *Being market-driven.* This means that the development of products is driven primarily by what the market demands, not just by the desire to implement the newest, hottest technology. Development- and technology-driven companies certainly can be successful and can have a strong customer focus; but being market-driven gives you an edge, because you don't have to shoot in the dark—that is, your products and marketing programs are driven by market research. Our development labs create products based directly on the customer/market research we do.

In this respect, high-tech companies can learn from some of the more traditional consumer products companies. I feel that Intuit is unique in the industry, because it has a heavy consumer products orientation and approach. Several Intuit executives and marketing people have backgrounds in consumer products, marketing everything from hair spray to kitty litter. They have a lot of experience in market research, expertise in tracking the results of their programs, and a knowledge of sophisticated merchandising techniques. They also tend to have a strong dedication to their customers and are experienced at communicating a product's benefits to them.

- *Basing decisions on data.* An important factor in developing a customer focus is having a philosophy about how to make product and marketing decisions. One way is to base them solely on subjective judgments, which often isn't the wisest choice. On the other side of the coin, decisions can be based purely on data.

  Basing decisions on data is the cornerstone of Intuit's corporate decision-making process. Although we recognize that not all decisions can be made this way, our goal is to reduce the gap between those based purely on judgment and those made with the available data. We're trying to assure that the controlling factors guiding us are customer and market information. Therefore, it is important to gather as much data as possible so that we have a sound, complete foundation on which to base decisions. We not only use the more traditional sources of market intelligence, but we also go to great lengths to get direct input from our customers.

- *Putting decision making into the right hands.* We think that it's necessary to empower those who are closest to the marketing and customer data to make major product and business decisions. In our organization, the product managers are closest to the data and the customers, so they make many of these decisions.

  Intuit views product managers as business managers. (This concept is based on a model successfully employed by some Japanese car manufacturers and other consumer-products companies.) Our product managers are charged with defining product needs, shepherding the research and development team, and generally galvanizing the company. Their goals: to elevate products to a dominant market-share position, to increase the size of the market and market penetration, and to do all this at a reasonable cost. They have the leverage and the resources—and the motivation—to do what needs to be done to meet these goals.

  Although everyone in the company is charged with being focused on the customer (and everyone makes a significant contribution to customer satisfaction), the people who are closest to the big picture are the product managers—and they make the decisions that have the most influence on the product and our customers.

- *Making sure that the customer focus permeates the entire company.* Our philosophy is that customer satisfaction is the charge of every employee, no matter what they do in the company. This means that everyone must learn what our definition of customer satisfaction is and what it means specifically to their respective jobs. One good way to do that is to put every employee in direct contact with customers. To do so, we've instituted a telephone contact program (see "Reach Out and Touch Them," in the next section), in which every employee has ample opportunity to speak directly to users.

PUTTING THE PHILOSOPHY INTO PRACTICE

Intuit has implemented several programs to get input from customers and, at the same time, communicate to them how important their input is. Here are just two of our programs.

Reach Out and Touch Them

Our telephone contact program is a critical element in our customer-focus efforts. Everyone in the company, including the CEO, is required to spend time each month talking with customers on the phone. (Imagine the surprise of the customers who find out that they're having their concerns addressed directly by the firm's CEO!) This program is so important that we've instituted a formal process to make sure that everyone participates regularly. We take this process very seriously, to the point of making those who miss a month do double the time the next month.

The telephone contact program has been in practice since the company was founded. It started when the company was very small; because the organization had only a few employees, each person had to get involved in many activities just to get the product out the door—from product box packing, to answering phones, to doing telephone product support. Now this practice serves as a constant "real life" reminder of why the company exists, and it keeps us focused on customers. Because it is a key priority in everyone's job, all employees come to understand just how important our customers are.

Follow Me Home

Our Follow Me Home program is particularly useful. As the name implies, we visit new customers' homes (with their permission, of course) and watch their first experience with our products.

We ask stores that sell our products to give us the names of customers who are willing to participate. Then everyone on the product team visits customers' homes and literally watches over the customers' shoulders as they install and use our product. We ask the customers to talk us through what they are doing and what they are thinking as they work with the application. We take notes and assess the situation: What do customers have problems with? What features seem to be easy or difficult to understand? Our main goal is to study the product in users' environments. (This process takes time; we have spent as many as five hours in a customer's home.)

One thing is sure: We learn a lot each time we make a visit. Some of the valuable lessons we've learned include the following things.

- *Users don't always read what's on the screen.* For example, we thought that it would be helpful to put a message at the bottom of the screen that prompts the user about what to do next; but by watching and listening as customers used the product, we saw that they often didn't notice the prompt. The lesson learned: You can't just throw something onto the screen and expect users to see it.

- *Consistent grammatical structure is a must.* For instance, the main menu of the DOS version of Quicken used to read:

> Register
> Write/Print Checks
> Create Reports
> Select Accounts.

   The items on the menu were not grammatically consistent, so many customers thought that "Register" meant "register the software" instead of "use register," which was what we had in mind. Therefore, we changed the menu to read "Use register."

- *Users don't look at all the menu options before they begin using a program.* One assumption we had made was that before using an application, users would look through the various menu options to see what the program could do. None of the customers we observed did this. They just started using the product right after they installed it.

Customers have been very receptive to participating in the program. From their point of view, our desire to get their input demonstrates that we truly care, that we are interested in their problems and needs, and that we value their comments.

THE FUTURE CHALLENGE

Intuit continues to grow, which we feel is a reflection of our concern for customer satisfaction. However, our growth also creates a challenge: how to keep a very strong customer focus as we broaden our product line and as our organization becomes larger and larger. (We now have hundreds of employees.) When the company was smaller, it was easier for everyone to stay abreast of what was happening in the entire company and of all its products. Now, the sheer size of the company and the complexity of managing multiple products on multiple platforms makes it harder for individuals to know much beyond the scope of their own jobs. We'll need to continue putting the internal programs and resources in place to make sure all employees stay close to customers and to ensure that our customer philosophy continues to permeate the entire company.

Also, while we have been changing, our customers are also doing so. The ongoing challenge will be to keep our finger on the pulse of our customer group and make sure that the pieces are in place to give them our all—and keep them 110 percent satisfied.

CHAPTER EIGHT

Understanding the Competition

HOW TO DISTINGUISH WHO YOU'RE REALLY UP AGAINST

By Frank Catalano, Catalano Consulting

Frank Catalano is the principal of Catalano Consulting, a market intelligence and marketing firm based in Sumner, Washington, and specializing in new software products and interactive technologies.

"**K**NOW your enemy." For centuries it's been a basic rule of the battlefield. Get into the opponent's mind, learn what makes him tick, and then you'll know his vulnerabilities. The same holds true in product marketing. Unfortunately, the personal computing battlefield is teeming with armies that don't always identify themselves with colorful banners. You have to use everything at your disposal to ferret them out and understand how they might capture your customers' hearts, minds, and money.

Competitive analysis is a crucial precursor to a marketing plan. It helps you position a product, choose channels, tweak feature sets, set pricing, and even decide if your product is truly viable. With a good understanding of the competition, you enter the market knowing who you're likely to encounter and which opponents you'll want to engage. But how do you begin the process of identifying competitors, especially if you're a small company with limited resources? Here are a few things I've learned about it over the years.

VIEW COMPETITORS THROUGH CUSTOMERS' EYES

When evaluating the competition, point of view is everything. You must step outside your own box and do some "outside in" thinking: Pretend you don't know *anything* about your company's development plans, marketing strategies, or importance to industry insiders. You should look at yourself as do your competitors and the industry overall.

But more important, you must view yourself as a mainstream customer would: as the provider of yet another tool for getting a job done or for filling some particular need. In general, mainstream users don't care if the application's core engine is a technological wonder; they're not the early adopters, the enthusiasts who thrive on getting (and understanding) the latest and greatest technology. Instead, mainstream users just want to be sure your product will fill their needs with a minimum of disruption, frustration, and headaches.

One of the most prevalent mistakes we all make at one time or another is ignoring how the competition looks *from the vantage point of customers.* They certainly view things differently than do the developers they buy from. Customers have a less segmented view of the personal computer business than industry insiders do. They don't always know or care about the finer points of product category differentiation (such as the distinction between high-end word processors and low-end desktop publishing packages). So your competition as defined by a customer could be anything from other Macintosh applications to a Nintendo cartridge to a pen-and-pencil set.

Instead of viewing competition by categories, customers tend to look at products as being a *continuum of possible solutions to a problem.* For example, if there's a rip in a chair's upholstery, the owner is likely to look for any possible way to fix it, considering everything from duct tape to a sewing needle to hiring an upholstery service. A customer in this situation doesn't necessarily (or consciously) look for a solution only within a particular product category, such as "adhesives" or "pointed metal objects." The point is that sewing needle manufacturers don't necessarily view makers of duct tape as competitors. But in this situation they do compete, even though the customer doesn't consciously distinguish between the two product categories. In fact, what might appear, to a vendor, to be a strange solution to a problem may be an entirely feasible solution in the customer's mind.

This is also true of mainstream personal computing customers. For instance, if users need to manage their household budgets, don't assume they will automatically turn to personal financial-management software. They may instead turn to spreadsheets (which, after all, are a logical choice for working with numbers) or electronic bill-paying services (if the services include monthly reports detailing where the money was spent).

Furthermore, how customers perceive product categories is likely to become even more blurred as personal digital assistants (PDAs) and other "hybrid" computing options broaden the number of possible solutions to a problem. As the range of choices increases, users begin to view your competition in ways that may not be obvious to you. Being aware of users' views of competition is an excellent first step in understanding the enemy.

Getting inside a customer's head is the next step. Try to define the problem as a customer would, and ask yourself the kinds of questions a user might ask in the search for a computing solution. Use your imagination. Write a description of your target customer: age, gender, education, income, computer sophistication (don't overestimate)—the works. Grab a magazine and clip out a photo of your "typical" target customer if that helps you visualize him or her. Then, as if you were the customer, ask yourself: What problem am I trying to solve? What do I hope to accomplish? Where would I seek advice to solve this problem? Is this something I really need or could I do without it? How much is the solution worth to me? Where would I buy it? If I can't find exactly what I want, what's my backup plan for solving the problem? How long or hard am I willing to look?

The answers to questions like these will help you understand, from the mainstream customer's point of view, who your competitors are and where they may lie in ambush.

TYPES OF COMPETITION

As you can see, competition comes from a variety of sources. And how customers view it can vary by the target group they belong to, the channels they buy from, or a plethora of other vantage points. You can divide the information into an almost unending group of competitive "sets" for your product. And as absurd as some competitive sets may seem, they are very real to customers.

However, there are some basic ways to distinguish the kinds of competition you're up against. Most broadly speaking, you can divide it into these categories: self-competition, direct competition, indirect competition, multiplatform competition, and "old-fashioned" competition. (While this categorization may appear to be based on common sense, don't underestimate its value—it's "common" precisely because it's been successfully used most often.)

Competing Against Yourself

As more software products enter the market, developers must try harder to maintain market share and shelf space. In crowded product categories, it's particularly difficult to maintain, much less gain, market share. The problem is exacerbated by fierce competition for limited retailer shelf space. Therefore, the tactics you use to get a leg up on the competition often end up making you compete with yourself.

There are several forms of self-competition. They're not necessarily bad, if executed properly and with a clear understanding of the risks and benefits. For example, cut-rate, direct-mail bundling deals with other developers can help you build market share—but not if the offer hits customers at the same time a reseller does a major push for the identical product, at a higher price. It could cost you a reseller relationship and impede long-term product growth.

You also compete with yourself when you market multiple products whose capabilities overlap. Imagine that you offer two drawing packages that are used for different purposes but have some key features in common. If you fail to significantly differentiate the two products by benefits or price, the customer may refrain from buying either package to avoid making the "wrong" choice from your product line. You lose that sale to a competitor whose choices are more clear-cut.

Offering customers an upgrade of an existing package is also self-competition. Almost every developer issues upgrades, but some don't recognize this as being self-competition. It is. You compete with yourself, for example, if you announce an upgrade more than a month or two in advance; an early announcement defers, and may cause you ultimately to lose, sales to customers who will want to "wait and see" what the upgrade has to offer.

Ditto for competitive upgrades, those pseudo-upgrades offered to a competitor's customers at a reduced price. In an uncrowded product category or in one with street prices that are already low, competitive upgrades can be suicide. More often than not, they result in a short-term return: You usually don't end up with additional market share, and you set new expectations for a lower price point in customers' minds. In addition, cut-rate competitive upgrades can reduce your profitability. Keeping a previous version on the market (with less-advanced features at a lower price) after you've introduced an upgrade can also create self-competition. The older version can "steal" sales from your upgrade if the new version's features aren't seen as being a significant improvement.

So don't overlook self-competition as you piece together your competitive picture. There are pros and cons to all its forms, and you should evaluate this kind of competition as seriously as you do competition from external sources.

Direct Competition

This is the most obvious competitive set. For example, if you offer a database, makers of other databases (sometimes for other platforms, if your customers are in a networked, multivendor environment) are direct competitors. However, it's not only current databases that compete; it's also the new or improved ones that will be on the market in the next 12 to 18 months. Keep in mind that if you do competitive research at the beginning of the development cycle, on the average your product will ship up to 18 months after you've done the analysis. Therefore, it's important to anticipate competitors' future releases and feature sets, because that's what is likely to be on the market when your product ships. Also, don't overlook shareware and freeware in your product category. Those products are also direct competitors than can eat away at your market share.

Indirect Competition

Because you may have to compete with products that aren't necessarily in your product category, it's important to develop your peripheral vision. For instance, if you're creating a specialized product, find out whether target customers are using a more general-purpose package to get the same job done. Ask yourself what would compel them to switch to your product, especially if you haven't provided a price or overwhelming feature incentive. For example, even if you could develop mailing-list management software that uses Apple Events and QuickTime, would users want to ditch their general-purpose flat-file databases?

Multiplatform Competition

Avoid having tunnel vision about your platform. As I mentioned earlier, your competition may not be only other *Macintosh* products. With the proliferation of multivendor environments and more developers creating products for multiple platforms, you may well compete with a product that runs on another kind of computer. Also, be aware that first-time computer buyers may not have decided what platform to buy, let alone which software product. Make sure you've assessed the direct and indirect competitors in the Windows and OS/2 markets. Consider also that your high-end product for a vertical market may cost as much as the hardware it runs on. Customers might just be willing to switch platforms if their choice of software doesn't run on and costs more than the platform they currently use.

The "Old-Fashioned Way"

Not everyone wants to use a personal computer for every task. Just because it's possible to put recipes on a Macintosh doesn't mean there's a burning need for replacing index cards and refrigerator magnets. The same goes for creating, for example, a program that can electronically mimic Post-It notes.

Sometimes the manual, low-tech method is perceived as the best way to get a job done. It'll be difficult to make customers switch unless you can sway them with an overwhelming benefit of using the Macintosh for the task. The key word here is "overwhelming." Offering an alternate way to perform a task that is only incrementally better probably won't overcome people's natural resistance to changing how they do things. Therefore, the "old-fashioned way" is sometimes a competitor.

INFORMATION SOURCES FOR THE BUDGET CONSCIOUS

Once you know what (or who) to look for, your challenge becomes gathering the necessary competitive information. There are lots of ways to get competitive data, and some companies spend hundreds of thousands of dollars (or more) on original research and analysis. Original research, although precise if designed correctly, is pricey. However, in many cases you don't need to hire a consultant or a market research firm to do some solid grass-roots qualitative research, and such research doesn't have to be expensive. For general competitive information, secondary or "informal" sources will take you a long way and will cost you far less than original research. The greater the variety and perspective of your research sources, the more likely your resulting marketing decisions will be on target.

A lot of what follows is common sense. However, you'd be amazed at how many people discount the valuable insights that could be obtained from some of these sources if they knew what they were looking for. Here's a sampling of sources that have served me particularly well.

- *Trade and consumer magazines.* The most obvious source of competitive information is weekly trade publications (*MacWEEK, InfoWorld, PCWEEK*) and the monthly computer consumer magazines (*Macworld, MacUser*). However, there's also valuable information to be found in the channel-oriented publications such as *Computer Reseller News* and *Computer Retail Week*. Most magazines publish quarterly or annual indexes, which also may be accessed through an on-line service such as Ziff-Davis's ZiffNet, available through CompuServe.

  From the scope and tenor of press coverage and product reviews, you'll get a good idea of how the media perceives your competitors. You can also get a good idea about competitors' advertising strategies from what their ads say. Are they focused on price? Availability? Features? Benefits? Are they spending a lot of money on ads? Buying a lot of ad space? Scrutinizing these issues will give you some interesting insights into competitors' marketing budgets, how they spend them, and whether this is an arena in which you can (or care to) compete.

- *On-line research.* A wealth of information is available from the commercial on-line services. For example, CompuServe has Ziff-Davis's Computer Directory and Computer Database Plus. These two databases allow you to search for products by category, title, developer, price point, or a variety of other methods. Computer Directory contains listings of more than 75,000 products; Computer Database Plus has abstracts and full-text articles from more than 130 computer industry publications. Ziff-Davis also makes the two services (combined as the Computer Library) available on CD-ROM. Other database services on CompuServe are available through the IQuest gateway. You can also access a similar product service, the *Redgate Macintosh Registry,* in the Third Parties folder on the AppleLink network.

To keep costs down, know what you're seeking before starting a search. IQuest, Computer Library, and other database services on CompuServe assess charges in addition to standard CompuServe connection rates. But if you know what you want, searches can be relatively inexpensive.

If you want to stay abreast of competitive developments as they occur, CompuServe's Executive News Service allows you to create up to three electronic clipping folders that automatically collect and store news stories from a variety of sources based on keywords (your competitors' names, for example). Another option is to simply scan a competing developer's on-line forum, special interest group, or icon on AppleLink, CompuServe, America Online, GEnie, or Delphi (politely, of course). This will give you an idea of how users feel about competitors' products. Also, hardware-specific discussion areas have libraries in which you can find shareware or freeware competitors.

- *Customers.* There's valuable information waiting in the stack of registration cards your customers return. Use it as effectively as possible. For example, pick a random group of customers and call each one; ask for their feelings about your company, product line, and competition. This won't yield quantitative information, but it's a great way to take the pulse of customers who feel strongly enough about your product to register it.

  Similarly, sit in on local user group meetings. Find out what products they're excited about. You'll get an idea of what kinds of features and benefits are "hot" in the user's mind, and you may also make valuable customer contacts.

- *Resellers.* It's surprising how many developers make marketing decisions without walking into a software store. Visit the front lines. Be a customer. Go into a store and ask the sales person what he or she would recommend for a particular use, and why. You'll gain insight into your competition and your own products, and you'll learn which key benefits are important to the sales people who recommend the products.

- *Industry associations and trade shows.* Finally, make sure that you get your money's worth from any industry association or trade show. Use them to gather literature from competitors. Listen to competitors' booth pitches, and pay close attention to what booth visitors ask them (don't be obvious, of course). Again, be a customer; ask about current and future product development and who they see as being their competition and customers. Touch base with trade associations such as the Software Publishers Association, and ask if they have published or know of any secondary research reports of interest to you.

How effectively and cleverly you use competitive information is as important as the information itself. But understanding the competition is the first step. It's one of the best weapons you can have in your arsenal: It gives you a target to shoot at, a basis for comparison, and a way to learn from others' mistakes. It can keep you from developing a product that doesn't meet market needs or that will be an "also-ran" pitted against a well-entrenched competitor.

Understanding the enemy won't win the battle by itself, but it will provide a secure staging area from which to launch your strategy, tactics—and ultimate victory.

PART FOUR

Communicating with the Market

Someone once said that in this business it's not enough to be *understood*; you must communicate with the market—with customers, the press, and other industry influencers—in ways that prevent your being *misunderstood*.

In doing so, point of view is everything. Chapter 9, "If We're So Smart, How Come We're So Dumb?: Positioning Your Message Using the Buyer's Perspective—Instead of Your Own," discusses a process for developing your perspective that applies to all our communications activities and perhaps even all of our marketing activities: how to step outside of *ourselves* and approach customers with messages that are understandable and meaningful to *them*—not just us.

In that same spirit: Have you ever been passed over by a product reviews editor or, maybe even worse, received bad or unfair reviews? Or are you just starting to solicit your first reviews and meet with industry opinion leaders? Chapters 10 and 11, "Influencing Opinion Leaders: How to Get High Impact for Low Investment" and "Getting the Maximum from Product Reviews: A Practical Guide for Creating a Reviews Campaign," seek to dispel some of the misconceptions you may have about capturing the attention of industry opinion leaders and what it takes to get the quantity and quality of reviews you want. They also describe how to create and execute reviews and opinion leaders campaigns.

If you've ever had to speak at a conference, seminar, banquet, or any other kind of business meeting, you won't want to miss Chapter 12, "Finding Your Voice: A Public Speaking Primer for Developers." Even if you've not consciously thought so, you yourself are a public relations vehicle. That chapter is packed with pointers about what to say at almost any kind of business occasion, as well as tips on how to avoid putting your foot in your mouth.

And depending on how you approach naming, Chapter 13, "How to Choose the Right Name for a High-Tech Product," would fit in a variety of places in the book. Some companies make naming the development or product management team's responsibility. Others consider product naming a marketing communications function. Regardless, a product's name is probably the first attribute of your product and your communications efforts that customers encounter. So, after due consideration, that chapter has landed here.

Other chapters focus on guidelines for creating packaging that will motivate customers to buy your products; how to get started in direct mail; the secrets to getting maximum sales from direct response advertising; how to evaluate agencies in your search for just the right one; and how to create demos that will help sell your product when you can't be at the customer's (or retailer's) side.

CHAPTER NINE

If We're So Smart, How Come We're So Dumb?

POSITIONING YOUR MESSAGE USING THE BUYER'S PERSPECTIVE—INSTEAD OF YOUR OWN

By Geoff Moore, Geoffrey Moore Consulting

Geoffrey A. Moore, a former partner at Regis McKenna, Inc., is the president of Geoffrey Moore Consulting, a firm based in Palo Alto, California, that provides consulting and education services to high-technology companies. He also is the author of *Crossing the Chasm: Marketing and Selling Technology Products to Mainstream Customers.*

I recently read "The Ten Commandments of Product Packaging: How to Create Packages that Sell," by Signe Ostby of Merrin Information Services [*Editor's note: See Chapter 14, "The Ten Commandments of Product Packaging: How to Create Packages that Sell."*] Each of Signe's commandments is, well, common sense (sort of like the original ten, come to think of it). The problem is, we often don't obey them (sort of like the original ten, come to think of it). Why not?

For example, let's take Signe's opening premise, as clear a piece of common sense as you would ever want to hear:

"The package's primary purpose is to sell the product inside it."

This statement is so obvious—particularly to people as smart as we are—that it wouldn't be worth making, except for the fact that so many packages simply *don't* sell the products inside them. If we're so smart, how come we're so dumb?

SPEAKER- VS. AUDIENCE-CENTERED COMMUNICATIONS

To understand this, consider that all "speech-acts," as some linguists like to call them, can be placed on a continuum between speaker and audience, depending on whose needs they are most focused on fulfilling. A very audience-centered message might be "Watch out!"—especially if audience members were standing under a falling rock, for example.

But what if the audience was deaf, and the speaker knew this fact yet still yelled, "Watch out!" Now what's going on? The speaker's speech-act is now a form of self-expression, a release of stress, if you will, something he or she just "had to do" even though the verbal warning could not communicate to the audience. The same thing goes for yelling "Ow!" when you stub your toe, whether or not anyone is in the room. Or singing in the shower. Or doodling in a meeting. These are all speaker-centered forms of communication.

These are the extremes of the speaker-audience continuum. As we move more toward the middle, the question becomes more problematic. If I write a software application and then tell you, "This is a really cool program," whose needs am I serving? Clearly mine, for starters—I can't wait to tell you, in fact; I'm just bursting with self-expression. But, if it *really is* a cool program, then I'm also serving your needs by letting you know that.

Now that works fine if we're friends. But what if you don't know me? How much leeway do I have for "self-expression"? How much do you want to hear from me? According to the research, you don't want to hear very much— indeed, you want to hear far less than I want to tell. And that's the problem we face in formulating the communications vehicles that carry our positioning messages to prospective buyers.

We know that we're supposed to be audience-centered, but when you look at our output, you see that all too often we've been unable to overcome the speaker-centered pressures that act upon us. To paraphrase the title of a popular self-help book, *Our Packages, Our Selves.* (This is actually but one title in a series, others of which include *Our Logos, Our Selves; Our Advertisements, Our Selves;* and the most popular of all, *Our Product Names, Our Selves.*) Unfortunately, "our selves" don't sell. Selling is about the buyer, not the seller. It is the buyer's self that sells, not ours. We need to resonate with the buyer's self, but we can't until we banish our own. So, to be painfully clear about this, it is not *our* package, or logo, or advertisement, or product name—it is *theirs.* And the issue is not whether *we* like it, but whether *they* like it.

Before the end of this chapter, I'll suggest some practical procedures for integrating this insight into your everyday communication efforts; but before I do that, we need to fully explore the dangers that surround you.

BEWARE THE DESIGNER

First of all, it isn't just you that has the speaker-centered problem. It's all of us. Take an ad designer, for example—author of *My Design, My Self,* subtitled with an appropriate Shakespearean echo: "A CLIO! A CLIO! My client for a CLIO!" (A CLIO is a prestigous television advertising award.)

Designers have agendas just as we do. I witnessed a public manifestation of this syndrome recently at an industry conference, during a panel on package design. A principal of a highly respected design firm was reviewing packages (in pairs) and pointing out the virtues of one versus the defects of the other. A slide flashed on, depicting a quite presentable box on the left, whose product name I don't remember (that, by the way, is what detectives call a *clue*), and on the right was the ever-memorable, phenomenally schlocky package for My Personal MailList (MPL).

For those of you who are so Mac-centered that you have never seen this box at, say, the check-out stand of your local superstore, the front panel portrays a prettyish, thirtyish '50s-style woman (Betty Crocker hairdo, June Cleaver facial structure), hands to her face in a golly-gee-whiz expression of astonishment as hundreds of letters rush out of her keyboard (which has been transformed into a mailbox) and into the postal system. Straight out of *Popular Mechanics* thirty-odd years ago.

The speaker was quite rightly praising the aesthetics of the box on the left and bemoaning the same for the MPL package, when someone from the audience had the temerity to note that MPL was outpulling the other product in the marketplace at a ratio of about 100 to 1—to which the response from the podium was: *Click. Next slide.* I believe this is what psychologists call *denial.*

The point is, since the MPL package violated even the simplest rules of aesthetics—and trust me, there's no doubt that it does—it violated the speaker's (a designer) value system, and thus *it could not possibly be good design.* The problem, of course, is that buyers didn't agree. They didn't have the "right" value system—so they ate it up. (Peasants!) In any event, this designer simply would not have it. No design like that would ever come out of *her* shop; it would ruin her reputation.

And the truth is, it might. But the problem is, this kind of design is what the audience in this particular market segment preferred. And if we're going to ask ourselves not to be speaker-centered in communications, we must be able to hold our design agencies to a similar standard (and not flog them when they deliver on it).

Now we need to bring another component of the communications problem into focus before we can move on to finding solutions.

THE FANTASY/REALITY MODEL

There is a second continuum in the realm of communications that cuts across the speaker-audience axis, and that is the one between fantasy and reality. In communications, this is a critical continuum to manage.

The role of fantasy in marketing is to communicate benefits that stimulate buyers' appetites. Customers expect some level of fantasy experience during the buying process. They want it. It's fun. It's why people browse in stores, even when they don't intend to buy anything. At the same time, customers don't like to be fooled. They know all too much about "buyer's remorse" ("Why did I buy that?"), so they want to be able to do a reality check before they make a purchase. How much reality checking customers need depends on how risky they perceive the purchase to be. In business-to-business sales, the scales tip towards reality. In entertainment products, they tip toward fantasy. The point is that it's the audience's call.

Moreover, the types of fantasy- and reality-based information that go on a package or into an advertisement should likewise be the audience's call. And so now we have the entire "message focus" model (Figure 9-1) to help us see where we go wrong and how we can correct it.

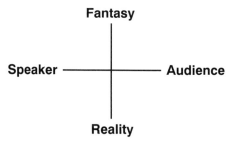

FIGURE 9-1   Message focus

The first principle of the model is that communications should be driven by the right side of the diagram (audience), not by the left (speaker). There are two forces that drag your efforts back toward the left. The first is the need to "self-express," whether it be on the part of the developer, the communicators, or the designer. The second is the desire to use a package, ad, or logo as a status symbol among your peers. Neither of these forces is legitimate, but both have power over you.

The second principle is that you should correctly weight the relationship between fantasy and reality relative to the audience's purposes. In a business-to-business sale, where the audience weight is toward reality, speaker-based fantasies are the worst communications sins. These are most often committed by vice presidents of sales. Being charismatic types, they're accustomed to creating reality distortion fields during sales presentations—and then holding them in place by sheer force of personality. They want that same distortion field to permeate all of product communications.

Print media communications, however, simply don't have the force to pull this sort of thing off. Moreover, in a situation in which the audience has real-world worries, fantasy-based appeals are often resented. Consider, for example, a recent Computer Associates ad showing wild horses splashing along the edge of a lake and captioned "No Fences. No Boundaries. No Limits. That's the Freedom of CA90s." This is an exercise in promoting a speaker-based fantasy that MIS directors aren't likely to share. CA90s are enterprise-wide information systems that require compromises to implement. My feeling is that audience members aren't likely to be attracted to this ad, and some may even resent it. (Just my opinion, of course.)

On the other hand, in the same magazine Sony ran an ad for its optical disks captioned "Write Once. Read Many. Worry Never." This is also a speaker-based fantasy, but it will probably work with the audience for two reasons: There is much less at risk in buying an optical disk than an enterprise-wide system, and Sony has a reputation for quality, probably more than CA does for freedom.

In most instances in business-to-business sales transactions, the vendor's reputation and credibility set the limits on how far the audience is willing to go along with such claims and therefore be charmed by marketing communications fantasy. To put this in perspective, let's turn to a consumer packaged-goods type of transaction, where the audience's expectations of communications pleas are tilted more toward fantasy. Here the worst communications sin is to indulge in speaker-based "realities"; this sin is most often committed by vice presidents of engineering. To avoid this type of error, you can put a fantasy on the front of the product package. However, you can also err simply by putting a *speaker-based fantasy* on the box instead of a *customer-based one*.

For example, recently the makers of the Aladdin game redesigned the package front, and sales shot up 30 percent. What happened? Well, the earlier box showed a movie poster image with Aladdin sweeping a harem maiden into a Rudolph Valentino embrace. The new box shows Aladdin all by himself leaping into the air and performing a kind of stylized Ninja kick. Now, which image do you think would have more appeal for a 9-to-12-year-old boy?

AESTHETICS AND SELLING

Finally, let's return to the matter of aesthetics. The aesthetics of your communications pieces send value signals to an audience. This creates a problem in high-tech marketing communications for several reasons. First, aesthetic values are inherent in all marketing communications, so they are present in all our transactions—regardless of whether we want them. Second, aesthetic values strongly correlate with perceived social status and class distinctions. This makes it very difficult for people, whether they're developers or designers, to opt for using audience-centered aesthetics because they think peers will make personal judgments about them based on their communications pieces.

The thing that was great about the My Personal MailList example was that its creators saw how a schlocky aesthetic could convey an appealing and reassuring marketing message, and they didn't hesitate to use it. The fantasy on the front panel of the package is ludicrous, but for anyone who has to type in mailing lists, it's certainly appealing. And the fact that it's done so schlockily means that the customer is not really expected to take the fantasy seriously.

Furthermore, this style conveys yet another message—cheap (as in inexpensive, not low quality). And that's exactly what MPL is, selling at well under $50 a copy. This cheapness is also reassuring because it implies that the product is not going to do very much (that is, it isn't complicated), and thus won't be too hard to learn or use. And finally, the '50s-style imagery is so old-fashioned that it is reassuring. This is a product, it says, for people who are not crazy about high tech, but who have to use it anyway. All in all, a very effective image.

Another issue relating to aesthetics further complicates the problem. High-tech marketing communications is usually a joint effort between engineers, who often lack an aesthetic sense, and designers, who have an overdeveloped one. These designers tend to believe it is their role to defend aesthetics against the assaults of the Philistine engineers; and designers can become so militant that even when their aesthetics are inappropriate for the product's audience, there is no way they can "hear" this feedback.

Worse, often a product with a package design that makes a great aesthetic statement simply does not sell, but instead sits on the shelf inertly, an impressive icon, but not something that attracts customers. So, for a variety of reasons, the aesthetic statements embedded in our communications are often out of sync with our marketing strategy. Business professionals who sense this are feeling increasingly irate about being held hostage by the value judgments of the designing profession.

THERE MUST BE SOME WAY OUT OF HERE

So, how do we proceed given that, for most of us, this whole business of graphics, packaging, communication, and aesthetics is not a strong suit? Here's my advice, formulated as seven admittedly California-ish beatitudes, in an attempt to add some extra balance to the admonishments of Merrin Information Systems' ten commandments.

#1: Blessed are the well-informed, for they shall not seek to drive to Hawaii. Read Signe's packaging chapter (Chapter 14). Every piece of advice it gives is sound.

#2: Blessed are they who know themselves, for they will not order pizzas for 20, all with anchovies. Before starting work on any communications piece such as packaging, form a clear image of your own personal style and that of any consultants or agency people you are working with. In the case of packaging, the easiest way to do this is to go to a superstore and simply point out to each other packaging that looks good to you. Or for ads, flip through some magazines together. Don't let this become a matter of right versus wrong; in aesthetics there really are no right or wrong answers, only matters of taste and class distinction. Instead, use it as an exercise in understanding each other's tendencies for self-expression.

#3: Blessed are they who are willing to know others, for they shall be able to distinguish windows from mirrors. Build a model of the audience, via a personal profile of an idealized target customer. Make sure this fictional person is clearly differentiated from everyone on the marketing communications team (unless you want to make one member of your team stand in for this person). Focus specifically on differentiating the target customer's values from your own.

#4: Blessed are they who are sensitive to the situation, for they will not throw to second base when there is a runner on third. Characterize the perceived risks and rewards of the buying situation from the target customer's point of view. Determine from this what kind of mixture of fantasy and reality he or she will desire. Capture that as a percentage ratio to be used as a test during communications/package evaluation sessions.

#5: Blessed are they who put things in their proper place, for they will be able to find the flashlight when the power goes out. In the case of packaging, allocate the front panel of a box to fantasy, the back to reality. The idea here is that the front hooks the customer into picking the box up and turning it over, and the back gives them permission to buy. (Like any general rule, this can be violated to good effect, but use it as a starting point and realize that when you do go against it, you are committing a violation.)

#6: Blessed are they who check themselves over carefully, for they shall not leave their credit cards in strange places. Make sure the fantasy is audience-centered and not speaker-centered. If it appeals to you strongly, make sure this is because you really do empathize with your customers and not because you have substituted your fantasy for theirs.

#7: Blessed are they who can walk in another's shoes, for they shall not have to go barefoot on pavement on a hot day. Make sure the reality information on the back

of a package is purchase-decision related. (The same applies to the body copy of your ads or brochures.) If it isn't something your customers need to know to help them buy, don't say it. It will only distract them from the information they do need to get.

If we go forward with these principles in our hearts, it shall come to pass that not only will we continue to be smart, but we will also, maybe for the first time, not be so dumb.

CHAPTER TEN

Influencing Opinion Leaders

HOW TO GET HIGH IMPACT FOR LOW INVESTMENT

By John Pearce, MediaMap

John Pearce is the founder and CEO of MediaMap. MediaMap, located in Cambridge, Massachusetts, provides PR research and automation systems to client companies in the computer industry.

W OULDN'T it be great if you had to sell only a few people to make your company's next product a success, instead of having to convince thousands or even millions of potential buyers that they should invest in your latest and greatest offering?

In very oversimplified terms, that's the idea behind an opinion leaders campaign. It's also why almost all successful computer product companies, big and small, make opinion leaders campaigns an integral part of their PR, product development, and product marketing process.

THE OPINION LEADERS' DOMINO EFFECT

The phenomenon of the "opinion leader" is recent and is largely a result of the special challenges facing buyers of computer products. Computer product buyers have a major problem: They have to decide what to buy in a complex market that sometimes defies their ability to make the best possible choices. The stakes of purchase decisions are often very high, and in many cases company productivity and profitability are on the line. But the technological details and pace of computer-product change leave buyers bewildered.

So what are buyers to do? They turn to sources of authority that they trust. These sources are "opinion leaders," and as I'll discuss later, they include a select group of industry analysts, editors, "gurus," and other experts. If, as a developer, you have the opinion leaders on your side, you have gone a long way toward influencing the decision-making process of your entire market.

Especially in more technical markets, there can be a dramatic domino effect. A few expert opinion leaders evaluate emerging technologies and products. Based on judgments of these experts, the most knowledgeable, active computer buyers tend to turn to a product. The real payoff for you, however, comes when the mainstream of the market makes its decision. And which product does the mainstream buy? Whatever everyone else is buying. In this model, the conclusions of a few experts end up driving the decisions of the leading-edge thousands who, in turn, ultimately shape the purchases of the entire market you are selling to.

There's another reason for making an opinion leaders campaign an integral part of your product's life cycle. In addition to having a direct influence on leading-edge buyers, the opinion leaders themselves represent a microcosm of your market. As such, they are more than just influential people to be convinced; they are also a test bed for your product concepts, your marketing messages, and your market intelligence.

As I'll detail later, even if opinion leaders had no impact on buyers at all, this golden opportunity to adjust your strategies before setting your company on a specific marketing or development path would be reason enough to build an opinion leaders campaign into your strategy.

The rest of this chapter examines the concept of an opinion leaders campaign. Because there are so few leaders for a given market segment—usually 10 to 40—the task of building these personal relationships and effectively initiating two-way communication is relatively manageable. When done right and as an ongoing part of your product development and marketing strategy, these campaigns can yield a high impact for a low investment.

WHO ARE THE OPINION LEADERS?

Opinion leaders vary with each market. In general, they include industry analysts, newsletter writers, prominent members of professional associations, leaders of market-focused special interest computer user groups, and editors who are prominent authorities in a market. In short, they are the sources of expertise to which your leading-edge buyers turn. They are also the sources of expertise to which the media turn: You can hardly read a *Wall Street Journal* or computer magazine story without seeing quotes from an industry analyst passing judgment on the moves of the company in question. For an idea of the diversity of these firms and how their focus differs, let's look briefly at three examples (of course, there are also many others).

Dataquest is a large research firm that tracks product developments in nearly every computer industry market segment. The company is built around industry service groups that cover 30 areas of technology, including semiconductors, systems and applications, telecommunications, peripherals, service and support, and more. Within each major group are as many as eight or ten subareas, with scores of analysts who are busy scrutinizing almost every part of the computer and electronics industry.

An example of a much smaller opinion-leading entity is *Soft•Letter,* a newsletter read by many leading software industry executives. Founder Jeffrey Tarter is an experienced, well-respected commentator on the software industry. Unlike Dataquest, Tarter isn't covering every development in every market segment; rather, he's looking for the innovation that indicates a new trend or the marketing strategy that is taking the industry by surprise. Very selectively, he writes about companies and the big-picture trends he feels will move the entire software industry.

Another kind of organization is Seybold Publications, a long-time opinion leader in a specialized market: electronic publishing. Seybold does a variety of things, ranging from publishing newsletters such as the *Report on Desktop Publishing* to putting on its industry-defining conferences.

WHEN TO START YOUR CAMPAIGN

Your opinion leaders campaign should be an ongoing part of company operations. It begins when your product is in gestation, not when it is born. Several months before you introduce a product, you should be developing relationships with key opinion leaders. After all, the very point of your opinion leaders campaign is to shape the market response to your company and product *before* your announcement, *before* you commit marketing resources, and *before* you're on a development track you can't alter.

Step 1: Target the Right People and Research Each One

Your essential first task is to create a list of targets, the 10 to 40 individuals who you conclude are the leaders of thinking, evaluation, and expertise for your market. By keeping your target group small, you can afford to offer the required personal attention to each one without making a big investment.

Targeting is easier said than done. Even choosing the right analyst at one organization can be a challenge. A company such as Dataquest has scores of analysts, only a few of whom should be on your list. The problem is exacerbated by how quickly staff members change roles in such organizations. For example, in the fourth quarter of 1991, our research revealed the following fact about a major research firm: Of the 20 most senior staff, 4 members were new to the company, and another 10 had significantly changed job responsibilities—all in a single 13-week period!

Once you've assembled your list, it's time to analyze the analysts. You must learn enough about them to conduct a personalized communication campaign with each one. As the above profiles of *Soft•Letter,* Seybold Publications, and

Dataquest should make clear, if you approach each without knowing what they're after, you may as well not pick up the phone. The job of selecting the key opinion leaders and then understanding them adequately is a task you can undertake yourself by calling the organizations and researching them. However, there are resources available to you (such as MediaMap) who constantly track and organize this information.

Step 2: Decide What to Say and Tailor Your Message

After you've chosen your targets, define your messages for them and prepare materials that convey those messages effectively. This doesn't mean writing press releases. It means tailoring the content of your communication to each person on your list.

The best way to influence opinion leaders is to find a way to help them do their jobs; you'll be successful if you make them successful. Remember, some research firms put on conferences; others publish newsletters and magazines. Most view their success in terms of whether they can anticipate market trends. They'll be more receptive if you can offer them advance knowledge or unique thinking about a particular market. If they plan conferences, your great idea for a conference topic or a speaker may well get their attention. If they thrive on being quoted in the press, advance briefings on your product plans and inside market data may be just what they're looking for.

In any case, never just send them a press release, alone. A press release, by definition, is a standardized communication to lots of people. An opinion leaders campaign is the opposite: It is an exclusive communication program tailored to the interests of an expert. Opinion leaders don't want to receive the same information the rest of the world is getting. The objective is to give them something that is insightful, exclusive, or unannounced.

Typical materials to prepare for a campaign include the following.

- Your interpretations of market trends: who's hot, who's not, sales data, the plans of major players, and how your plans relate to them.

- Positioning. How you position your product compared with its competition, and your view of the potential of each market segment.

- Beta-test data, including benchmark test results, user experiences, and other information.

- Company background. The crucial differentiating aspects of your firm, its principals, its capabilities (here, brevity is best).

Whatever form these materials take, make sure they don't look like materials for mass distribution.

Step 3: Make Contact

The next step is making contact. You basically have two choices: meeting your opinion leaders in person or working through phone and mail. It's by far more effective to meet them in person. Like anyone else, analysts or other key contacts value personal relationships and, despite efforts at impartiality, will give greater "share of mind" to people they know.

One of the best ways to make personal contact is through a product tour, generally conducted months before your product launch. Product tours may seem expensive; they take time to prepare, and you have to spend a week or so trekking around the country (usually Boston, New York, and Silicon Valley are adequate). But if well executed and conceived, a product tour can be one of the most effective uses of your time and money.

To set up the tour, start with a phone campaign to arrange appointments. Before making the calls, put together a pitch for each person on the list. That's why, as previously noted, your background research on each analyst, editor, or other target contact is so important. Tailor a few key points designed to arouse the individual's interest. For instance, a newsletter writer who covers end-user trends will probably be interested in seeing a demo of the specific technology and hearing unannounced test data and reactions of beta users. These are the key points to make in the pitch call to that person. In short, you need to give analysts and other opinion leaders a clear idea of why they should care about meeting with you. They're busy, and they have seen more than a few product demos in their time.

During this call, you should also set expectations about nondisclosure. Most analysts and other opinion leaders respect nondisclosure agreements; but don't take nondisclosure for granted, especially with editors. Although signed nondisclosure agreements often are unnecessary, make sure you are explicit about the terms under which you are informing your contacts of your unannounced plans. With editors, be explicit about dates until which coverage should be embargoed.

Step 4: Meet the Opinion Leaders

Once your appointments are scheduled, it's time to get your presentations together and hit the road. A good presentation is an art form. It is credible, reasonably entertaining, well paced, and clear. It is short, with a few key points established effectively, followed by an open-ended discussion. Let the opinion leader's questions, reactions, and interests drive a good portion of the meeting.

Here are some tips to help make your tour more successful.

- *Take the right people from your company.* You need people with two kinds of skills on your tour: someone who is a communicator and someone who is technically knowledgeable. They don't always come in the same package. Often your top technologist will be hopeless as a communicator. You'll need both skills at your disposal; if that can be one person, great. Otherwise, splurge: Take them both.

- *Create an opinion leaders database or file.* Before your tour, create a database or file with information on each of your targeted opinion leaders. Your dossier on each person should include all contact data, what clients they serve, what publications they produce or conferences they put on, where you've seen them quoted, their preconceptions about your company that should be addressed, and a few hot buttons and specific objectives for the appointment.

- *Brief your team.* Before each meeting, use your file on each opinion leader to brief all the people on the tour about the analysts or editors they will speak to. The more you know about whom you're talking to, the easier it is to tailor your remarks to their interests and needs.

- *Brief one analyst or organization at a time.* Analysts live by creating unique added value to information in the form of insights and exclusive knowledge, neither of which are available as they sit in a crowded room with their competitors. Let analysts succeed by forming their own perspective and adding their own value to your information. In-person presentations are far more conducive to two-way exchanges, relationship building, and the kind of exclusivity analysts prefer.

- *Make your points concise and clear.* Analysts are very busy, have heard hundreds of developer presentations, and may be predisposed to a rather bored skepticism. After a very brief introduction, focus on the three or four key points of product differentiation or market interpretation that are the most important. Don't use precious time waxing philosophical about the bios of company principals or other extraneous information. Get to the heart of your messages, and leave time for questions and reactions.

- *Demonstrate that you value their input.* Like any of us, opinion leaders want to be taken seriously. If they have concrete reactions, are skeptical, or make suggestions, make a note of what they say. Make it clear that you are listening as well as talking.

- *Debrief and follow up.* After each meeting, debrief your team about what you've learned. The debriefing can be informal, even in the car as you're driving between meetings. Ask yourselves specific questions: Did our messages play well? How should we adjust those messages based on the contacts' input and reactions? What features did they react to particularly well, what features did they react to poorly? How do their marketing interpretations compare with ours? How should we follow up (what information was promised, initiatives suggested, contacts to be made, review copies to be shipped, and the like).

- *Update your opinion leaders database or file.* When your tour is finished, update your files on each contact. This should include their reactions to what you have said, what you have promised them, any issues you need to address with them, and any suggestions they may have made. This data will help you fulfill your commitments, steer media toward sympathetic analysts, and better understand the preconceptions of your target contacts in the future.

- *Take the results back home.* Last but not least, be sure that you convey the conclusions you've reached on your tour to your company's marketing and product-development staffs or departments. This feedback is critical if your organization as a whole is to be fully in touch with the experts whose opinions will have such a bearing on the success of your products. It will also underscore the value of your opinion leaders campaign, establishing the return on this unique marketing investment.

Above all, keep two factors in mind: First, your meeting should be a two-way street. Certainly you want to persuade opinion leaders of the value and importance of your product and convey a sense of authoritative reliability; but you also should listen, as well. Even if an opinion leaders campaign ends up having no impact on sales—which is hardly conceivable—it is a golden opportunity to test your product and marketing message on a microcosm of your market.

If you listen and carefully note what works and what doesn't, your meetings will indicate your strengths and warn you of possible problems. If you're lucky and receptive, the input you get can help you avoid major missteps in marketing message, market interpretation, and product features. And if the tour does result in your redefining product features or marketing messages, you'll have obtained that input at a time when you can actually do something about it. Also, listening carefully tells you who is likely to comment favorably on your product and company, which will be useful information when you announce your product.

Second, view your relationship with each opinion leader as a long-term investment. The meeting is not an end in itself, but is the beginning of an ongoing process. This means that your credibility is crucial, so it is very important to convey objective expertise in each presentation. Opinion leaders have heard every line in the book, and even if you manage to fool them, they won't appreciate it the next time around.

The ideal relationship is a friendly, expert interaction based on mutual respect. You help opinion leaders with insight and advance information on important industry developments, and they help you refine your product, messages, and marketing approaches; find potential marketing alliances; and shape market acceptance of your product.

An opinion leaders campaign is a small company's least expensive route to getting mindshare in its market. The campaign can help you refine your business and disseminate your message to the few most crucial evaluators of your company's products. In short, your opinion leaders campaign helps take the suspense out of your company's product announcements. After an effective campaign, the market's response—and your company's success—should be considerably more assured.

CHAPTER ELEVEN

Getting the Maximum from Product Reviews

A PRACTICAL GUIDE FOR CREATING A REVIEWS CAMPAIGN

By John Pearce, MediaMap

John Pearce is the founder and CEO of MediaMap. MediaMap, located in Cambridge, Massachusetts, provides PR research and automation systems to client companies in the computer industry.

ALTHOUGH the product review is only one of many kinds of product press coverage, it is probably the single most important element of a product publicity program. From the standpoint of getting the right kind of information to the right people—that is, the chief buying influencers for your products—the impact of the product review can't be equaled. Because of the function, content, and readership of reviews, their impact dwarfs that of news stories, flattering profiles of your company executives, and corporate image pieces (although those types of stories certainly have their place).

Reviews hit the bull's-eye of the market for a specific product, the real buyers: the small group of individuals that evaluate your product and either recommend it to others in their organizations—or recommend your competition. When you look at it that way, you see that all coverage is not created equal and that product reviews can have an impact that's completely disproportionate to the number of column inches of ink you get, or even the number of readers you reach.

For example, at our company one person makes the product purchase decisions for all our requirements. He doesn't read news stories; he thinks they're fluff, and they're not what he's looking for. He may glance at trend stories, but he does his own thinking about what products will meet our needs. And he completely ignores the personality profiles and such because he doesn't care if someone in the industry has a colorful personality or not. What he does care about is whether a product will meet our needs. And most often he gets that information from product reviews. He's only one reader, but he buys for 20 people. He's your bull's-eye.

WHERE ARE THE OPPORTUNITIES?

There are literally hundreds of review opportunities for computer-related products, not only in our own industry's publications but also in other media. In the United States, roughly 70 publications dominate the computer trade press, and many of them run reviews. But although many developers limit their thinking to the trade press, there are scores of opportunities beyond the obvious ones.

National Press

One often-neglected media category is the national press, which includes major magazines and newspapers, syndicated columns, radio and TV shows, and wire services. These can be a gold mine. One example is "Ask Dr. John," a column picked up by hundreds of papers of every kind and size across the U.S. Those newspapers reach literally millions of readers, many of whom are potential customers for home-use products. Because the column isn't in the computer trade-press mainstream, it's easy to overlook, but it's well worth the time and effort to pursue.

Another personal favorite is the Associated Press syndicated column "CompuBug," which runs product reviews that reach more than 400 newspapers throughout the United States. One of our software company clients was reviewed in CompuBug; the review was picked up by hundreds of those papers—and the company was deluged with thousands of inquiries. Now, that's cost-effective marketing!

Computer Industry Newsletters

These provide even more opportunities for reviews, especially for the more technical or leading-edge products. Newsletters usually have a very small circulation compared with that of consumer publications, but they can make a huge impact. Many are expensive to subscribe to, so the subscribers—who include most of the computer industry's opinion and market leaders—are very likely to pay attention to the newsletter's review opinions.

Roundup Stories: The Ultimate in Reviews

The roundup story is probably the most important kind of product review because it is a comparison of multiple products in a given category—and usually points out the best. If you come out on top, you'll really make an impact on potential buyers. There is no more powerful way to work with the press to help position your product. But a word of caution: As powerful as roundup stories are, if your product gets savaged or mispositioned, it can be a severe blow. As we'll see later, avoiding such damage is ordinarily within your control or at least your influence.

Sometimes roundup stories are scheduled and listed on editorial calendars, so be sure to get the editorial calendars for all your key publications. Find out who will write the story by calling the managing editor (or referring to a resource such as MediaMap). Once you've made the right contact and ascertained the direction and theme of the story, it's time to help the editor understand how your product fits into the publication's mission. Comparison tables honestly contrasting and positioning your product versus others in your category can be a good way to get empirical and even subjective information across to a roundup-story editor. In any case, take personal responsibility for ensuring that the editor truly understands what your product is and is not.

Most often, however, roundup stories aren't formally scheduled on editorial calendars. Instead, editors look for hot market segments to cover without being constrained by a calendar planned months in advance. That's a golden opportunity for you to pitch a roundup-story idea, one that is especially welcome when your company isn't making any "news." However, you must proactively find and act on the opportunity. This is particularly true in the national press—especially the end-user press—because it isn't hooked into the moment-by-moment news of our trade. The key is to find a way to group your product with others and give the reviewer the appropriate information. In doing so, you help the journalist by providing a good market niche to report on, and you help your company by pitching a good story that positions your product accurately.

HOW TO ATTRACT REVIEWERS' ATTENTION

At MediaMap we define public relations (including getting product reviews, of course) as "helping the press do its job." To do that, you must understand that job and make your strategy dovetail exactly with it.

One of the biggest mistakes developers make is assuming that getting a publication to review a product works the same as getting an editor to read and run a press release. This is not true at all. The product review process varies widely from publication to publication, and each one may periodically change its policies and procedures. The key to getting good product reviews is understanding the differences in the product review process and editorial mission between publications.

To succeed, you must understand (and keep up with) the process for each target publication and make sure your efforts complement the publication's review process. Otherwise you'll be very frustrated. You'll send boxes of products into a black hole and wonder why you're not getting reviewed. Most of the time, it's because your approach and methods are on a different wavelength than those of the publication. For example, if you don't do your homework for a particular magazine, you may not discover that in a given case the "product review editor" is not an active product reviewer but is instead a front-end person or administrator, someone who receives calls from developers and says, "Yes, thank you very much, please send us your product." The actual reviewer may be sitting on the beach in Malibu with a portable computer.

It's also useful to know such things as whether a publication uses a testing laboratory. Knowing that and understanding the lab's evaluation process is the key to getting a review in such publications. For example, the *Infoworld* review process is unique. *Infoworld* doesn't use a process in which you send a package to somebody who opens it, looks at the product, and decides what the review will say. Instead, the executive editor of reviews coordinates the activities of five review teams, a testing lab, and a reader survey operation.

Each team is responsible for specific kinds of technologies, and within each team the members have designated responsibilities. The testing center works with the review teams and other editors to determine review goals. The results of the review are combined with results from a survey of 1,000 readers to determine users' hot buttons. Needless to say, simply having a slick pitch on the phone isn't going to dovetail with the entire process.

Learn the Format, Content, and What to Send

You also should be familiar with the format and review content of a publication so that you can better position your product when you send it for review. Use that information to select the hot buttons you'll press when dealing with that publication.

Your interaction shouldn't be "Gee, won't you review our product?" It should be something more along the lines of "I hope you'll consider our product for review. Since you serve readers in the hog-farming industry, we've put together a little package of information relevant to your readers' interests, including how we stack up against manual hog-accounting techniques...." and so forth.

We did a major survey of the media for a client. Many editors told us that they particularly appreciate receiving a well-thought-out package of supporting materials with review copies of products. Such materials position each product against the other products in the same niche and personalize the product features and benefits for the specific publication and audience. You can also include backgrounders about the technology or your company. This is similar to the press-kit concept, but it's designed specifically for a product reviewer.

CREATING THE PROGRAM

Getting reviews takes planning, foresight, and some degree of commitment. Rather than approaching them helter-skelter and opportunistically, you should consider using a campaign approach. Putting a working system in place and getting the first review is the most arduous part of the process (especially for smaller companies whose resources are stretched) and the most resource-intensive.

As is true with most PR efforts, the most needed resource is usually staff. But pay that price, and you're in a great position: The incremental effort to get the next review is much smaller, and when you get the machine going and your fifth, tenth, and twentieth reviews come in, you'll realize the full power and incredible cost effectiveness of a good product review campaign.

Start by making someone directly responsible for the campaign. That person will plan and systematically execute the campaign and do the needed record-keeping and contact work. Then determine how many opportunities you will pursue and in what priority and order. With more than 200 review columns to choose from, you *must* be selective; base your decision on who your target market is, whom the publication reaches, and the relative impact of each publication. In most markets, it's reasonable to choose 20 to 50 publications; but, of course, it depends on your goals and resources and how many publications reach your market.

After selecting your targets, you must research each one's review process. As I said before, each process is different—and that difference is crucial to your success. Depending on your resources and time, you may opt to do this research yourself or you can refer to research services. (For example, every 13 weeks we issue a new report that describes the review process of hundreds of publications.) If you opt to do it yourself, you can contact the publications and find out what their review process is by talking to the managing editor, reviews editor, or even editor-in-chief. This will take time, but you need this knowledge before you shape your strategy.

Information Necessities

You need to create a record-keeping system that tracks every review target on your list. Depending on your needs and resources, your system can be as simple as a form for each publication or as complex as a full-blown relational database integrated with your other PR activities. In any case, here's some of the information you need to record.

- For this publication, who is the audience, what is the editorial mission, and what kind of editorial posture does it generally take?

- Who are the product review contacts? What are their names, addresses, phone, and fax numbers? What is each person's role? Who are the primary versus the supporting players?

- What kind of system does the reviewer use? What computer, what operating system, what version, and what media format does the editor need? (Reviewers are not terribly inclined to rave about products they can't use!)

- What's the lead time for reviews in this publication?

- Does the publication honor nondisclosure agreements? If so, under what conditions? What are the implications for any product-announcement schedules you may have?

Your form should also include space for notes about each conversation you have with editorial contact people so that you'll know when you've spoken to whom and what they said. A callback date tickler function is also very desirable for tracking your commitments to editors and for reminding you to take needed steps.

With this information in hand, you're almost ready to go. Using this information and your product positioning, tailor your message to each publication's special mission and audience. Then you'll be ready to contact the editors.

STEPS TO SUCCESS

There are several steps to initiating the review campaign, all of which should probably be check boxes or blanks on your record-keeping form for each target publication. You must make the initial contact with the editor, determine whom to ship the product to, follow up to make sure the material was received and is in good working order, and find out if the reviewer needs additional information and support. If appropriate, send reviewers guidelines or support materials, and test various approaches. Throughout the process, don't forget to keep notes of your conversations and any reactions you get from reviewers.

In addition, be sure the person responsible for your campaign has good in-house support. If the person isn't capable of handling all the responsibilities, identify and brief all the appropriate individuals, especially a technical support expert, a marketing/positioning expert, and an administrator who knows or can ascertain the status of your interaction with each target publication. These in-house players must be reliably available when needed by a reviewer.

Your campaign should also include a systematic evaluation program, which is a plan for making use of the feedback you get from reviews and reviewers. If you listen, there are many benefits: First, you may head off an unfavorable review before it ever sees the light of print. Second, you may get realistic feedback that will help you tailor your approach with the next reviewer or revise your support materials or messages. Third, you can regularly report incoming reactions back to marketing and product development so that they can make adjustments in their thinking as well. Putting reviewer feedback to good use punctuates the whole process.

Timing Review Campaigns

For a new product, reviews are probably the most important press coverage you can possibly get, and you should plan your review strategy months before the actual announcement. For each target publication, devise a plan that takes into account lead times as well as nondisclosure and embargo policies.

Editors will be candid about their embargo policies (that is, agreements not to release information until a given date), and you should make the agreement explicit if you expect them to hold the review until your announcement date. Although many editors will refuse to sign formal agreements, they almost always honor their commitments; an explicit verbal agreement that you follow up with a letter stating your understanding of the agreement is usually adequate. Editors who break such agreements are quite uncommon, but misunderstandings can occur if communication is not clear. Remember also that many publications, especially newsweeklies, explicitly do not agree to embargoes; without an explicit agreement, there's no such thing as being "off the record."

The best approach is to handle the timing issue by conducting a preannouncement product tour—anywhere from a few weeks to a few months before the announcement date—featuring nondisclosure presentations to key reviewers, news editors, and analysts (again, make sure that agreements are clear). Such face-to-face interaction helps you build credibility, even in advance of your having any news to announce.

When Not to Solicit Product Reviews

It's not reasonable to expect a full review about a marginal product change. And if you cry wolf by launching an all-out product review campaign around such an upgrade, you run the risk of blowing your credibility for future efforts.

A good alternative for a less substantial upgrade or release is simply to announce it with a press release and "phone-athon" to news editors. Limit your pitch to the two or three key upgrade features that have the greatest market impact. If the upgrade is too minor to make the news pages, you can still get substantial coverage because most publications have a column for product upgrades and minor product announcements.

DEALING WITH "UNFAIR" REVIEWS

Often, developers become frustrated or irritated because they think they've been unfairly reviewed. In spite of how it occasionally seems to an enraged product manager, editors are rarely out to kill products; they're in the business of trying to describe them accurately.

In truth, when a developer feels wronged by a review, three of every four times the responsibility rests with the developer rather than the reviewer. Your responsibility is to make sure the reviewer *can't* misunderstand the product. A good example is a very high-end application—a power-user product—that gets panned by a reviewer because it wasn't easy to use. In such a case, the reviewer probably didn't understand the product's positioning. The developer must take the responsibility and invest the effort it requires to help the editor understand the product.

But if you feel that you've done all the right things and the review is still negative, squelch the natural desire to give the reviewer a piece of your mind or to take retaliatory action such as canceling your advertising in that publication. Don't forget that you're in it with the press for the long haul, and act accordingly. If you feel that a reviewer has incompetently reviewed your product, by all means take action, but do so rationally.

Deal with your problem through the appropriate channels; convey your concerns to the people in charge (such as the editor-in-chief) in a reasonable and objective way. Be very specific and concrete about how you feel your product was misrepresented. Also, many publications provide some kind of feedback forum, such as a reviews-response or letters-to-the-editor column. Take advantage of it. And realize that in the longer run your calm approach will work: If editors are incompetent, they won't be around long and you'll still have a good relationship with the rest of the editorial staff. If they are competent and have simply made a mistake, they're quite likely to bend over backward to avoid a similar error in the future.

When the Reviewer Is Right

Another thought: View a less-than-glowing review as a unique opportunity to acquire useful market feedback. Usually the editors who review products *do* know what they're doing, and sometimes a product is criticized because it actually has a deficiency. If you consistently get hammered in a certain area, take it as a signal. One of your toughest jobs is telling your executives that perhaps the reviewer is right and that your company should act on the feedback.

Here's a story about a bad review that has a happy ending: A year or so ago, a company got a particularly bad review. Instead of getting huffy, the company examined every criticism, went back into the labs, fixed the problems, and one year later got an editor's choice award from the publication that had panned it before.

Reviews are the driving force behind the development of the market's consensus opinion about your product. If you properly manage the process of getting reviews, the quality and quantity you get will increase dramatically—as might your sales, company standing and image, and competitive position.

CHAPTER TWELVE

Finding Your Voice

A PUBLIC SPEAKING PRIMER FOR DEVELOPERS

By Raymond Nasr, Apple Computer, Inc.

Raymond Nasr is an executive speechwriter in Apple Computer's worldwide corporate communications department. This chapter was adapted from his presentation at Stanford University's Graduate School of Business, where he teaches a workshop on corporate speechwriting.

YOU'VE spent months preparing your product for market. All the pieces are in place—the distribution and marketing plan, production schedules, the PR and advertising strategies, your opinion leaders campaign—and now you're getting requests to speak at various meetings and functions. How persuasively you deliver your messages can quite easily dictate the future course of your organization.

Regardless of the kind of forum, speaking publicly is not only a powerful marketing tool, but it's also an excellent PR opportunity for your company. It's an occasion to convey that you and your company are knowledgeable, interesting, and worth listening to—and gives the impression that you are in demand. (Consider how important this can be for a startup!) Putting your best foot forward on these occasions is critical to advancing your company's image; you'll not want to take any chances.

Woody Allen once said, "Eighty-five percent of life is just showing up." This is also true of public appearances, but you'll want to make sure that you're doing the right thing during the other 15 percent of the time. Whether you write your own speeches or work with a speechwriter, it's important that you find "the right voice" for each occasion. This means tailoring your words and developing your messages to meet the audience's expectations. Delivering powerful speeches takes a lot of practice, both in preparing and in presenting them. Even veteran speakers often return to the basics to make sure they arc on target. To help you "find your voice," I'd like to offer a few basics, or rules of thumb.

GENERAL RULES OF THUMB

There are several important, yet fundamental, things that will help make your speaking engagement a success. First, a speech is designed to be heard, not read. Keep in mind that you are writing for the ear, not for the eye. Accordingly, like a piece of music, speeches should make full use of rhythm, cadence, and punctuation, and have the same kinds of interludes, such as pauses, crescendos, and tonal shifts. Also, it helps to use simple, graphic, and concrete language that lands easily on the ear.

Another simple rule: Make sure the objective of the speech is clear and relevant to the audience; tailor every speech to the audience and occasion. A "boilerplate" speech is seldom successful. Every audience has different expectations and levels of familiarity with the speaker and the subject. Although the main messages may remain consistent from speech to speech, the ways they are expressed will vary with each audience. In every case, knowing an audience's expectations is the single factor that puts you into a position to exceed those expectations.

These rules of thumb apply to every kind of speech you can make. However, every occasion also demands a special touch. What follows are some tips to help you find the right voice for each speech you'll give.

THE SPEECH OF INTRODUCTION

When you are introducing another speaker, the speech contains three main points: the other person's name, title, and the subject of his or her speech. Of course, no one ever wants to stop here, and it would be pretty boring if they did. Audiences want to hear about the personality of the speaker you're introducing—and in small doses this frequently makes the speaker feel more welcome and gives the audience some helpful background. Here are a few things to keep in mind when preparing a speaker introduction.

- *Keep it brief.* "Brief" here means 30–45 seconds. As a courtesy to the audience and to the speaker you are introducing, the less time spent introducing the keynote speaker, the more time there is for the rest of the program. This is especially true of evening or banquet-style events, which should never run later than 10:00 p.m. This is your chance to keep the program on schedule.

- *Remember who they came to hear.* The audience came to hear the keynote speaker, not your introductory remarks. Make sure that whatever you say is low-key, understated, and not overly dramatic; it's not your show.

- *Try to avoid clichés.* By using such phrases as "...without further ado..." or "...the next speaker needs no introduction...," you risk coming across as being insincere or too lazy to prepare something thoughtful to say. Instead, try to diplomatically convey how delighted you are that the speaker has accepted the invitation to speak. You can do this by beginning with a comment like, "I know we're all interested in hearing what our guest has to say, so please join with me in welcoming...."

- *Never preempt the speaker's subject.* It's rude to do this to your guest. And never read the speaker's résumé; it's okay to include a few highlights from the biography—in fact, it's almost required—but do so briefly, in only the most narrative of ways.

CEREMONIAL SPEECHES

When giving this kind of speech (such as for dedications, promotions, site expansions, farewells, and so forth), try not to burden the audience with troublesome—or taxing—ideas. This is an important event, and you don't want to run the risk of bursting the ceremonial bubble by talking about an indiscreet subject (that is, stay away from politics, religion, and money). A few guidelines work for all types of ceremonial speeches.

- *Pour on the praise.* Don't hold back. For example, if the event is to commemorate Henry's 25 years of service to the organization, then go ahead and comment on Henry's courage, endurance, and commitment to quality: "In my professional life, I've met very few people who are as conscientious as Henry...."

- *Back it up with specifics.* Speaking concretely about Henry's accomplishments demonstrates that you actually know something about him.

- *Personalize.* Offer anecdotal comments that throw light on the person and what he means to you. Of course, this is difficult to do if you don't actually know the guest of honor. But here's an easy solution: "I've not had the privilege of knowing Henry until this evening, but his supervisor said...." Saying something like that shows that you have taken the time to get to know a few things about Henry.

PRODUCT INTRODUCTIONS

Ideally, months before the new-product launch, the marketing department will have "fleshed out" the key marketing messages for your new products. Once these messages are carved into stone, here are four key ideas for your product-introduction speech.

- *Keep it snappy and inspired.* The most important concern is to transmit your enthusiasm not only for the specific products but also for the organization's long-term vision.

- *Don't make the statesman a "demo dog."* As Guy Kawasaki comments in *The Macintosh Way*, "Have the person who knows the product the best, not the highest-ranking, do the demo. Just because a president or vice-president is at the event doesn't mean he has to do the demo."

- *Invite a host of luminaries to comment on how great the product is.* It is always better to hear the words "This is a spectacular product" from a credible industry commentator than from a person representing the company who made it.

- *The audience should "glow and tingle."* The single most important objective is to make audience members feel as if they cannot live without the product. When the speech is over, they should want to do nothing but get their hands on it and feel the magic themselves. (If you'd like more information about this, see Paul Sherlock's book *Rethinking Business-to-Business Marketing.*)

ANALYST MEETINGS/REMARKS TO SHAREHOLDERS

There's a formula for both of these kinds of speeches: The chairman delivers the "big picture" overview presentation, the president gives a report on the operations side of the business, and then the chief financial officer delivers the numbers. This is what the audience expects, so try your best to meet those expectations; of all the audiences in the world, the investment community is not one to play games with. The first two speakers—the chairman and the president—should be honest, optimistic, and confident about the future. The audience expects the CFO to give the numbers and to illustrate his or her remarks with lots of charts.

Also, make sure you are up to speed on the Security Exchange Commission rules that constrain these types of presentations. As one would expect, there's not much room for creativity. The speeches may sound boring, but remember that audience members want to hear about the return on their investment; they didn't come to be entertained. You can make these presentations a bit spicier by adding a product demonstration to the speech; but, again, the challenge is to create a positive feeling about the company's competitive position without sounding overly optimistic about the future. The analysts want consistency, and the press wants the latest scoop. That's a tough combination to deliver in a single speech.

THE VIDEO PRESENTATION

The videotape presentation—in lieu of an actual speaking appearance—has become commonplace on the executive presentations circuit. It saves you the hassle of traveling to Salt Lake City to address the National Association of State Directors of Transportation Districts—and it still gives your company a presence there. (The secret is, of course, knowing when you should be there and when a video will suffice.)

Again, meeting the audience's expectations is paramount. People seated in front of video monitors expect a Peter Jennings–style of address, not a 20-minute keynote-style speech. Also, as Edward R. Murrow once commented, when television is used effectively, it can educate, enlighten, and even inspire. When used unwisely, it is nothing but "a box of lights and wires." Here are a few tips.

- *Brevity is the viewer's friend.* The longest you ever see Peter Jennings on the screen at one time is about a minute. No one wants to hear more than one minute of a talking head, primarily because they're not used to it.

- *Use the tricks of the TV trade.* A good director, a tightly written script, and a telegenic speaker can make a three-minute spot a blockbuster. Changes of camera angle, charts or visuals, and a video "field report" effectively break up the talking-head portions of the video and give the production a professional look.

- *Conduct teleprompter-reading practice sessions.* Many speakers are not familiar with the teleprompter. If you're not given several opportunities to practice, you can appear awkward, stilted, and uncomfortable on the screen. If you feel ill at ease, then it is very likely that the audience will, too.

THE KEYNOTE ADDRESS

A great political philosopher once said, "Talent is hitting the target that everyone knew was there. Genius is hitting the target that no one knew existed." If you want to deliver a presentation that is "a work of genius" (even at the most basic level), there are few helpful suggestions that will help you structure your keynote address.

First, keep it brief. Blaise Pascal once said, "I apologize for writing such a long letter, but I didn't have time to write a short one." The same holds true for speeches. Speeches measured by the hour die by the hour. The Gettysburg Address ran for 3 minutes and 10 seconds, and yet it advanced some of the most powerful ideas in the history of humanity. Generally, if you can't reduce your remarks to 20 minutes, people will perceive that you don't know what you're talking about. Keep it simple, succinct, and entertaining.

Next, every keynote speech should have these three elements: an introduction (including the thesis), the body, and a conclusion.

The Introduction

This part of your talk should be witty and brief and should draw the audience into the speech. This is a perfect opportunity to win audience respect and trust. However, breaking the ice is often the most difficult hurdle for a speaker. Mikhail Gorbachev once said that the most difficult part of perestroika was knowing where to start. Similarly, launching into a speech is often the most difficult challenge a speaker faces. Here are a few tips that will help you break the ice and begin to "soften" the audience.

- *The honest compliment.* Finding something that the speaker genuinely appreciates about the audience can be a powerful force. For example, John Sculley delivered a speech in Washington state a few years ago in which he commented on how delighted he was to be in the apple capital of the world. "Although we could never compete with the number of apples you ship out of your state each year, we're giving it our best shot...." However, be careful how you use this tactic. After all, as one speaker once pointed out, "A pat on the back is only a few vertebrae higher than a kick in the butt...."

- *The common bond.* This is an easy way to establish empathy with the audience, provided the common bond is genuine. The speaker can say, "I happen to have a similar enthusiasm and respect for the Future Farmers of America. I grew up on a farm in Iowa and still have several close relatives living there...."

- *Humor.* Effective use of humor can put an audience at ease. Here is an example from David Rockefeller, then chairman of the Chase Manhattan Bank, speaking at the Commonwealth Club of California: "This is the second time I have had the good fortune to address the Commonwealth Club of California which, if little else, certainly testifies to your indomitable courage!"

- *Surprise openings.* You can use a device, prop, or something unexpected to grab the attention of the audience. It's risky, though, because if it's not "just right," it can fall flat. Before using something, try it out on a few people to see if it works.

- *Illustration.* Starting with an attention-grabbing story builds a "curiosity" factor into the speech. It's also fun to weave a story in and out of the speech as it progresses.

The introduction should also include your thesis—the single most important idea the audience should take away from the speech. State it simply and with conviction. Here's an example of how John Sculley presented his thesis in a 1989 speech to school-district superintendents (the italicized sentence represents the heart of the thesis): "The world is undergoing dramatic change, where the economy is going to be, in many ways, very different from anything we have experienced in the past. *Today, I'd like to give you a perspective of this changing world from the vantage point of a CEO running a corporation that may add to your perspective as leaders and CEOs of your school districts....*"

The Body

The body of the speech should begin where the thesis statement left off. It should contain these elements.

- *The main points.* These serve primarily to corroborate the thesis (no more than three main points, please).

- *Amplification of the main points.* This is basically an expansion or special treatment of the main points.

- *Materials that support (or prove) the main points.* Just as a lawyer in a courtroom offers a proposition and supports it with concrete evidence, you should define your thesis and follow it with specific supportive ideas. Support can come in many forms, such as examples, illustrations, metaphors, anecdotes, statistics, and quotations. Although I won't elaborate on each of these, I'd like to say just a few words about numbers and quotations. Round off numbers, always voice them to your advantage, and use them frugally. For example, instead of saying "four-point-seven percent," it is better to say "five percent." Or instead of saying "Twenty percent of the U.S. population...," say "One in five Americans..." Also, be careful with numbers. Most people come to speakers' forums for entertainment, not number crunching. It's easy to lose an audience in the numbers.

    Using quotations and expert opinions, especially when they're not expected, adds a refreshing dimension to public presentations. A few rules for using quotations: Never use more than 3 per 20-minute speech; they are to be savored and delivered with reverence; and a good quote is usually pithy—the audience should be able to absorb it in one earful.

- *Transitions.* Transitions between main points (such as "in addition, in contrast, on the other hand, yet, additionally," and so forth) let the audience know that you are moving from one idea to another. They define the beginning and end of the "modules of thought," indicate the relationships between the main ideas, and remind you that you are moving from one idea to the next.

The Conclusion

Once you've said, "In conclusion" or "To summarize," the audience will stay with you for only about another minute. This is the perfect opportunity to help the audience recall your main points. There are several ways to end the speech in a short, punctual, and entertaining way. You can restate the core idea, challenge the audience to action, offer a closing quote or story, or use any of several techniques. I also recommend that you end with "Thank you very much." Although some people feel this isn't necessary, I always use it. If nothing else, it lets the audience know when to clap.

Whether you're a seasoned veteran on the speaking circuit or are just starting to find your public voice, applying some speechwriting basics and really paying attention to the needs of your audiences will make the difference between a memorable speech and a humdrum one.

A final word: If you can wield any influence over choosing the menu for the banquet, make sure they're serving something good because "A well-fed audience is always less critical."

CHAPTER THIRTEEN

How To Choose the Right Name for a High-Tech Product

By SB Master, Master-McNeil, Inc.

SB Master is president of Master-McNeil, Inc., a firm located in Berkeley, California, that specializes in product and company naming and nomenclature systems.

IN a time when high-tech products are produced with the frequency of baby rabbits, developers must use everything at their disposal to distinguish their products from the rest of the pack. Choosing the right name for your product can be the element of distinction that determines whether customers give your product a try.

But finding an appropriate name can be a serious test of character for a marketing team. Recent revisions in trademark law and the overwhelming number of new products entering the market have made finding a suitable *and available* name more difficult than ever. However, by following a well-organized naming plan and allowing yourself enough time, choosing a product name can be rewarding—and even fun. This chapter outlines the basic principles of product naming and defines a process for helping you match your great new product with a truly stellar name.

WHAT A NAME WILL DO FOR YOUR PRODUCT

Once you realize that a powerful name can play a key role in launching a product in the right direction, the energy required by a serious name development effort will be easier to justify and your efforts will be more rewarding. But how does having a good name affect a product? The following list summarizes our view.

- *Good name, bad product.* A great name can help kill a bad product. A great name will encourage people to try a product, and they'll thereby find out sooner that the product is bad.

- *Bad name, bad product.* This one is obvious: Forget it; save your time and money.

- *Bad name, good product.* A great product can usually overcome a bad name, but a bad name can slow down trial and acceptance. Why burden your great product with anything less than a great name?

- *Good name, good product.* This is the best situation you can hope for, and is definitely worth the effort. We should all seek this powerful conjunction of product and name.

KINDS OF NAMES

There are two basic categories of names to choose from: names that are real words (Apple, Sun) and those that have no intrinsic meaning (Exxon, Abex). Between these extremes is a wide variety of hybrids with more or less intrinsic meanings.

Which category of name is right for your product depends on the qualities you need to convey, who your target market is, how crowded your product category is, and the size of your marketing budget. The following paragraphs describe some things to think about as you consider what kind of name will work best for your product.

Real-Word Names

Many companies use real-word names for their products. There is a single-word form of this (Apple, Radius) and a combined form (AppleTalk, ColorSync, After Dark, HyperCard). These real-word names have the advantage of being immediately recognizable and understood, and they go a long way in establishing what a new product has to offer. Well-chosen real-word names use simple vocabulary, so they usually retain their meaning worldwide, no matter what language they are built upon.

The problem with real-word solutions, however, is that the more descriptive, relevant ones are often already being used by someone else. The less descriptive, less relevant ones are less desirable because you need to spend time and money to help explain, establish, and attach an image to them. However, real-word names are worth a lot of serious creative exploration. If you can find a relevant real-word solution that is unique and effective, it will be among the easiest of names to establish it in the marketplace.

Coined Names

At the other end of the spectrum are made-up or "coined" names. As the number of new products increases, finding an available real-word name solution is becoming increasingly difficult. As a result, companies are increasingly turning to coined names to identify their products.

Coined names can be subdivided into arbitrary/obscure and meaningful categories. Some examples of the arbitrary might include Synovus Financial, Allegis Corp., Ceridian (the Control Data spin-off), and perhaps Pentium. These are all examples of coined words that on their own mean little if anything to anyone. However, they can work. One way is to spend a lot of money establishing them. One example might be Exxon.

Coined names that work best, however, are those built on large enough "chunks" of language that the resulting names have intrinsic meaning. The best of these combine intrinsically meaningful, relevant roots into whole new words. Some examples are Navistar, Unisys, and Televangelist.

Why are these kinds of solutions worth pursuing? Primarily because of legal realities (more on that later in this chapter). It's becoming more difficult to get legal approval for new names, and software seems one of the most difficult categories of all. We believe the latter group of names, the intrinsically meaningful "coined" ones, will be the place where many companies increasingly find candidate names that pass legal scrutiny.

CHARACTERISTICS OF A GOOD NAME

One of the most commonly asked questions in the naming business is what separates good names from bad ones. This isn't really the relevant question; what really matters is whether the name communicates the right messages to the right people. Thus, the crucial first step in creating a product name is determining exactly what you want your name to express, and to whom. These qualities will be embodied in your naming objectives, described later in this chapter (defined in Step 2 in this chapter under "Creating Your Name").

Whatever kind of name you choose, it must meet all of the following criteria.

- *Good names are easy to pronounce.* An effective name rolls off the tongue. (Can you imagine having to provide a pronunciation guide in your product introduction literature? Some companies actually do that.) But even more important, the name must be difficult to mispronounce. This point can't be overstated. If you give customers an opportunity to mispronounce a product name, chances are they will. Or, even more fatally, they won't talk about your product at all because they fear the embarrassment of mispronouncing the name. When this happens, you stand to lose one of the most valuable, yet least expensive, communications media available to marketers: word of mouth. The pronunciation of your product name must therefore be totally without ambiguity.

- *Good names are memorable and appealing.* When it comes to choosing one product over another, all other things being equal, the product with a name that sticks in the customer's mind will probably be the stronger candidate. Ease of pronunciation can be evaluated objectively using linguistic principles, but memorability and appeal require subjective judgments.

  Some names are definitely more memorable and appealing than others. These names are not only easy to pronounce, but they also tend to be fun to say, to be spelled conventionally, and to relate in some manner to the product category or benefits. A totally arbitrary name that has nothing to do with anything and that is unpleasant to say is often unappealing and not memorable. But a name that strikes a responsive chord, or that manages to attach itself to an existing "hook" in the customer's mind, and slips easily off the tongue, is likely to be more memorable and appealing. Some good examples of memorable and appealing names are SimCity, FinePrint, QuickDraw, FreeHand, WriteNow, PostScript, Persuasion, and Timbuktu.

- *Good names are free and clear of legal problems.* You need to ensure that a name is available for use in all your key markets. A name should be trademarkable or should be so descriptive that you don't need a trademark for it. (Names that are very descriptive often use words in common use in the language and often aren't trademarkable.) Get advice from a trademark attorney.

- *Good names should be effective worldwide.* To be effective worldwide means that beyond being legally available in all key markets, a name should be pronounceable, have no negative meanings, and have no embarrassing connotations in the countries, cultures, and languages in which it will be used.

  You should consider this issue for two reasons, even if you have no immediate plans to market internationally. One, even if you intend to market only in your home country, there usually are large numbers of potential customers who speak languages other than your native tongue. Two, if your product succeeds, you may eventually want to market it outside your home country. It is far more cost effective (and better worth the time and effort) to build a worldwide identity for your product than to change its name, country by country.

  There are a variety of considerations regarding what makes a name appropriate in multiple markets. As Lauri Jones of Intracom, Inc. points out in Chapter 36, "Avoiding Cultural Mishaps During Localization," most technical product companies keep a product's original name when changing markets. This hasn't always been true of more consumer-oriented marketers, but it's becoming more common. So, it's important to ensure that as you take your name from country to country, it does not take on negative connotations in other languages. A classic example is General Motors' attempt to market its Chevrolet Nova model in Latin America. *No va* in Spanish means *doesn't go*.

A cost-effective way to check the multiple language associations of your chosen name is to review it with native speakers of various languages within your company. Quick checks by electronic mail or phone with foreign associates also work. Be sure to talk with native speakers, not just someone who happened to take a few years of the language in college; you need to be aware of slang, archaic, regional, and street language associations as well as textbook or dictionary meanings. To be truly safe, you should consider enlisting the services of localization experts to evaluate your name in foreign markets.

CREATING YOUR NAME

Now you're ready to begin creating your name. A key consideration is when during product development to start the naming process. Set up a schedule working backward from the date the name is required; typically this will be the date of the initial product announcement or the date you need to drop a name into product manuals or packaging. If you are a startup company, you may need the name much sooner: When talking to investors, your product concept will seem much more tangible if the product has a name.

How much time to allow for naming depends a lot on the size and culture of your company, how many people need to participate, and how many levels of approval are required. Generally, a 12-week schedule should be adequate to take you through the naming process described later in this chapter.

Step 1: Organize a Naming Team

Setting up a naming team is the first—and often overlooked—step in creating an effective name. While a one- or two-person team might make the decision process easier, you'll eventually have to defend your choices to a larger group and you'll lose the time you saved. A team effort is better: It leads to increased participation in the naming process and a more diverse range of opinions about what the name should convey. You'll end up with a happier staff and with more people having a pride of ownership in the name of their new product.

A naming team should include six to eight employees who represent a variety of viewpoints and job functions; the team should include at least one person who is likely to be a key participant in the eventual implementation of the name, such as someone from public relations, marketing communications, or advertising. Team members ideally should include a mix of mid- to high-level employees, all having some degree of familiarity with the product.

If there is someone in the company who is likely to hold widely divergent or controversial views and who has the potential to veto or slow down the process, don't put off the confrontation—include that person on your team. Believe me, this works better than isolating dissenters and then later trying to convince them of your wisdom. By having a variety of viewpoints and job functions represented on your naming team, you'll go a long way to getting the necessary buy-in from the company as a whole.

The naming team's job is to carry out the steps that follow. Team members will also play a role in explaining the project process and results to fellow employees.

Step 2: Develop a List of Naming Objectives

The team's next step is to establish a list of naming objectives. These should reflect the marketing objectives for the product, including such things as who the target audience is, how competitors are positioned, pricing, distribution plans, and relationships to existing company products.

Naming objectives define the ideas or characteristics the name should convey. In high-tech companies, objectives often encompass such concepts as innovation, efficiency, dependability, speed, or high quality. The naming team must establish a list of the most important goals specific to your name. What do your potential customers need to know to make them consider your product? What key words or concepts already exist in your product category—and do you want to leverage or avoid them? Will the name need to stretch over any other products? These key thoughts should be embodied in the naming objectives.

Why is it important to conduct this objective-setting exercise? Because once you have agreed on a list of objectives, you can use it to evaluate the candidate names.

For objectives to be useful, they must be specific, discrete, and unemotional. Try to keep the list short, and establish a priority order. For example, a set of objectives for a new family of software utilities could be

- to suggest an "umbrella," a family of products

- to suggest utilities, tools, assistants, aides—not complete solutions

- to suggest increased efficiency, productivity, and speed.

Note that these objectives are dry, rational, and unemotional. They do not overlap or contradict each other. They lend themselves to the kind of name evaluation you'll have to do later: Does the name suggest a family of products—yes or no? Does it suggest a utility or a complete solution? And so on.

In contrast, next is an example of a less useful set of objectives. They are confusing, unspecific, contradictory, and there are too many of them. They don't lead the team in any particular creative direction and they will give you little help when evaluating names:

- to be catchy, something that grabs you, or funny

- to suggest innovation, the leading edge

- to suggest the mainstream, a safe choice, reliability

- to suggest leadership, importance

- to suggest friendliness, approachability, a helpful quality.

I think you'll agree that these objectives are vague, inconsistent, and less useful than those in the first list.

Step 3: Develop a List of Naming Criteria

Naming criteria function as technical specs for the name. They dictate how your name will express the ideas stated in your objectives. For example, here is a set of criteria to accompany the objectives for our family of software utilities. The name must

- fit in with other products in the existing product line

- contain no more than two syllables (must be short because it may be combined with company name and individual product identifiers)

- avoid use of terms used by competitors, as in power, mate, multi, set

- be pronounceable and legally available in the countries in which you plan to market the product (list them specifically).

As with objectives, criteria should be simple, specific, uncontradictory, and few in number.

Step 4: Initiate the Creative Work

Once team members thoroughly understand and agree to the objectives and criteria, you're ready to begin the process of creating the name itself. Don't underestimate the effort needed at this point in the process; while it can be fun, developing names is more difficult than it appears.

To give team members confidence and to help focus their creative efforts, provide the team with a synopsis of competitive naming practices, and discuss whether competitive names make sense or represent directions to avoid. Also provide the team with lists of word parts from English, Latin, Greek, or other relevant languages to give them raw materials for expressing your objectives in less obvious ways. These word-root studies are excellent springboards from which team members can explore new directions for names.

To construct the list of roots, start with key words from your objectives list and explore both where those words come from and how other languages express those ideas. The resulting names will not all be easy to understand (not all of the roots have easy connections to English), but many will make for unique and interesting name alternatives for your product. For example, from the software utilities objectives, a root study of the word *speed* would include such word parts as *agilis* (Latin for quick), *celer* (Latin for swift), *presto* (Italian for quick), and *tachos* (Greek for speed). These could all be used to construct new names.

Each team member will interpret the word parts from a different point of view, yielding an expansive list of coined but intrinsically meaningful names that are less likely to be already in use.

Also, construct a list of any names that the team and other company employees have previously suggested. Discuss what about those names made them interesting (tone, meaning, balance, character), and try to create more names in those same categories. Finally, provide your team with dictionaries, thesauruses, directories of existing products, competitive promotional litera-ture, and anything else you think might help.

Then, turn the team lose. Ask each person to develop a long list of names. Encourage team members to continually refer back to the original objectives and criteria to help them stay on target.

Step 5: Review Creative Work Together, Then Do More

After the team has had time to work independently, you should get together for a team meeting. How soon? Probably after team members have each devoted at least eight hours of focused effort to name development (ideally spread over three to five days). The objective for this meeting (which everyone should know before you start) is to review the creative work with an eye toward establishing preferred *naming directions*, highlighting interesting ideas for further exploration, and uncovering any new revelations.

Open the meeting by reviewing your naming objectives and criteria to ensure that everyone remembers the goals they've agreed upon. Then explore the creative work, highlighting the positive and avoiding any judgment or ridicule. Create a feeling of progress, of zeroing in on the ideal name. Agree on which ideas are promising and worthy of further attention and which ideas have been adequately explored.

Then, send the team away for a second round of creative development. Team members should explore the preferred naming directions, exploit new information, and probe more deeply into the creative possibilities suggested by the objectives. This will lead to an entirely new list of names.

It is often this second, more focused and educated push, that results in the most interesting name alternatives. Continue the process of creative exploration–team meeting–creative exploration until you think the objectives have been exhaustively explored. You could easily end up with a master list of a thousand or more name candidates.

Step 6: Narrow the List

Each subsequent step from here is a gradual convergence on the best names from your master list, carrying forward only the best alternatives. Review the master list and select the most promising candidates. These are the names that, in the team's judgment, best express the objectives and meet the criteria that were agreed upon earlier. Though it may take a few fist fights (or some bribery), the team should agree on a smaller list of 40 to 50 names before taking the next step: a preliminary search to determine if the names are already being used in the marketplace.

Step 7: Preliminary Searches for Market Presence

The preliminary search for market presence can be done in several ways. In the United States, the simplest and, in general, most effective method is to use an on-line database such as TrademarkScan that lists current, pending, and canceled U.S. trademarks.

There are a few key pitfalls to avoid when conducting these searches. One potential problem is spelling variations. Trademark law is designed to prevent confusion among products in the marketplace; two names that are spelled differently but pronounced similarly may be rejected. You'll need to check similar spellings and plural versions of your name, as well as exact matches. A name such as LaserWriter, for example, could be spelled LazerWriter, LaserRighter, or Laser Writer. You need to think of and check all of these.

You also should consider multiple trademark classes. A trademark may be registered within one or more classes, each class representing different product types. You need to search not only the class into which your product falls (electronic goods and services, for example) but also other potentially overlapping classes such as entertainment, telecommunications, and printed matter. To do this, you'll need to consider the product categories into which the name might eventually grow, not just where it is today. One example is the software that became a television program, "Where in the World Is Carmen Sandiego?" The advent of multimedia products has made it even more important to check name availability in multiple product categories.

A third pitfall is prematurely discarding name candidates. While it's true that the previous existence of a name in the market can cause problems for your candidate name, information gathered through preliminary searches is not always accurate. Many products that show up as potential conflicts may have been discontinued long ago. Their parent companies may have disappeared. The product may have never been introduced. Some names may be for products different enough from yours to avoid any conflict. Or names may be owned by very small or nearly defunct companies, who might not object to your using their names, particularly in exchange for a small fee. Therefore, it's important when examining the results of your searches to keep a close eye on all the information provided, and investigate the companies listed as using your name candidates. Many excellent candidates will otherwise be tossed out.

Once you've put a list of names through the preliminary search process, you can learn even more about their potential availability by checking some other readily available databases. The United Kingdom version of TrademarkScan, which tends to turn up major European trademark users, is now available on-line. Other useful methods include literature scans, which search for articles in industry journals that might mention your candidate names; the Electronic Yellow Pages, which turns up companies of all sizes using your candidate names as company names; and the Companies And Their Brands database, which shows products whose names owners may not have bothered to trademark.

Step 8: Select Your Finalists

You now must decide which of the names that have passed scrutiny are the most worthy to pursue. By this stage, all the remaining names will have passed many tests. But you'll probably still have too many names. How do you decide which ones to take forward?

Go back to the objectives and criteria one last time; consider the names' longevity, extension possibilities, and potential international acceptance. Some names may express one particular objective well but leave others somewhat neglected. If so, your team must decide which objectives carry more weight and which tradeoffs make the most sense. Through this process, select a group of five to seven names, any one of which would be a good solution.

Step 9: Have an Attorney Conduct a Full Trademark Search

A full search for a name's legal availability should be turned over to a trademark attorney. The attorney will need to do a full U.S. search, as well as international trademark searches in key markets.

Review the results with your attorney. If only one of the names submitted is available, you have found your name. If more than one is available, your last step is slightly more difficult, but still straightforward: Choose one.

If you were unfortunate enough to lose all of your final candidates to existing trademarks, don't panic. Review your most promising name list (or the original master list, or even do a third round of creative work) and select a new batch of names that meets the objectives and criteria. Then submit these names to a preliminary search and continue the process through doing a full search.

BUILD IN-HOUSE SUPPORT FOR YOUR NAME

As if finding a legally available and appropriate name weren't difficult enough, you'll now need to convince your associates that you have found the best name. This task will be easier if your team was constituted as I recommended earlier; members representing various departments and interests will probably have kept their colleagues somewhat informed as to where the naming process was going, so its outcome won't be a complete surprise.

Depending on your organization, who needs to be informed, and when, will vary. The first task is to get approval for your selected name at whatever level your organization dictates (such as the vice president of marketing, for example). A formal presentation (though the definition of "formal" varies) is recommended. In your presentation, the naming team should review the process it followed; it's important that people understand and appreciate that your name recommendation is not being made lightly. Show the steps you took, the people you talked to, the competitive practices reviewed. Spend time on the objectives and criteria—why you chose them, which ones you left out. Review any international or customer input, linguistic issues, and legal results.

Finally, present your recommended name, and demonstrate how it meets the objectives and criteria. You may wish to present some mocked-up packaging or product brochures that use the name prominently. Repeat the name in your presentation as many times as possible. Your goal here should be to help management feel as comfortable as you do, both with the fairness and professionalism of the naming process and with the name itself.

Once the name has been approved by management and before you share it much more extensively, you should ask your attorneys to file an "Intent-to-Use" application. This will reserve the name for your use. Actual name roll-out should be coordinated with all other aspects of your product announcement and introduction plans. In conjunction with PR, promotion, and advertising activities, your new name should be prominently featured in all product introduction events.

The final step: Pat yourself and the naming team on the back for a job well done. You've done everything possible to give your product a name that will set it apart and help it reach its full potential in the market.

CHAPTER FOURTEEN

The Ten Commandments of Product Packaging

HOW TO CREATE PACKAGES THAT SELL

By Signe Ostby, Merrin Information Services

Signe Ostby is an advisor to Merrin Information Services, a Palo Alto, California, company that offers full-day practical marketing seminars on improving in-store merchandising, increasing sales through better packaging, and other topics.

I'M sad to say that few developers treat product packaging as seriously as they do their advertising. Most companies deliberate for days, even weeks, over advertising strategy and objectives. However, few of us develop objectives for packaging beyond those needed to protect the product during shipment.

This lack of attention can severely handicap a product that will be sold in shelf-oriented stores. The reason? Shelf-oriented stores—computer superstores, office product superstores, warehouse membership clubs, consumer electronic stores, and discount department stores—currently account for about one-third of all software and peripheral sales and 25 percent of all hardware sales, according to research conducted by Merrin Information Services. And if industry analysts are on target, those figures could double during the next two years, as more software and hardware find their way into these kinds of stores. The increase in number of these kinds of stores will probably happen mainly at the expense of the traditional computer dealer. At current sales rates, one computer superstore does the same volume of business as at least 100 traditional computer dealers.

The tremendous growth of shelf-oriented computer stores is making packaging one of the single most important parts of your product marketing and communications plans. In fact, packaging is likely the make-or-break marketing element of your product in this selling environment. We believe your package is as important as your company's advertising. There are four million shoppers—four million potential buyers—walking the aisles of shelf-oriented stores each month. What advertising media can deliver that kind of audience?

So how do you create a dynamo package? Read on.

SELL, SELL, SELL: THE PACKAGE'S MAIN PURPOSE

The package's primary purpose is to sell the product inside it. All other objectives are secondary. Thus, each element of the package design should be evaluated in the context of how it helps sell the product inside. Anything that compromises that purpose will limit sales. You can have a good- or even great-selling product without good packaging, but good packaging sells even more product.

To provide developers with guidelines for good package design, Merrin Information Services has formulated ten guidelines of product packaging based on extensive research in the packaged goods industry. These "commandments" of product packaging are not meant to be rigid, constraining rules that inhibit creativity. Rather, they are designed to help you evaluate your packaging needs, challenge your thinking, and channel your creative efforts.

I. THOU SHALT HAVE A STRONG, PROMINENT WHY-TO-BUY MESSAGE

The "why-to-buy" message is your positioning statement boiled down to a succinct, catchy, competitive, and compelling phrase. Although you may know this as the product "tag line," we prefer the term "why-to-buy" message because it more accurately describes its role on the package's front panel. Its job is to tell customers why they should buy your product. After all, if you don't tell a customer why he or she should buy your product, who will?

A *succinct* message is five to nine words long. A *catchy* one rolls off your lips like a good jingle; the words have a natural yet intriguing flow. The *competitive* element of the message can be either implicit or explicit. An explicitly competitive message more directly references the competition, as in "works faster than brand X" or "no other product delivers faster performance." Implicitly competitive messages state a reason to buy that implies that the competition doesn't work as well or in the same way. For example, the Kid Pix tag line (see below) implies that all other painting programs are not designed especially for children. A *compelling* why-to-buy message addresses the customer's key need that your product fills and compels them to take action (buy your product) immediately.

Here are some examples of effective why-to-buy messages:

- *"The easiest way to improve your writing."* Grammatik by Reference Software.

- *"The paint program just for kids."* Kid Pix by Brøderbund.

- *"The easiest way to fax. Period."* SatisFAXtion Board by Intel.

II. THOU SHALT BE REALISTIC ABOUT THY COMPANY'S NAME AND LOGO

Putting your company name on a package is important, especially if the name is well recognized. However, it should never be the major element of the package design—unless it's the best reason for a customer to buy the product.

It's easy to communicate your company's identity without overpowering other design elements. A classic example from the consumer packaged-goods industry is Nabisco, which uses its red logo in the upper corner of all its products. The rest of the package is devoted to selling the product, not the company. A caution: Don't use the package to make your logo or company name better known. If your product becomes successful, people will begin to recognize your logo and company name. The reverse does not hold true. Examples of packages that do a very good selling job without using an over-powering company name or logo are Symantec, Brøderbund, and Claris software.

III. THOU SHALT NOT USE THY PRODUCT NAME FOOLISHLY

Some names help sell the product that's inside the package, and others don't. In general, if a product name is either extremely well known (such as Lotus 1-2-3) or is very descriptive (such as LaserWriter), then it can be the major package design element. If the name does not clearly convey product benefits or if you can't change the product name to one that is more descriptive or sales-oriented, it should not be the major package design element.

IV. THOU SHALT USE PRODUCT INFORMATION AS A COMPETITIVE TOOL

The purpose of the product information printed on the front and back panels of the software package is to *sell*, not merely *inform*. Usually, there are only two or three functional benefits that make a customer decide to buy your product instead of a competitor's. To know what those are and to determine what related product information to use on your package, you must understand the target customer very well.

You must phrase the product information on the package in a way that directly and competitively addresses these issues. Don't merely state that your product performs a certain function or has a particular feature. Instead, sell the customer on why your product performs that function better than the competitor's product does. In other words, emphasize the product benefit, not the feature. (See Table 14-1 for examples of feature- versus benefit-oriented package copy.) On the other hand, don't overload customers with too much data. Make your key points, and then stop.

Table 14-1 Samples of Feature- versus Benefit-Oriented Copy

Product	Feature-Oriented	Benefit-Oriented
Calendar software	Wide variety of printing options	Prints all major appointment-book formats so that you can take your schedule with you
Scanner	32 gray-scale	32 gray-scale for superior image quality
Monitor	640 x 400 bitmapped graphics	Screen is easy to read and easy on the eyes
Disk compression	Disk caching	Disk caching for speedier software performance

V. THY PACKAGE SHALL HAVE HIGH VISUAL IMPACT FROM TEN FEET AWAY

Customers cruising the aisles of shelf-oriented stores are usually three to four feet away from shelves and are scanning shelves up to ten feet ahead of them as they walk. They skim them quickly from top to bottom, until something makes them stop and look more closely. Your package has about one second to catch a customer's eye, urge him or her to stop, and pick up your product. Therefore, it's crucial that your package be very easy to read.

Color

Color is critical in achieving high impact. The consumer packaged-goods industry has spent millions proving that day-glow red, orange, and yellow have the most shelf impact. Next time you're at the grocery store, look down the laundry detergent or cereal aisles (the two most heavily researched aisles in grocery stores) and note the effect and impact of these colors. The same holds true for any computer product package.

Placement of Key Design Elements

For most software and peripheral products, the highest priority design elements (chosen from among the why-to-buy message, product name, company name, graphics or visuals, and product information) should be on the lower half of the front panel. The reason: In most superstores, it is extremely difficult to see the tops of packages that are placed on lower shelves, especially when stock is low and packages are not "shelved out," that is, placed on the forward edge of the shelf. This rule is even more critical for software products because some stores (Egghead, for example) overlap shelves. A shelf overlapping the one below obscures whatever is printed on the upper third of the package on the lower shelf.

Many developers put the product name on the top half of the package; a name in that location will be completely hidden by the shelf above it at stores that overlap shelves. In those cases, there is no way a customer can locate your product by name, except by peering at the small type on the store's shelf tags.

VI. DESIGN THY GRAPHICS TO COMMUNICATE

If an uninformed customer cannot immediately and easily understand what the product does simply by glancing at your package, you should scrap your design and start over. If you choose to make a graphic or other visual a major element on the package's front panel, make sure that target customers can easily recognize or figure out, at a glance, what the visual element is or represents.

VII. THY PRINTING SHALL BE READABLE

Customers won't read that which is not easy to read. Thus, your fonts must be instantly legible to a customer who is four to ten feet away from the package. In general, sans-serif fonts are easier to read from a distance. (That's why most freeway signs use easy-to-read sans-serif fonts.)

This doesn't mean that your fonts need to be dull and uninteresting. Kid Pix is an excellent example of a package that uses creative sans serif fonts that are easy to read and that uses bright printing on a light background. Legibility is also increased by having the maximum amount of contrast between type color and background color. Consumer packaged-goods research has proven that, in general, dark or bright printing on a light background, rather than the reverse, is the easiest to read quickly, especially when there is a lot of text. (There are, of course, case-by-case exceptions to this rule.)

VIII. THOU SHALT USE EVERY AVAILABLE SURFACE TO SELL

You never know how a store will place your product on the shelf. It could be placed front panel out, side panel out, stacked on its back (and thus bottom panel out), or whatever. To make sure customers can see, at minimum, your name and why-to-buy message, these should be prominent design elements on all panels.

If you've done a good job establishing in-store merchandising programs, your products may be placed on an individual display. The most common of these are in-aisle displays. In most cases, products on an in-aisle display are simply stacked on the floor or are otherwise separated from the store's other products rather than being mixed with other software on shelves. Unless the display is always stacked to chest or eye level (something you can't control), the package surface that the customer sees most frequently is the top panel. If your selling message isn't there, you're wasting a sales opportunity.

IX. THY PACKAGES SHALL BE DESIGNED TO FIT ON STORE SHELVES

This guideline seems so obvious, but it is frequently violated by attempts to be clever, distinctive, or just different. Most shelves in superstores are a standard height. Take this into consideration when designing your software package; an average to use is 10 inches. If your package is too tall for standard shelves, your product will be relegated to a less visible location or stacked on the shelf in a less than optimal manner.

For example, if your product is taller than standard shelves, the stores will stock it on the bottom shelf or tip your product onto its back. This is the problem with one well-known graphics application. Inside the package is an 8½" by 11" page, which makes the package taller than the normal shelf. Thus, in superstores the product is normally stacked on its back on the bottom shelf. On the other hand, Brøderbund, for example, has tried to minimize the effects of this problem by using very bright yellow-orange colors to improve the box's shelf impact in a substandard shelf location.

Unusual package shapes also run the risk of not working well in this channel, where products are often stacked on top of each other. For example, if your box is triangular, you can't stack another box on top of it, which limits the display height to one box—a very puny display with low impact.

Unusual shapes (a package that comes to mind is a painting application in a creative paint-can type package) can help a package stand out on the shelf, if the packaging is also functional. But your package must be able to stand on its own without support, and you must be able to stack another package on top of it without toppling the stack or obscuring the key selling messages. If you can achieve this using a creative package shape, go for it—but understand what you'll be up against in the store environment. (Some developers have provided stores with special shelf holders for their unusually shaped packages; but this is a very expensive proposition, and stores might not even want to use them.)

X. THOU SHALT VIEW THY PACKAGE ON A STORE SHELF BEFORE COMMITTING TO A DESIGN

A package's ability to sell is relative to the environment it competes in. No package can be evaluated by itself "out of context" in your or your art director's office. What appears to jump off the shelf of the white bookcase in your office can disappear on the store shelf. A red package could look dynamite in your conference room; but if your competitors also have red packages, yours won't stand out. Furthermore, lighting and shadows in stores can make some designs less noticeable than others.

There is no substitute for taking a package prototype to a store, placing it in a couple of shelf locations, standing at least ten feet away, and evaluating what you see. Make sure you do this during the design stage—before you have spent substantial money on package inventory.

WHERE TO START

How do you start the process of creating the ultimate package? Approach it as you would any other marketing communications strategy: with a plan. Before you begin a package-design project, make sure you develop a package-design brief that includes:

- target customer description
- product marketing objectives
- key product features
- most significant reasons for a customer to buy
- why-to-buy message
- description of the top three to five competitors
- priorities for front-panel design (why-to-buy message, product name, company name, graphics or visuals, and product information).

I can't emphasize enough how important this plan is. It serves several purposes. The planning process itself forces you and those you work with to carefully think through, articulate, and agree on key marketing information—and how it relates to your package. The plan also serves as a communications vehicle between you and the designer; if well written, it provides clear, concrete direction that will increase the odds that the package design will meet your objectives. It also gives you some basic criteria with which to evaluate the various artistic solutions that will be offered to you.

If you already have a package, give it the ten commandments test. If it doesn't sell, sell, sell, consider going back to the drawing board. And if you're just starting to design the package, we hope these guidelines will help you create what will be, for your product, the ultimate package that sells.

CHAPTER FIFTEEN

How Direct Mail Saved Our Company

By Dave Johnson, Working Software

Dave Johnson is the president of Working Software, Inc., a productivity software developer based in Santa Cruz, California.

Editor's note: For reference, this chapter was written in mid-1992.

IN 1989, Working Software was broke, few of us were getting paid, we owed a lot of money to other people, and we couldn't seem to sell anything. (Does this remind you of any startups you know?) Within the following two years, we'd turned things around so dramatically that in the final quarter of 1991 we mailed more than one million pieces of direct mail, sold thousands of units of product, and pretty much broke even—despite the recession that was in full swing.

This chapter is about how direct mail saved our company—what our challenges were and what we learned in overcoming the fear of channel conflict.

FROM GROWING REVENUES TO HARD TIMES...AND BACK AGAIN

Working Software was formed in 1985; we first sold Spellswell at the January 1986 Macworld Expo. By mid-1988, we were selling an entire line of products through most major distributors and retail chains. When our sales took a major downturn in late 1988, we were perplexed. We were receiving a lot of great press coverage and our products were getting very good reviews. Existing customers told us that they liked the products and the company. But we weren't getting orders. We didn't realize that the Mac software marketplace had changed, and we didn't correctly understand who our customer was. The situation wasn't really that we couldn't sell any software; it was that we were trying to sell software to retailers—and the rules for selling to that channel had changed. Only later would we learn that our true customer is the Macintosh user, not the retailer.

Does the following tale sound familiar? Smaller stores couldn't afford to keep a large number of titles on their shelves, which was bad news for a small company such as Working Software. Most large retailers wanted a substantial amount of cash up front before they would carry our products. They also preferred to carry higher-priced products that yielded a higher profit per unit sold. And they wanted "spiffs"—fees the salespeople receive for recommending one product over a different, possibly superior product. Furthermore, catalogs wanted money to list us. Magazines were asking almost $20,000 a page for ads. (You have to sell a lot of software to pay those prices.)

This meant that for a small company such as ours—six products, fewer than ten people, and less (far less) than $1 million in sales—it was becoming too expensive to sell in the retail channels. (I also don't think any of these tactics were doing the customers any favors; the results were often decreased selection and higher-priced products being recommended to customers for the wrong reasons. But that's another dissertation.)

By the end of 1989, we were literally down to our last dollar. We had just revised Spellswell and had received quite a few upgrade orders. We decided to put a coupon offering our Lookup and Findswell products at half price into the upgrade package. To make a long story short, we sold a lot of copies of Lookup and Findswell. Almost 10 percent of customers who received those coupons also bought one or both of the other products. It occurred to us that all might not yet be lost.

At about the same time, *MacUser* magazine asked if it could mail subscription offers to our customer list and, in return, offered to let us make a mailing to an equal number of *MacUser* subscribers. We decided to try it. If retailers started calling us, we would tell them it was only a test. The catch: We were so broke that we had to scrape to get the money to mail 200 test pieces.

The mailing, made in plain envelopes with only the company name and address on them, included a two-page letter and fliers (all photocopied) for each Working Software product. The offer: Buy each of our products at a 40 percent discount. It cost about 60 cents to produce and mail each piece (we did it all ourselves)—a total campaign cost of $120.

The test was successful. Enough orders came in to finance the mailing of several hundred more pieces to the *MacUser* list. So many orders subsequently came in that we dramatically expanded our direct mail effort. We began printing rather than photocopying fliers and offer letters; we tried different messages on the outside of the envelope; we tested different prices. And we sold more and more products. Within four months of the first mailing, we were sending offers to the entire 250,000-plus names on the *MacUser* list.

By mid-1990, we were mailing as many as 60,000 pieces a month—and by the end of the year, we were mailing that many per week and making a healthy profit. The response rates reached 4 to 5 percent, almost no matter what we offered or how the direct-mail piece looked. (However, response rates have dropped since then.)

THE EFFECT ON OUR BOTTOM LINE

In 1990, our gross revenues were 600 percent of those in 1989. In 1991 our gross revenues doubled the 1990 figure, allowing us to develop several new products and upgrade the existing ones. We have also been able to develop a new technology, the System 7 Apple event Word Services Suite, which allows any application that uses it to access any spelling or grammar checker or other word service—as if it were a built-in menu item.

Our registered-customer list has grown to more than 70,000 buyers of direct-mail products (and we rent our list to others, which provides another source of income from our direct-mail efforts). Our products have received so much exposure from the mailings that we are also once again pursuing—believe it or not—retail channel sales.

The most important thing we learned was this: You have to reach the end user to sell your product. We discovered that people wanted what our products had to offer but had not been able to find them. For us, selling directly to the customer was the answer.

OVERCOMING THE FEAR OF CHANNEL CONFLICT

Why hadn't we tried direct mail sooner? Maybe for the same reasons other companies have steered clear. I had thought about it for years but had always been told that it was important to avoid "channel conflict."

Many people in the software industry have traditionally believed that if you use direct mail, retailers will think you are competing with them and will refuse to carry your products. Why? There are various reasons, not limited to the fact that you *are* competing with them. The retailer loses its percentage of that sale, and direct mail requires using some tactics such as offering a low enough price to convince customers that the "sight unseen" purchase entails an acceptable risk.

However, the reality is that as soon as you sell your products through more than one outlet, you have the potential for channel conflict. For example, if you allow more than one store in a given city to sell your product, they will compete and there will be channel conflict. Of course, individual resellers will want exclusive rights to sell your products. But the fact is that some kinds of sales organizations do a better job than others in selling to a given customer segment, and you have to use what works for you.

I was afraid of channel conflict. Even when we were down to our last dollar, we were afraid to put that half-price coupon into the package with upgrades—but we convinced ourselves to do it. After all, these were already our customers and we were not selling many Findswells and Lookups through stores anyway, so what could it hurt?

I must admit that our use of direct mail did cause problems with retailers. However, now that more and more software companies are using direct mail, I think that retailers are beginning to adapt—they'll have to. And the customer will be the ultimate beneficiary.

THE BEAUTIES OF DIRECT RESPONSE

Direct mail was once considered a less than desirable, risky way to buy a product. This image is changing. Have you noticed the increase of toll-free numbers used in advertisements from major companies? An *ADWEEK* article discussed the movement of major advertisers to direct-response marketing, including Proctor & Gamble's experiments with this concept; it said that P&G is even considering compensating its advertising agencies (and eventually the advertising media) based on the replies it gets to direct-response TV and magazine ads.

Using direct mail is an excellent way to reach customers. Although you are competing with other mail, you aren't buried in a magazine cluttered with many other ads, competing with heavyweights who have more money than you do. The same holds true for store shelves, where you compete for space and for the retailer's attention. In the customer's mailbox, your sales potential is equal to anyone else's. Also, with direct mail you know exactly to whom you sent the offer and exactly who responded; you can have more space than you would in an expensive magazine ad to tell your story.

The real beauty of direct mail is that it is measurable. You can test everything. You know what the response is to different things you do. If you put the right tracking procedures in place, you can find out exactly, to within a thousandth of a percent, if changing the offer by $5 increases the response rate or if printing your letter in blue ink makes a difference.

IF YOU DECIDE TO TEST THE WATERS

Here are some key considerations about using direct mail and some suggestions about how to proceed if you decide to use it.

- *It requires a change in thinking.* Direct mail will change the culture of your company. It certainly changed the way we look at our business. Direct sellers don't seem to worry as much about "corporate image" or "strategic positioning"; they worry more about getting orders and making sure checks clear. This is probably because direct-mail response is immediately measurable. You quickly discover what does and doesn't work, and there isn't a lot of room to get away with silly stuff. In my experience, there is a lot more common sense involved in direct mail than in other forms of advertising.

- *Margins may be lower.* The margin on products sold through direct mail can be much lower than those sold through retail channels. (But remember, if you've tested the offer and the list, you'll likely know how much risk you face.) To be successful in direct mail, you have to make a very good offer to customers—often at a price point well below what you've offered at retail. If you are doing well in retail or other channels, you should consider that the offer you make directly to customers must be good enough to prompt them to buy through the mail rather than running down to the local store. And that means that you are competing with retailers—and with your own products on store shelves.

- *Start slowly.* Learn the ropes. In our case, the growth from a few hundred to 60,000 mail pieces a week did not just happen. It evolved. It was a learning process, fueled first by an empty cash register and then by the positive reinforcement of a revitalized cash flow.

    We—Mark Galvin (our former marketing manager) and I—read every book and magazine article we could find on the subject and attended seminars. Also, one of the most useful things we did was to examine carefully every piece of response mail we could find; we scrutinized the design, content, wording, placement of graphics, envelope messages, and even the label placement. Imagine reading all your junk mail every day! In addition, we had to learn about printing costs, postage classes and rates, and how mailing houses and list brokers operate.

- *Should you do it yourself?* We did it all ourselves because we didn't have any money. It turned out that we had a natural knack for it. But I would not recommend this approach. Direct mail done the wrong way can be much more expensive than hiring a good consultant. Many very good direct-mail consultants are available.

- *Give it an honest try.* Don't hedge: Don't fool yourself into thinking that you can send a letter and a flier with no order form in an attempt to direct customers to the retail store that carries your product; if customers want your product and can't order it via your mailer, when they run to the store to buy your product, the salesperson may very well "switch" them to a competing product.

So don't just make the offer; take the order—give customers a chance to order right then and there. Furthermore, you have to be willing to make a good offer; make one that customers can't refuse, and you'll find that the orders will flow in.

- *Test, test, test.* With proper tracking procedures, you can test everything. Since you can directly measure the results, use that to help you create the most effective campaign possible. Test your offer. Test your list. Test the format and/or presentation of your offering. Testing is the most important factor in the success or failure of your direct-mail campaign.

- *Be realistic about response rates.* What's acceptable? The response rate that matters is one that makes money. You may have heard a rule of thumb: 2 percent is the acceptable response. Don't get hung up on it. If you are offering something for $500, you need fewer orders to make money than if you are offering something for $10.

GETTING THE RIGHT OFFER TO THE RIGHT PERSON

What determines the response you'll get to your direct mail offer? Experts say that 50 percent of the response depends on the list, 35 percent depends on the offer, and 15 percent depends on the perceived quality of the mailing piece (that is, the production quality).

Direct mail is about getting the right offer to the right person. The ideal situation is to find a list of people who have a *desire* to buy and the *ability* to buy—people who have been looking for a product just like yours and who get large tax returns the day before your offer arrives. And when you begin using direct mail, you will tend to spend a lot of time trying to make the artwork (the letter, brochure, and order form) look nice and read well. Of course, you want to put your best foot forward, but don't do so at the expense of fine-tuning the offer and the list.

To illustrate how important it is to make the right offer to the right person, consider two scenarios.

- *Scenario 1:* You're a Macintosh developer, all your equipment is Macintosh-oriented, and you really want a laptop. You get a poorly written letter from a guy who says he wants to sell two PowerBook 180s for $1,000 each, still under warranty—if you call him right away. You *will* call him right away. This demonstrates the power of making the right offer to the right list. (The poor production of the mailer probably won't stop you from taking advantage of the offer.)

- *Scenario 2:* You get the same letter, but the seller is offering Toshiba laptops for $1,000 each. You don't call. Great offer, wrong list. The list made the big difference. Junk mail is in the eye of the beholder. A piece of direct mail is "junk" only when it makes an offer you aren't interested in. When you're spending a nice chunk of change on a direct mailer, you begin to understand that you have a huge incentive to get the right offer to the right person.

Finally, have you ever noticed that many direct mail pieces look the same? There is a reason: Direct mail experts test everything—they find out what works, and they stick to it. For example, almost all direct mail letters use the Courier font. (Don't ask me why, but it works, and I don't want to spend the money to try a different font.)

IS DIRECT RESPONSE RIGHT FOR YOU?

That's a tough question. Direct mail can more than pay for itself when it works. But when it doesn't, it teaches some very expensive lessons. (We've learned a few good lessons, such as don't drop 250,000 pieces a week before a war starts; don't commit to mailing 1 million pieces just before the president says we are in a serious recession; and don't accidentally send a great Mac product offer to a list of IBM PC owners.) Also, you must decide for yourself what constitutes channel conflict and what is acceptable, given your circumstances.

In our case, direct mail was the right thing to do; it saved our company. And the feeling of control over our own success that comes from being able to measure and track the market's response to different things we try has made this business fun—and profitable—again.

CHAPTER SIXTEEN

Selling Off the Page

GUIDELINES FOR CREATING SUCCESSFUL DIRECT RESPONSE ADS

By Leigh Marriner, Marriner Associates

Leigh Marriner is the managing partner of Marriner Associates, a firm located in San Rafael, California, that develops competitive strategies and marketing programs for personal computer software companies.

ADVERTISING is often the first thing that comes to mind when a company develops a marketing plan for a product. At first glance, it seems to be a natural, high-profile choice. But let me go on the record saying I believe that automatically relying on advertising as the foundation of a marketing plan is a lazy—or uninformed—approach. Advertising does play a useful role as part of a *balanced*, carefully crafted marketing plan. One thing advertising can accomplish is raising customer awareness of your company and product (creating an image). However, this kind of advertising can be expensive because to create significant awareness—and see a tangible result—you must run an ad many times during a relatively long period. Therefore, if your total marketing budget is under $100,000, awareness advertising will eat such a large piece that it may not be a wise allocation of your money.

But another kind of advertising may make more effective use of a small budget: You can sell products directly "off the page" using direct response ads. These ads are intended to close a sale and give customers a way to place an order (such as by using a mail-in coupon or toll-free telephone number). Well-executed direct response ads that are run at the right times in appropriate publications can give you a tangible, immediate result—revenue. And when used in tandem with other communications strategies, direct response advertising can contribute to building product and company awareness. Of course, choosing the most appropriate publications in which to run an ad and having an adequate infrastructure to handle inquiries and orders effectively are a must for a successful direct response campaign. But the foundation for a successful campaign is *an effective ad.*

The details of what makes good direct response ads would fill a book. However, there are some rules of thumb that can aid you in evaluating the quality and potential efficacy of the ads you produce. To help you do this, here are two groups of "rules" (there are always exceptions, of course). The first group focuses on how an ad looks without any consideration of content; these rules therefore apply to most ads, not just direct response ones: the role of the headline, visuals, and copy, and the purpose of the ad. The second group of rules addresses the specific elements that make up a successful direct response ad.

ACHIEVING "THE LOOK"

The following set of guidelines about how ads should look applies to both awareness and direct response ads.

Guideline #1

Ads shouldn't be art for art's sake. The purpose of a direct response ad is to create desire for a product and generate an order—not showcase artistic creativity. There's nothing wrong with running an ad that is aesthetically beautiful or unusual, *as long as* it sells the product. But if a prospect can't read the name of your product, or thinks "My, what a beautiful picture" and then turns the page, or doesn't understand the message, you won't accomplish your objective.

This is one of the most difficult lessons to learn. The experts whose advice you most heavily depend on—ad agencies or freelance graphics and advertising professionals—usually lean toward being highly creative: Their orientation and training are usually geared to creating interesting or beautiful ads. Your job is to help them remember that the purpose of your advertising is not to be pretty, unusual, or to win awards, but to sell. Your agency should try to temper its natural bent toward creativity, artistic trend, and visual beauty with a clear understanding of an ad's marketing objective. (Even the best agencies sometimes lapse into creating sublime form at the expense of function.)

Guideline #2

Make sure the headline conveys the main point, and does so in the form of a well-defined customer benefit. The headline's purpose is to grab the attention of as many people as possible and coax them to read the ad. This is important because the statistics say that most readers won't notice your ad at all; some people will look at the headline or visuals, very few will read subheads, and even fewer will read body text. If the headline, alone, captures readers' attention and communicates that the ad is about a product that will solve a problem they face (that is, if the headline describes the user benefit), they'll be more likely to continue reading. For example, if your drawing application is particularly easy to install and learn, a headline such as "It's a piece of cake" doesn't give readers a clue about whether the ad is about something they need. On the other hand, "Complete your first drawing within one hour of installation" broadcasts a clear benefit message.

Guideline #3

Headlines shouldn't require mental effort on the reader's part, and headline language should be clear. Most readers just page casually through a magazine, and often aren't looking for anything in particular. If they don't immediately grasp that your ad is about a product of interest to them, they won't stop to read it. Headlines such as "Don't seek and you shall find" can be annoying and propel readers right past your page.

Likewise, use clear language. Don't brag, use cute plays on words, or be indirect and still expect readers to follow you. "We sell straight lines" tells readers nothing except that the ad agency was trying to be clever. Instead, refer back to the preceding rule: Make your main point in the headline.

Guideline #4

Short headlines aren't always best. If clearly stating a well-defined user benefit requires three lines of text, and the wording is as clear and concise as possible, so be it. The objective is to stop readers as they flip by your ad and entice them to read more of it.

Guideline #5

Good headlines often mention a product by name. This helps build and reinforce reader awareness of your product. It is also a cue to interested readers who have already heard of your product that it may be worth the effort to read on.

Guideline #6

Use visuals that complement the headline. The headline and visual each should clearly communicate your main point, and they should work together to reinforce the user benefit. For example, a photograph of a handsome man or beautiful woman holding your product doesn't give readers information about the product's value, unless it's an ad for such things as clothing, hair care products, or a dating service. On the other hand, a picture of someone climbing out of a combat tank, dirty and smiling, speaks volumes if your product is a World War II tank-simulation game. Visuals that have a problem-solving, storytelling quality are most effective.

Guideline #7

The body text should communicate information directly and clearly. Readers approach an ad with an innate skepticism about its honesty. To help counteract this, your choice of words should be honest, realistic, and clear. Don't use lyrical prose or boastful verbiage. If you give readers any reason to think you're exaggerating or overplaying your hand, they'll flip the page. For example, telling readers that your product will "make your personal computers do all those wonderful things you expected them to do in the first place" won't convince them of anything except that you and your product proposition are naive. In that case, you've paid good money to give the reader a negative impression.

Guideline #8

Body text should provide adequate information and benefits. It's difficult to err by giving readers too much information, as long as the ad is easy to read. Tell readers all the sales points and benefits needed to kindle or confirm their interest, but be specific about product facts. If you have won awards, show them; if you've done research demonstrating that using the product increases productivity, cite it. However, make sure not to rant on; there's a fine line between giving readers information they need to make a decision and bogging them down in too much irrelevant detail.

Guideline #9

Make the text easy to read. If an ad is hard to read, most people won't go to the trouble to do so. The danger signs include text that extends from the left margin of the page to the right margin without a break, lack of either white space or subheads between blocks of text, and white text on a black or dark background. Blocks of unbroken text are deadly, no matter how well written the ad or how much white space it contains. Use subheads to break up the text; they are easy for readers to skim, and subheads help them decide if it's worthwhile to read the entire ad. Using subheads also gives you an opportunity to call attention to a major point.

Although white type on a black background (called "reverse type") occasionally works for a headline, this combination is less legible than black-on-white. Reading an entire block of text in reverse type can give people headaches. Also, it's tempting to reduce the type size so that you can squeeze in more text. When you feel the temptation, don't give in. Instead, prioritize the product benefits and eliminate a few from the ad.

GUIDELINES SPECIFICALLY FOR DIRECT RESPONSE ADS

The guidelines just given apply to almost any kind of ad, including direct response ads. But as you'll soon see, when it comes to direct response ads, looking good falls lower on the priorities list; conveying the specific information needed to sell a product is the primary objective. Here's how you can accomplish that.

Guideline #1

Don't go it alone; hire an individual or agency with direct response advertising expertise. The purpose of a direct response ad is to convince readers to order your product. As you can imagine, since an ad's text, not its artwork, conveys most of the key information, art direction is less important than copywriting. And because direct response copywriting is a special skill, a good, general advertising copywriter or agency is definitely not right for this job. Instead, I suggest choosing an agency or writer who is experienced in direct response techniques.

Likewise, it wouldn't make sense to try to create these ads yourself. The elements of effective direct response advertising are specific, and the details can make the difference between success and failure. If you don't have the budget to pay for good direct response talent, don't do the ad; you'll probably waste your money.

Guideline #2

Make sure the ad contains all the necessary elements. All good direct response ads contain some common, necessary components. Here are the elements that are mandatory for an effective direct response ad:

- *A thorough yet concise description of the product and the user problem it solves.* It's important to offer sufficient information for readers to make up their minds. Most people are somewhat hesitant to buy a product they haven't actually seen, so anything you can do to offset this misgiving will work in your favor. (For example, a photo of your product usually works well.) Give readers plenty of information to help them make a decision, including all key benefits, features, specifications, and hardware and software requirements. Try to address any objections customers may have. Also, don't assume readers know more than they do. For instance, don't try to advertise an add-on product without describing what the base product does.

- *A substantial promise about product performance or user benefit.* Back your promise with facts that are focused on your target audience and the benefit and value you offer. For example, if your promise is that your product compresses files "on the fly," tell users that they can save 50 percent of their disk space and also open files as fast as they could if the files weren't compressed.

- *Price.* Display your price prominently. Don't frustrate potential customers by making them search your ad with a magnifying glass to find the all-important product price.

- *A money-back, full-satisfaction guarantee.* Offering a guarantee is crucial to fostering a feeling of customer confidence. It implies that you have confidence in your product and that purchasing it is a no-risk proposition. Successful direct response ads remove all barriers to purchase, and a guarantee will eliminate a lot of customer hesitation. If you're not confident enough in the product to offer a guarantee, then your product will probably fail regardless of whether your ad is effective.

  In some geographic areas, federal or state regulations dictate whether you must offer certain terms to mail-order customers, such as a money-back guarantee. Ensure that your policies are in tune with these regulations (and those of other countries or states, if you're shipping across borders or state lines).

- *A special offer.* Give readers a reason to believe they are getting an especially good deal if they buy your product now. Most successful direct response ads rely, in part, on impulse buying, and a special offer can help close the sale. Make sure it is somehow related to the product and that it appeals to your target audience. However, if you also sell this product in retail channels, don't make the total offer (the product plus the special offer) much better than what the retailer can offer, or you'll hear complaints from the channel.

- *Magic words.* Use language that will tempt customers to buy and that reduces the perceived risk of ordering "sight unseen." Examples of effective wording are "free," "no risk," "special offer," "guaranteed," "limited-time offer," and "breakthrough." (However, make sure that what you say about your offer is true.)

- *A call to action.* Be clear about what response you expect from the reader. Come right out and ask for the order. Use motivational phrases such as "Yes, I want to order Product XYZ!"

- *A toll-free telephone number for placing orders and making inquiries.* Studies show that offering a toll-free telephone number increases the response to an ad. It's important that readers be able to interact with your company or sales agent immediately (while the desire to buy is high), so contacting you to order or make inquiries should be easy. This is especially important if your target customers are home or small business users, who must foot the bill for a telephone call themselves.

- *Multiple ways to order.* To make ordering as easy as possible, offer as many options as you can, such as telephone, fax, and mail.

- *Information that will facilitate the purchase.* Let readers know everything needed to place an order. For example, there should be no question of what days and hours your telephone line is staffed; from what countries or areas the toll-free number can or can't be used (for example, most U.S. toll-free numbers can't be called from other countries, and vice versa); what forms of payment you accept; and the product stock number (if required by your sales center when customers order). Also, if customers are purchasing upgrades and will need to offer proof-of-purchase such as a serial number, tell them up front.

- *A code that will allow you to track where responses come from.* In direct response advertising, as in direct mail, you have an opportunity to determine if you are achieving the needed return from your investment—probably the most important part of a campaign. For example, you can put a code number somewhere on the order form (coupon) or add a bogus extension number to a toll-free telephone number. It doesn't matter what the code is, as long as it corresponds uniquely to each ad placement. In other words, an ad run in November would have a different code than the same ad run in December, and ads in *Macworld* magazine would have a different code than the same ads placed in *MacUser.*

  With the appropriate tracking system, the first time you run an ad you can determine if it is generating sufficient orders. After you gain experience, six to eight weeks into a campaign you'll be able to predict the total revenue that will be generated. Tracking responses is particularly important when you've placed your ad in more than one trade magazine or run it in more than one issue of a publication. You'll need to know which publications draw the most customers (or what months of the year work best) and alter your strategy accordingly.

Guideline #3

Don't overlook other elements that can help the ad sell. There are several additional elements that can be especially effective in selling off the page. You don't need to use each one in every ad, but you should use these as the situation dictates:

- *A coupon.* Consider including a coupon—a mini-order form—in your ad, even if you don't expect readers to order by mail. It identifies the ad as a direct response one—an important visual clue for readers. The coupon also gives you a place to summarize the offer and ask for the order and tells readers what information they'll need to give you when they call to place an order.

- *Photo of the product package and its contents.* Magazine readers don't have the opportunity to hold your package and examine it. A photo of the package and its contents will help readers to visualize what they are buying.

- *Screen shots or samples of printed output.* These things will help customers visualize what they are ordering. The more information you can give and questions you can answer, the more likely customers are to buy your product.

Guideline #4

Give your proposed ad the acid test. Before you sign off on a particular layout and text, test your ad—even if you do so informally with a few company outsiders—to determine if it meets your objectives. Generally, you should determine the following.

- Does the ad follow the guidelines suggested here?

- Does it contain all the necessary elements?

- Does it drive home the one main selling point?

- Overall, does your ad make people want to do business with you?

If you can't answer these questions affirmatively, it will be well worth your time and effort to correct any problems. But if you can truthfully, objectively answer "yes" to each question, you're probably ready to launch the ad.

As you can see, you may get the most from a small advertising budget by using direct response ads in lieu of awareness-building ones. If you clearly understand the product benefits that will "sell" your customers—and effectively communicate this information to them—selling off the page can be a winning strategy.

CHAPTER SEVENTEEN

Making Sense of the Glitz

HOW TO EVALUATE DESIGN AGENCIES

By Dee Kiamy, Open Door Communications

Dee Kiamy is president of Open Door Communications, a strategic communications consulting practice located in San Jose, California, that serves high-technology and entertainment companies. She also developed and edited this book.

DURING a product's early life, marketing communications pieces—data sheets, sales brochures, point-of-sale materials, and the other pieces that are usually known as "collateral"—become almost as important to your success as your product's code. You didn't trust just anyone to program your application, and you likewise shouldn't let just any communications firm handle your collateral work. The reason: Along with your other communication efforts—such as public relations and advertising—collateral materials contribute heavily to establishing your company's public image.

Choosing a design firm or agency to handle these critical items can be confounding the first time around. Early in my career, I planned collateral and promotional strategies (often with as many as 40 to 50 projects on the drawing boards at any given time) for a large company and was responsible for choosing the agencies and designers for the jobs. A steady stream of designers scheduled presentations of their wares, and I soon became dazzled (or was it razzled?) by all their six-color, multifold, scored, perforated, three-dimensional, award-winning glitz. In that overwhelming paper parade, every firm looked good to me.

However, the task of selecting the "right" designers really wasn't so daunting once I realized a simple fact: There was a wealth of information about each firm contained in the pages of its portfolio. The portfolio is simply a collection of a design firm's creative work, and, together with its client list, is the firm's stock in trade. It is probably the single richest source of information about the caliber of a firm. From it you can glean important information about how the firm does business, the kind and quality of work it produces, the range of services it provides, and its clientele.

When I began asking the right questions about what I saw in the portfolios I reviewed, I broke the code. The result was a much clearer picture of each firm's talents and expertise and, most important, whether it was a good match for my needs. This chapter is not as much about how to *choose* the right agency as it is about how to *evaluate* what you see and hear while examining a firm's portfolio.

BEFORE THE SHOW

A portfolio presentation will do no good if it doesn't address your particular needs. So before designer and agency presentations, take a little bit of time to help them prepare to meet with you. Otherwise, you may end up sitting through spiels that fail to deliver the kind of information you need to make a decision. However, a small investment of time up front can help prevent wasting it later. Ahead of time, the firms you review should understand the general nature of your company, your product, and the communications job you'll need. They'll need answers to questions such as these: Is this a new product introduction? Are you trying to break into a new market? Or do you simply need to develop a '90s look for your packaging?

If you clearly define your project up front, the agency can prepare better and will be more likely to bring the right items to your first meeting. Also, by knowing your needs ahead of time, the agency can forewarn you if it doesn't offer the particular services or expertise you're seeking. For example, suppose your project involves designing product packaging; if the agency you're considering instead specializes in creating promotional brochures, you'll want to know that up front.

UNVEILING CAPABILITIES

The portfolio's contents can reveal a lot about a firm's capabilities, especially if you ask questions to establish the exact nature and extent of the contribution a firm made to the work you see in its portfolio. Try this test: Choose some brochures or other pieces from the portfolio that you find particularly striking, and ask questions such as these: What role did you play in the creation and production of this work? Did you create pieces from scratch, or did you act as a project manager and contract the projects (or large portions of them) out? Did you come up with the concept? Direct the photography? Do the writing? Manage the printing and mailing? How much did it cost? What was the purpose or use of the piece? What role did the client play in the process? Did the client offer any after-the-fact feedback about how successful the piece was? Also ask what, in retrospect, the agency would have done differently.

The answers to such questions can help you evaluate whether the agency may have the specific expertise to meet your needs. For example, firms often use existing photography received from clients or licensed from photography "banks." If your project will require extensive original photography, you should be on the lookout for pieces that demonstrate an agency's ability to direct photography. The same applies to copy writing. In most cases, it's not a negative if an agency didn't do everything from scratch. Being able to draw from a pool of outside talent allows a designer or agency to purchase very specialized talent as needed by a project (such as an illustrator with a specific style or a photographer that specializes in filming certain kinds of products).

However, if a firm must subcontract out a lot of the work, you in essence become subject to the subcontractors' schedules. Although in principle that should be the concern of the firm you've hired, in practice it doesn't always work that way. How well the firm manages its subcontractors can affect whether it can meet deadlines. It's important to understand the role the firm played in each aspect of its work so that you get a more accurate picture of its capabilities, strengths, and weaknesses.

As you flip through the pages of a portfolio, ask designers which pieces they are most proud of and why. What do they feel they do best? Ask them to point out examples. You should also inquire if the creative person or team responsible for this work is still employed at the agency. Agencies and design firms tend to have a tremendous talent turnover, and today's creative team (or person) may work somewhere else tomorrow. If a firm consistently produces good work, it's probably able to hang onto its talent, or is good at hiring the right kinds of people, or is well managed—or a combination thereof.

Make sure that when reviewing the portfolio you pay particularly close attention to examples of work that are conceptually or functionally similar to your project. Find out what was involved in producing those pieces—how the agency worked with the client, the approximate budget, how long the project took from start to finish. You'll not only learn more about the agency, but you'll also develop insights into how the designer approaches the creative process and how this approach may apply to your project.

However, even though you may need a specific service, don't ignore the other kinds of work a firm has done. By reviewing a variety of pieces (including direct mail campaigns, promotional brochures, advertisements, corporate image pieces, and so forth) that are representative of the firm's creative range, you'll get a feel for a designer's overall creative range and style.

DISTINGUISHING QUALITY FROM GLITZ

When you examine a portfolio, try to get a feeling for whether the firm can produce quality work on a limited budget. The issue here is distinguishing quality from glitz, quality in this case meaning effective design that meets your marketing communications objectives while portraying the right image for your company—without budget overkill. (Of course, there's a difference between shoddy workmanship and quality, budget-conscious—but effective—work.)

From scrutinizing the portfolio's contents, you can determine whether a designer or agency can tailor itself to a range of needs and budgets or produces only very upscale (read: expensive) work. Face it: Sometimes you need a Lexus, and sometimes you need a Hyundai; sometimes you need luxury, and sometimes economy. If your budget is tight, recognizing what you really need to accomplish your communications objectives and hiring a design team that can accommodate you can mean the difference between bringing in a project on budget and blowing not only this quarter's money but also next quarter's—on one job.

Some firms do have a proclivity for producing only expensive work. They prefer to push the creative envelope and develop designs that use the latest and greatest in color, imaging technology, paper stock, and the like. But if they can't (or won't) produce a marketing communications piece that meets your needs within budget, then you should look elsewhere. For example, your data sheet design probably doesn't have to feature a hologram and be printed in four colors on exotic paper. That's an extreme example, but the point is that many times your collateral pieces need only be "what they need to be" to accomplish your communications objectives. I've seen lots of four-color brochures that, with a little bit of clever, well-executed design, writing, and production, could have been excellent two-color pieces that still met their objectives. Of course, much of the burden also falls on you, the client, to recognize what's needed to meet your objectives—and to stick to it even when the temptation to increase the glitz factor is strong.

Also, remember that the design fee itself is just one portion of the total cost to produce a piece of collateral. Printing, collating, and mailing can also be real budget eaters. Even if a designer's bill is well within your budget, you may still blow your pot of money if the resulting piece requires expensive printing and production; the same is true if the piece is so unusually shaped that it requires special inventory storage (say, in the case of product packaging) or a highly customized mailing envelope (in the case of a brochure, for instance).

Many firms tend to show you only their more glitzy, top-drawer pieces. Showing you only ultra-slick work in the portfolio may be a tipoff to an agency's proclivity toward glitz. However, a firm may simply want to show you "its best." Inquire about it, and probe designers for their viewpoints on the tradeoffs between creativity and communications function. If they try to skirt the issue, that should send up a red flag. Also, ask to see several more modestly produced pieces, too. (Tell designers ahead of time so that they'll know to bring these things to the presentation.)

AWARDS AND CREATIVE BEAUTY: WHAT'S THE REAL PRIZE?

Speaking of glitz, agencies and design firms are deservedly proud of the awards they've won and will probably mention these kudos when showing their portfolios. Awards can give you important information about the firm; it's important that when awards are mentioned, you do a little bit of investigating about them.

In design, advertising, and public relations, there are more award competitions than you can shake a stick at. (This mirrors the TV, film, and music industries; how many awards ceremonies have you heard of or seen recently?) However, it would be a mistake to categorically discount the awards a firm has garnered just because there are so many of them to be won. When designers speak about awards, ask which awards they are most proud of and why. Ask to see the pieces of work the awards were for; inquire about the specific accomplishments the awards recognized, who the competitors were, and what the judging or selection process was.

Asking these questions will help you gauge the caliber of a designer's work as perceived by "experts" or peers. It also gives you an opportunity to applaud your potential partner and thus signal that you are interested in its work and would value its particular skills. (A quick aside: Buying a creative service isn't like purchasing office supplies or equipment parts. Instead, you are buying brainpower—creativity—just as you do when you hire programmers, and you should be sensitive to what motivates creative people. Just like everyone else, the agency's artistic team wants to create things that they can show off with pride, and they want opportunities to produce work that speaks well for their talents. They also want to make money.)

On the other hand, beware if a firm unduly emphasizes its long laundry list of awards, because some companies inadvertently produce award-winning art at the expense of accomplishing communications objectives. The real prize, as far as you're concerned, is meeting your communications objectives. What Leigh Marriner said about direct response advertisements in Chapter 16, "Selling Off the Page: Guidelines for Creating Successful Direct Response Ads" also applies to almost any piece of collateral or promotion: It shouldn't be art for art's sake.

I think the point is so important that it bears repeating here: The main purpose of a marketing communications piece almost always is to promote a product, not showcase artistic creativity. There's nothing wrong with creating a communications piece that is aesthetically beautiful or unusual, as long as it achieves your communications objective. But if prospects can't read the name of your product, or are so distracted by a brochure's artistic beauty that they fail to remember what product or company was being promoted, or don't understand the message, you won't accomplish your objective.

Ad agencies or freelance graphics and advertising professionals generally lean toward being highly creative: Their orientation and training are frequently geared to creating interesting or beautiful work. However, your agency or designer should be capable of tempering its natural bent toward creativity, artistic trend, and visual beauty with a clear understanding of your marketing objective. This ability (or its absence) will become apparent as you discuss the portfolio—if you watch for it. Be on the lookout for awards for work that was evaluated on its creative merit as well as how well it met marketing or communications objectives. The answers to questions you ask about each piece's communications purpose will give you some of the best hints. For example, if the agencies' responses to such questions are couched in terms of how their brochures met marketing objectives or increased customer inquiries or reached a particular audience segment—something of that nature—it's a sign that they may be clued in to your *raison d'etre.*

THE CLIENT LIST

The client list is another indicator of what is important to a design firm, as well as the caliber of work it creates. Who a firm works with (or doesn't work with) can give you clues about whether it may be a good match for you.

After reviewing a portfolio, you'll probably want to ask for references to a firm's clients. Although of course you'll probably be referred to only its happier clients, as you review the portfolio you can also make a mental list of other ones. You can also note such things as whether the firm focuses on particular-sized companies and on companies in your industry, other industries, or a mixture. Has the firm worked with your competitors? With companies whose communications efforts you respect or feel have been successful? This kind of information lies within the pages of the portfolio.

UNDERSTANDING A FIRM'S BUSINESS PHILOSOPHY

Finally, the portfolio and tenor of the presentation should give you a sense of what a design company's business philosophy is. It also doesn't hurt to ask such outright questions as "What's your philosophy about client service?" and

"What's your business objective or mission statement?" When a firm stammers and stutters and can't directly address the question, you've probably either hit a nerve or the company isn't focused enough to give you a good answer. But if it responds with a well-defined answer about how it prefers to do business, you'll know you're on the right track.

Successful client/agency interaction is as important—maybe even more important—than its creative abilities. Some years ago, I was considering a small but up-and-coming agency for a particularly important job. During the presentation I asked the agency to cite an example of how it had overcome strong client objections to what the agency felt was effective work. The answer prompted me to inquire about the firm's client service philosophy, and the agency responded straight and to the point: "We're here not only to fill your desires, but also to meet your needs." The agency representatives went on to explain that they preferred building the kind of business relationships in which they wouldn't be relegated to being "yes-men." Although this agency acknowledged that usually what the client wants is what the client gets, it wanted the freedom to point out (diplomatically, of course) the instances when fulfilling our desires was getting in the way of meeting our needs—and to know that we'd listen and accept the input in the spirit that it was offered.

I learned a lot about this firm during that discussion. It (a) was clued in to the need to meet communications objectives, (b) employed people who were likely to be good communications problem solvers, and (c) did some thinking for itself. (By the way, I did hire them; we certainly had some interesting meetings, and the resulting ads and campaigns handsomely met our objectives.)

You can learn a lot about a design firm or agency by closely scrutinizing its portfolio. If you ask probing questions about its work—and read between the lines of what you see—you'll be better able to make sense of the glitz and distinguish which firms are best for handling your collateral materials.

CHAPTER EIGHTEEN

Selling Your Product When You Can't Be There

HOW TO CREATE A DEMO THAT SELLS SOFTWARE

By Tom McLaren, McLaren Associates, Inc.

Tom McLaren is the president of McLaren Associates, Inc., a Portland, Oregon, company that specializes in creating software demos for sales and user training.

IN her monthly *ADWEEK* "Marketing Computers" column, Kristin Zhivago once said, "Buying software without a demo is like buying a car without taking a test drive. Most people want to get a feel for it." This is absolutely true, but I'll add a caveat: to sell software, the demo has to be a *good* one.

I have boxes full of demo disks from over the years, disks intended to sell software—demos that supposedly explain and convince and give a feel for the product. My guess: No more than a handful were successful. Many of them are poor examples of marketing communications. Haven't you sat through more than your share of bad demos? In this chapter, you'll find out why a good demo is important and how to make sure your next demo sells your software.

DEMOS DEFINED

This chapter focuses on demos that are used to sell a product—the pre-sales demo. However, there is plenty of overlap between this kind of demo and others, such as post-sales tutorial and help systems; much of what you'll read here could apply to most demos. In fact, any tool that helps people learn about your product will increase sales, since a product fully and successfully used gets good reviews and lots of word-of-mouth referrals.

The next time you create a sales demo disk, ask yourself how you want to use it. There are two ways to use demos as sales tools. A *direct response demo* is intended for a single viewer who doesn't have the benefit of someone to hold his or her hand or answer questions. The demo might be mailed to someone who has responded to an ad, or it might be used in a telemarketing campaign. A *point-of-sale* demo is a one-to-many people vehicle. It works well at trade shows and in stores.

Demos for Direct Response

A few types of demos that work well in the single-viewer environment are the simulation demo and the trial-size demo. A *simulation demo* (such as a self-driven "tour") can give users a feel for your application without allowing them to wander off-track and without requiring lengthy setup and orientation. Also, since you "control" the demo, you have a much better chance of ensuring that the customer feels some satisfaction after completing it. Indeed, a good simulation demo gives users a sort of self-substantiating proof: They'll believe the software works the way you claim it does; consistent prompting and feedback ensure that users understand how each feature works.

If your software generally demos well in person ("live"), it will probably show well in a simulation demo. Simulation demos work best when the software accomplishes a concrete goal that gives the user instant results. For instance, "Do operation A, then do B, and voilà! Report C prints out—all the documentation the banker will need to process your loan." A simulation can be part of a point-of-sale demo, but since it requires a high level of involvement and interaction with the user, it works best as a direct response tool. The user can sit down with the demo in his or her own environment and explore your product more fully. This, of course, is more difficult to do in a retail environment.

If you anticipate difficulty simulating your software or if it is difficult to do a "canned" demo in person, your product probably isn't a good candidate for a simulation demo. Likewise, if your product can prove itself only when people use their own data, a trial-size demo may be your best choice.

A *trial-size demo* is used almost exclusively as a direct-response tool. This kind of demo uses a "quick start" book and a limited (or "crippled," to use a less appealing but more common term) version of the software. A trial-size demo must be accompanied by a compelling, clearly written book and bullet-proof sample data to make sure that people get the software up and running successfully. The last thing you want is a potential buyer trying your product, getting lost in the installation process or the application itself, and deciding that your product is too hard to understand—or takes too much time to use. Lose the customer there, and he or she will probably never come back for more.

Point-of-Sale Demos

The heart of a point-of-sale demo is the *attract loop*, a self-running presentation that draws passers-by to a computer and engages them in an interesting discussion of your company and product. Using compelling visuals and sound, this kind of demo helps the viewer associate an upbeat message with your product and company. Attract-loop demos work well in situations where salespeople need help. For instance, at a trade show when your sales representatives are swamped, the attract loop can give browsers an overview of your company and product while they wait for your representative to talk to them.

GOOD DEMO, BAD DEMO

Making sure your demo is a good one is paramount to converting a customer's interest in your product into a sale. And a bad demo isn't only an ineffective waste of money; it can hurt you. A customer who has a bad experience with the demo will be left with a negative impression of your product, company, or both. Not only will you lose that sale, but probably others, as well. Remember, friends tell friends....

So it's important to take the time and effort to create a really good demo. Good demos are based on audience needs. Most of us have had it drilled into our heads: Stress the benefits, not the features, of our products. (This is sometimes easier said than done. For instance: "Our printer is 50 percent faster." Is that a feature or a benefit to the user?)

Think of your demo as a story that must prove that your product meets your audience's needs. If you can't convince people of a product's benefits in a way that is meaningful to them, you probably won't make a sale. Needs-based demos keep your audience's interest with a concise story and compelling conclusion. Likewise, a good demo is targeted at a very specific, well-defined audience. Of course, the demo may be useful to other people, but to be successful it must be focused on one particular audience.

In contrast, bad demos are usually based more on your love of the product's features and technology. They often are formless, overwhelming, and opaque and are characterized by lengthy feature lists and no particular movement forward or conclusion. They try to reach everyone rather than a specific target and end up communicating to no one.

Good demos are succinct, with a brisk pace appropriate to the subject. If you go into too much detail, you'll lose your audience. Think of what's going on when you drift away from a book, a TV show or, heaven forbid, a magazine article. Good demos, like any communication, move quickly enough to hold interest but linger long enough to cover essential information. Don't make your demo too long. For example, if the demo includes laborious company and product positioning followed by glowing descriptions of all the features, it's probably going to lose the viewer, who is thinking, "Hey, get to the part that involves *me*!"

On the other hand, don't make the demo too short. Sometimes a developer assumes that a list of features will convince me to buy the product—but it won't if I don't even understand half the terms on the list. If your product requires it, give me enough education to get through the demo comfortably.

Good demos are thoughtfully designed—in terms of both graphics and user interface. A good demo always tells users where to look and what action to take. Bad demos confuse the user and fail to distinguish clearly between demo messages and the software that is the subject of the demo. Good demos use the fundamentals of good visual communication to increase the power of the presentation. Bad demos use distracting graphic doodads that may be great whiz-bang attention-getters but will confuse the audience.

Good demos don't require any special installation process. (The user should be able to pop the disk into the drive, double-click on its icon, and be off and running.) Bad demos, on the other hand, undermine customers' confidence in their abilities to use your application.

Good demos are software- and user-tested. Use the same thorough, sound testing methods on your demos that you use on your products and your other sales and communications tools. Ask yourself such things as: Does the story work? Does the screen design work? How easy is it to install and use the demo? What message did it deliver? Did it reach the intended audience? This process is very important; bad demos reflect poorly on your design and development expertise.

Ten Most Deadly Demo Traits

To help you put the good demo/bad demo comparison in perspective, here is my brief synopsis of the ten most deadly demo traits:

#1: Talking to several audiences at the same time. *"I think they started to lose me when they spent all that time talking about the output speed to 3-D rendering devices...."*

#2: A long-winded features-based story. *"Gee, I'm only on screen 5 of 9—maybe if they supplied a glossary I'd actually understand some of what they're talking about...."*

#3: Not being clear about where to look or what do next. *"Perhaps it's just me, but I can't tell if I should click here, or watch the flashing dog icon, or just wait for something to happen...."*

#4: Too long. *"Silly me, here I am thinking I can learn about mailing-label software in under an hour...."*

#5: Too many choices of what to do next. *"Hmmm...should I choose, Benefits, or maybe Quick Tour, or maybe Easy Reports, or perhaps Executive Summary? Or maybe I'll come back to this when I have more time...."*

#6: Cluttered windows. *"This is exactly what I'm looking for in an application—something even more unappealing than my desk on its worst day...."*

#7: Condescending, idiotic sample data. *"Hoo-boy, this is truly real-world, an inventory example featuring the short-people's stilt company...."*

#8: Difficult installation. *"Well, I'm ready right now to order software from a company whose demo I can't even install...."*

#9: Carrying simulation to a fault. *"I'm tired of typing in phone numbers. Is this actually a typing proficiency test...?"*

#10: Offering unclear info about hardware requirements. *"Jeez, Marge, the demo shut us down. I guess our system just isn't good enough for their demo...."*

In the end, *you* are actually the best person to decide what makes a good demo for your product. My best advice: Call some 800 numbers, order some demos, and see for yourself what works and what doesn't. Pick them apart, see why you like or don't like them. Look at demos for competing products as well as new, unrelated products. Look at games, too. They're great at getting and holding attention.

DEFINING AUDIENCE NEEDS

As I said earlier, a good demo is based on audience needs. If you start the demo creation process by defining and specifying audience needs, it will be much easier to decide on content, pacing, and design. If you do a good job defining audience/needs, the rest of the pieces should fall neatly into place. (I'll add that if you hammer out audience needs for your product communications programs—your marketing messages—as a whole, your advertising, PR, and demo messages will also fall into place.) In fact, both the look-and-feel and message of your demo should dovetail with all your communication pieces. Examine your software, logo, stationery, brochure, spec sheets, and ads—and company image overall—and be sure the demo fits.

The audience for your demo is a subset of the audience for the product. Even if your potential customer base is made up of various kinds of users (such as engineers, system administrators, and managers), each demo should focus on just one category.

How do you decide which group to focus on? First, ask yourself which group has the most purchasing power and which group will respond best to the demo. Sometimes the first and most obvious choice for your demo audience may not be the best. For instance, we created a demo for a networking product. Even though system administrators had the purchasing power, we realized end-users were the primary influencers; thus they were our audience. They were most likely to read our ads, and they were most open to getting the message in a simulation demo. For that matter, although a system administrator might not use it for a technical evaluation, the end-user demo would help him or her to explain the purchase and get buy-in from everyone else involved in the sale.

Next, create an audience profile that will help you design the demo. Be specific: What's the audience's level of computer expertise? Level of interest in this software category? Knowledge of competing products? Usual method for purchasing software? Typical hardware configuration? Because audience needs will determine which features you demo, ask questions such as these: What basic need does your product meet? Will it allow people to spend less time doing something tedious? Does it do something that results in better job performance? Whatever the answer, demo the product in a way that clearly shows the user how it will meet those needs.

Also, instead of thinking in terms of your *product* ("my product saves you time at the fax machine") think in terms of your *audience* ("you need to reduce the time you spend on tedious, repetitive faxing"). Along the same lines, a demo that stresses that a product is fast and easy to use is not directly addressing customer needs. Even if the speed of your product is its selling point, you must craft the message in terms of the specific needs of your audience. "Speeds up screen redraws" is not an effective message. "Spend less time waiting for your display" is a more appropriate one. A demo that clearly shows that the user will wait less time is more likely to close the sale.

Although having a product that is more convenient to use may be a need of some of your customers, the concept of convenience itself is too general and too relative to be the basis of a good demo. For that matter, just because your application is easier to use than other software products doesn't necessarily mean that using it is easier than doing the same thing manually. Ideally, you should come up with needs that are so pronounced—so compelling—that if you can prove you meet them, you will make a sale.

Needless to say, defining audience needs is an important, painstaking process that may take awhile. Everyone, from your engineers to your warehouse manager, has strong ideas about the product and the audience. But once you decide on a primary audience and its most pressing needs, you'll be able to create a successful demo.

CREATING THE DEMO'S "STORY"

Once you've settled on the primary audience and its needs, here's how to translate that into a story for the demo. First, examine the needs list and determine exactly how to prove that the product meets these needs. Then double-check the steps needed to perform an operation. You may find that some features or processes just don't demo well. It's acceptable to skip a few of the non-essential steps, but avoid misrepresenting how basic operations work.

Next, create a story based on a normal project or chain of events that features your product in the starring role. Think about how your primary audience would approach this project, and then create a scenario that proves that your product can do the job.

You may want to provide a "step-by-step" tutorial. These can be extremely effective, but such tutorials have a down side as well. On the up side, some people need to feel they are really giving a product a workout. A step-by-step tutorial accomplishes this by taking users through the actual menu choices and keystrokes required to perform a key task with your product. Also, a tutorial is effective in helping users believe the product really works the way you say it does. And the more interactive the demo, the more your prospect is involved in the sales process. On the down side, your audience may not wish to do such a rigorous evaluation, and a tutorial may be a bit too detailed for them. (You can see how understanding audience needs and targeting the right people is critical.)

DEMO VERSATILITY

Demos are versatile tools. If you plan well, you can use them in a variety of ways. They aren't useful only for the near-term; demos can also work with long-term marketing programs. For instance, if you're rolling out several new products in the next two years, consider creating a modular demo that can be easily updated.

With minor modifications, demos can be used in some very creative ways. I urge you to get the most out of your investment by thinking about all the ways you might use demos. For instance, if you're increasing co-op advertising with resellers, think about how to tie a demo to a special promotion—such as contest disks. In a contest disk, users are given an incentive to go through essential parts of the demo. One way might be to reward them for matching three graphics; that is, at the beginning of the demo they are given a graphic. If they find two other graphics during the demo that exactly match it, they can return the disk to the developer and receive a prize.

Also, direct response demos are used not only in conjunction with ads ("call this 800 number for a free demo") and direct mail campaigns, but also as handouts at trade shows and as leave-behinds for salespeople. They can be bundled with other products and can even be bound into magazines.

Demos can also be customized to feature bundling or comarketing arrangements. For example, a label company customized the demo of a leading database application to showcase the section about how to run labels. They bundled an offer for the demo inside their label packages. Also, point-of-sale demos can be used as props (and prompters) for salespeople. By replacing text with bullet points, the demo becomes a salesperson's portable presentation.

PROJECT MANAGEMENT AND TIMING

A demo is a unique communications medium—a hybrid of software, print, and video. A successful project leader should be able to focus on the customer, be familiar with software development cycles, and manage review cycles involving both marketing and technical people. And most important: The project leader must nurture the underlying communications goal and keep it intact throughout the process.

Manage the creation of your demo as you would a software development project. Demo development works best when you follow a plan through prototype, interim versions, and tested golden master. And make sure to leave time for both software testing and user testing. Early on, your tests should determine if consumer action goals are being met and if the interface works properly. Later in the process, testing should focus on software functionality and compatibility with all target hardware.

Think long-term. If you design a modular demo, it will be easier to upgrade next year. If you might eventually localize it for use in other countries, think about what you can do now to facilitate that process when the time comes.

To estimate development time, consider these ranges and the size of your project. During the R&D stage, you learn a development system, build tools for your job, or both. This may take a couple of weeks or even up to several months. For scripting and prototyping, allow a minimum of a week; four weeks or more is probable. For building a first full version, allow two to eight weeks. Each iteration (new version based on review feedback) takes anywhere from two to eight weeks. The total development time (excluding R&D) is anywhere from 5 to 20 weeks. The low number is very ambitious and the high number is not too high for a large job.

However, sometimes you're under pressure to get the demo to market and must do whatever you can to shorten the cycle. If you must compress it, do so carefully. If you "throw together" a demo, it will be clear to the audience that this is what you did. You should carefully weigh the possible consequences of getting an ineffective demo to market quickly against taking a little more time to produce a demo that will sell software.

It's important to approach demo project development as seriously as you would any software project, but design it using communications goals just as you would for a brochure or other communications piece. If you concentrate on the audience and its needs—and avoid the ten most deadly demo traits—you'll end up with a demo that will help sell software.

PART FIVE

Distribution, Licensing, and Antipiracy

Getting products into customers' hands is where the rubber meets the road. No distribution (or the wrong distribution), no sales. Channels continue to change rapidly, and the right path isn't always obvious. Needless to say, related issues such as licensing and piracy are no picnic either. Mastering the intricacies of the distribution demon is, shall we say, an ongoing challenge for all of us.

If you're approaching a national distributor for the first time or feel you've experienced rejection too many times, Chapter 19, "Understanding U.S. Distribution Realities: How to Approach a National Distributor," and Chapter 20, "The Distributor Product Review Process: A Typical Scenario," are the ticket for you. Straight from the source, you'll hear what makes national distributors tick, how to approach them, how they review products, why they often say "no", and how to make them notice you.

Chapter 21, "The Changing European Distribution Channels: Sorting out the Options," is an overview of European distribution channels. It discusses the many (and changing) options, offers a prognosis for them, and describes a model to help you determine which channels to consider for your products. In addition, it compares, in some detail, the distribution path that a product takes in the United States versus Europe and subsequently explains why U.S. software costs so much more in Europe.

If you've been mulling over the pros and cons of site licensing and could benefit from a discussion by someone who's been there, have a look at Chapter 22, "The Advantages of a Site License Program: Secrets of How and Why Site Licenses Can Be Effective." It describes one developer's reasons for choosing this route and how it creates a win-win situation for everyone involved.

If piracy has been a thorn in your side, Chapter 23, "The Ways and Means to Fight Piracy," and Chapter 24, "How to Discourage Piracy: How AutoDesk Makes Back Two Dollars on Every Antipiracy Dollar It Spends," are chock full of practical antipiracy suggestions from fellow developers who are grappling with the problem of "unauthorized" customers.

Finally, if you've ever considered selling directly to customers through the mail, take a look at Chapter 15, "How Direct Mail Saved Our Company." (It's in Part IV.) It describes one developer's experience in overcoming the fear of "channel conflict" and using direct mail as an alternative to retail selling.

CHAPTER NINETEEN

Understanding U.S. Distribution Realities

HOW TO APPROACH A NATIONAL DISTRIBUTOR

By Barry Evleth and Jeff Davis, Ingram Micro

Jeff Davis is the senior director of products and technology, and Barry Evleth is the senior manager for product evaluation for Ingram Micro, a computer products distributor located in Santa Ana, California.

UNDERSTANDING how a U.S. national distributor chooses which products to carry—and why—is sometimes confounding and frustrating. However, distributors really do want to carry your product. In our case, if we don't pick it up, it isn't because we think the product doesn't have serious merit or that your company lacks vision. Instead, it's often simply a matter of timing: Developers, whether based in the United States or elsewhere, often approach us too early in their product's life cycle. "Too early" means before products meet the criteria necessitated by the distributor's business needs.

The reality is that the noise level—the sheer number of products competing for distribution—is high. Distributors feasibly can carry only a finite, albeit large, number of products. For example, Ingram Micro carries more than 13,000 items from more than 650 vendors (300 of which have a Macintosh product). We receive more than 100 new submissions every month. Therefore, we must set criteria that will help us choose products that best fit our high-volume, mass-distribution model.

With this chapter, we'd like to help you understand these criteria and how we evaluate products, give you a clearer idea of the right time to approach national distributors, and provide insight into a distributor's mindset to help set your expectations. We also hope to reduce the potential frustration when you first approach distribution and increase your chances to create a win/win relationship with a company like ours.

WHEN TO SEEK A DISTRIBUTOR

The real key to successfully approaching a distributor is timing—where your product is in its life cycle. The best time to begin a relationship with a national U.S. distributor is when your product has already begun making solid inroads into the market. Like most other businesses, distributors must carefully balance perceived risk with potential gains. To strike that balance, we usually seek products with proven track records and companies who have established relationships with resellers and users.

Every distribution company has its own business model and the accompanying requirements for profit margins, sales run rates, and return-on-investment. The reality is that to meet our business objectives and succeed as a company, we must be able to move products out the door relatively quickly. Although there's no set-in-stone minimum required volume, on average, if we think we can sell a software product at a rate of $25,000 a month (wholesale) or more, we'll be more likely to carry it. The amount can be somewhat higher for hardware items, depending on support requirements, size, weight and other product handling issues.

The timing is right when you have:

- created a degree of market demand

- penetrated two or more reseller segments (such as computer specialty dealers, VARs, mail-order firms, aggregators/chains, mass merchants/retailers)

- developed an ongoing relationship with dealers or resellers in more than one geographic region, and

- demonstrated that end users accept the product.

If your product has been newly introduced or if it's in the "chasm" between early market acceptance and adoption by the mainstream, it's probably too early for you to approach a distributor.

Editor's note: In case you haven't yet read it, Chapter 3 "Breaking into the Mainstream: How to Move from Early Success to Mainstream Market Leadership," is an informative—and unusual—discussion about what constitutes the chasm.

There is, of course, an exception to the rule. Maintaining our competitive position depends somewhat on our ability to anticipate what will be hot in the reseller market. If you can show that your product is ahead of market demand, that it is part of a budding market, or that it takes advantage of a new or emerging Apple technology, then we may be more willing to take a risk on it. For example, we might be willing to consider a product that takes advantage of some hot new technology, such as QuickTime, or is one of the first to incorporate O.C.E. (Open Collaboration Environment). The burden is on the developer to demonstrate that the product is part of an emerging trend and that it has market potential. Convincing a distributor that a burgeoning demand is just around the corner reduces the perceived risk and makes your not yet established product more attractive to us.

WHAT WE ARE, WHAT WE AREN'T

An important part of working with a distributor is understanding exactly what its business is and isn't. The role of a distributor varies, depending on whether your products are for new or established markets. But overall, our role is to broaden and/or accelerate penetration into the reseller channel—not (usually) to create initial market demand. In a new market (such as pen computing), the distributor's primary function is to broaden channel penetration by generating visibility with resellers, providing reseller education, doing promotions, and creating buying incentives. In established markets, our role is primarily to provide product availability and quick delivery; assume credit risk; and give leverage to a developer in the form of our large reseller base, economies of scale, and targeted marketing and sales programs. We call this the "leveraged model." In this model, the distributor acts as an extension of the developer; the developer gains additional marketing leverage by partnering with a company (the distributor) that has an established marketing and distribution infrastructure and the accompanying resources.

A caution here: It is important not to view a distributor as the final sale. Developers with this view tend to expect a distributor to generate channel and user demand; they structure their businesses without focusing on creating the necessary pull and product exposure needed to generate demand. This is a mistake, given what the distributor's role is. The key is to remember that the final sale is a transaction *between the reseller and the user*, and the developer must play a role at every level.

Historically, distributors outside the United States often have played a more extensive role, dictated by market conditions in their locales. They sometimes offer marketing programs, localization assistance, and other services beyond what is generally offered in the United States. This is particularly important to non-U.S. developers who wish to enter a national distribution relationship in the United States. Be aware that the role the typical national U.S. distributor plays—and the services it offers—can be different than that played by distributors elsewhere. This means a developer must demonstrate that its product has a presence or track record in the United States.

HOW TO SUBMIT A PRODUCT

We use a standard process for reviewing products. *[Editor's note: For a general explanation of the reviewing process, see Chapter 20, "The Distributor Product Review Process: A Typical Scenario."]* Understanding this process can help you better prepare for what's ahead and, we hope, save you time and spare some frustration. What you submit and how you submit it is as important as the process itself. Of course, distributors want to see the whole product—disks, packaging, documentation, "the works."

Another important part of your submission is a vendor profile (see Step 3 in Chapter 20, "The Distributor Product Review Process: A Typical Scenario"). This is a snapshot of your product and company that helps us gauge whether you present a "business case" that is consistent with our objectives. The profile gives us important information, such as what and how much product you sold last year and the year before, and your competitive position, competition, and immediate plans for producing and marketing the product. Its primary purpose is to give us a feeling about who you are and put your company in perspective with others like it.

The exercise of completing the vendor profile also can be useful to the developer. It can help you better understand what we're looking for. It may also raise questions that you haven't yet addressed in your business plan, possibly indicating that it's still a little early to seek a national distributor.

Paint the Big Picture

In addition to submitting a complete product and vendor profile, it's important that you send us a proposal that clearly paints the big picture for your product. How is it positioned in the market? *[Editor's note: You might want to try using the process outlined in Chapter 2, "Positioning Your Product Using the 'Elevator Test': How to Nail It in 14 Floors—or Less."]* How does it compare with the competition? What is your overall marketing strategy? What are you doing to create product awareness and visibility? Has your product been reviewed? What did reviewers and analysts say? Send us reviews, copies of ads and information about response rates, articles about your products written by outside parties—anything that can help demonstrate that we can sell the needed volume of your product.

This picture will help us determine whether we can successfully distribute your product. It also helps identify potential opportunities for us to offer bundles that are complementary to your product or to piggyback on existing advertising or promotional campaigns, road shows, and so forth.

Tried-and-True Ways to Turn Off a Distributor

In summary, here are several sure-fire ways your approach can turn off a distributor. Generally speaking, if you can avoid these, you're more likely to have a more satisfying experience.

- *Submitting a me-too product before you've generated sufficient market demand.* Unless your product is on the cutting edge, the distributor is looking for an established sales record and existing relationships with customers. Without demand, it's difficult for the distributor to move a product off its shelves, which does no one any good.

- *Sending a beta version.* Again, the distributor is looking for a proven track record. If you're in beta, you're not yet out in the market. The exception is if you have a technology/product that is especially innovative or that takes advantage of a new or emerging Apple technology. For example, if you have a product that truly takes advantage of O.C.E. or QuickTime, it's likely (but not guaranteed) that the distributor will want to see the product in the beta stage.

- *Using a hard-sell approach.* Once you've made your submission, let the distributor do its job. Try to squelch the urge to phone the distributor every other day to "follow up" on your submission or to continue pitching the product. Although that may be considered a good sales practice in other circumstances, in this case it's a proven way to turn off the distributor. Have faith that the distributor is giving your product its due. If you've done a good job preparing your submission, your product and company track record will speak for themselves.

    Another way to look at this: Don't view the distributor as the "final sale." The best possible way to look at a distributor is as a partner or provider of services, a distribution mechanism, as opposed to being a customer. Save your final-sales tactics for the reseller or user—your true customer. Remember, a product is not actually sold through to a user just because it's on a shelf in the distributor's warehouse.

- *Sending a "brown-bagged" product.* Sending a product before its packaging is complete is an unmistakable sign that the product isn't already on the market. Also, the distributor is looking at your product's market appeal as a whole, not just its technical merits—and that includes how effective the packaging is.

- *Sending inadequate documentation.* A "whole" product includes the manuals. Your documentation should be complete and bound, if not shrink-wrapped.

- *Focusing on how big the distributor's opening order will be.* From the distributor's viewpoint, developers that dwell on how big the opening order will be betray their misunderstanding of what a distributor's role is. A better topic for discussion is what the product's long-term success will be. The distributor's job is to ascertain what level of stock will be required to fill its customers needs; its buyers are expected to have the right amount of stock needed to fill the demand and will work with the developer to create the proper flow of product.

ANTE UP: MEETING PRODUCT EVALUATION CRITERIA

Once you've submitted your product, the distributor's real work begins. The process of choosing which products to carry is one of convergence: We start with a very broad base of offerings and eventually narrow them to the few that we'll actually carry.

Most distributors have concrete criteria against which they evaluate submissions. Our new products committee reviews both the business aspects and the technical merits of a product. Table 19-1 is a list of the various aspects we consider.

TABLE 19-1   Business and Technical Considerations

Business	Technical
Market size, need, demand, perceived value	Features and benefits
Current marketing budget	Ease of set-up, understanding, and use
Marketing fit w/Ingram Micro	Competitive products
Overall salability, pull-through	Customer appeal
Industry positioning, developer reputation	Packaging quality
Support required	Documentation
Price vs. competition	Error handling
Gross margin, estimated monthly volume	Overall performance

Based on what we learn, we can determine whether your product meets our business model criteria. (See Figure 19-1.) The more criteria you meet, the more appealing your product is to our company.

The criteria are sorted into three main categories. The bottom third of the pyramid represents what is needed to rise above the *noise level*. Products that meet criteria on the levels just above that have what we characterize as a *good chance* to be picked up by Ingram. Those that meet the criteria in the very narrow tip of the triangle are what we call the *slam dunks*—products that are the strongest candidates. These are often mainstream vendors with established products who do not currently use a national distributor (such as Apple Computer before 1992). We spend a great deal of time proactively pursuing them.

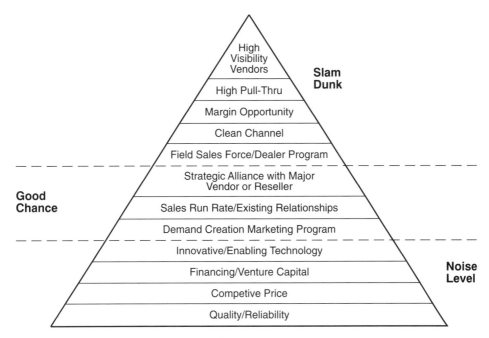

FIGURE 19-1   Product selection criteria

Rising Above the Noise

The bottom section of the pyramid represents the opening ante; products that don't meet these criteria basically don't make it beyond the initial reading of the vendor profile. The reason: Almost every product we receive fits the bottom two criteria—quality/reliability and competitive price. Likewise, most of these companies can demonstrate that they have adequate financing or venture capital. However, innovative or enabling products (as we discussed earlier) are usually on the upper fringes of the noise level.

To rise above the noise, products must exceed the expectations set by the criteria in the bottom tier of the pyramid. This is particularly important because as the market for Macintosh-related hardware and software grows, distributors are literally bombarded with products. To give you an idea of what the noise level is, consider these numbers, which generally apply to most national distributors.

- On the average, in a slow month we receive about 100 submissions. In a busy month we get as many as 200 or more products. This means that in an average month we receive about three to four submissions per day. Generally speaking, two of those are Macintosh products. Of those total submissions,

80 percent are unsolicited by us, and the rest are products we have actively pursued.

- About 20 to 25 percent of those products make it through the first cut, which is a process of eliminating products that are obviously not a good fit. We generally can discern this from an initial letter, fax, piece of literature, or phone call. The kinds of products that are weeded out early are things such as computer furniture, monitor shades, keyboard covers, or laminators. It may be tougher to get an initial reading on products in a crowded category, such as a monochrome monitor, a backup utility, or yet another canvas bag for a Macintosh PowerBook.

- Products surviving the first cut are then reviewed for technical merit and business proposition. Each month approximately 15 products pass that milestone and are then reviewed by the committee. (See Step 7 in Chapter 20, "The Distributor Product Review Process: A Typical Scenario.")

- Approximately 80 percent of those, or about 12 out of every 100 products we receive (12 percent), end up on our shelf.

Good Chance

If the product is a "me-too" one, the ante is much higher; to even be considered, it must meet the criteria that are in the good chance section of the pyramid. Products that have a good chance of being accepted have a track record in the marketplace; they have a demand-creation marketing program and a healthy sales run rate (and therefore existing relationships with customers). These companies also have created strategic alliances with major resellers or dealers.

Because distributors generally don't create user demand, developers must establish their own programs to generate it. Having a good sales run rate, something that is measurable, is important because it demonstrates that there is a market for the product and indicates that the distributor should be able to move the product adequately. Having a strategic alliance with a major reseller, for example a regional distributor, is a plus but not a must. Quantifiable success stories about sales through any kind of resellers go a long way toward differentiating your company.

The Slam-Dunk

Products that meet the criteria in the pyramid's upper tip are usually high-visibility ones. In fact, if you meet the top two criteria, chances are that we will be calling *you*. Companies that meet these criteria have already invested in the channel in some form or other and have a field sales force of some kind. They offer a good margin opportunity, have a high pull-through (have created a significant customer demand), and are highly visible, well-recognized players in the industry.

They also offer the distributor a "clean channel," that is, a pricing model that clearly differentiates between two-tiered distribution (resellers and end users). There are exceptions, such as when a product offers us a strategic opportunity; but as a rule of thumb, the higher up the pyramid you go, the more likely you are to be a fit for a company such as Ingram.

"NO" ISN'T A DEAD END

If a distributor must decline to carry your product, don't view the outcome as a dead end. Instead, use it as a learning experience. Ask the distributor to explain why your product isn't a match, and, in that context, ask for suggestions for improvement or change.

Remember, *timing is everything.* Even if you have a solid product, you may have approached the distributor when its resources were focused on other opportunities or when other products in your category were already a part of its marketing mix.

Understanding the distributor's role and taking the appropriate steps to implement a channel strategy before you approach national distribution is critical to your success in working with a distributor. Trying to establish national distribution too early in the product life cycle can be a costly and frustrating experience. There are tremendous opportunities to accelerate your penetration into the channel by using national distribution to extend your reach into the market—at the appropriate time.

CHAPTER TWENTY

The Distributor Product Review Process

A TYPICAL SCENARIO

By Linda Kazares, The Ambit Group

Linda Kazares is president of The Ambit Group, a channel marketing, sales, and development consulting firm located in San Francisco, California.

EACH distributor, such as the one described in the previous chapter, has its own process for accepting and evaluating product submissions. However, to help give you an idea of what is involved, here is a typical scenario for a distributor working for the first time with a developer.

Step 1: Developer contacts distributor by telephone, fax, or mail.

Step 2: Brief telephone conversation ensues; distributor receives overview of company and product(s).

Step 3: Developer completes a vendor profile form and returns it to appropriate distributor contact.

Step 4: Distributor approves or rejects profile. If approved, it will request product for evaluation.

Step 5: Developer mails or personally delivers product for presentation/evaluation.

Step 6: Distributor evaluates product (see Step 7) and notifies the developer of the evaluation status. The evaluation process can take from two weeks to six months, or longer. The less suitable the product is, for any reason, the longer it will take to evaluate. A distributor with strong doubts about whether it can sell a product may nonetheless put the product through a lengthy evaluation to learn about the market and acquaint itself with product issues.

Step 7: If the product passes the initial evaluation, it is presented to a committee within the distributor organization. This committee meets formally once or twice monthly at a predesignated date and time. It may include VPs from marketing, new products, sales, purchasing, and possibly director-level representatives from the same departments. At the meeting, the product reviewer makes a case for or against the product. The developer does not attend this meeting.

Step 8: If the product reaches this step, the committee often makes its final decision during this meeting. However, one out of every ten products is held for a decision because the committee needs additional information about the technical or competitive environment. If the product is rejected, the distributor will telephone or mail the notification to the developer.

Step 9: If the product is accepted, the developer will receive a boilerplate contract within a short time, usually one week.

Step 10: Contract negotiations begin. They can take two weeks to six months and are usually paced by the distributor.

Step 11: Once the contract is approved by both parties, the developer will be handed off to its permanent contacts in marketing and purchasing. Then, a purchase order is sent to the developer. Depending on the complexity and type of product, the developer may be scheduled to conduct brief sales and technical training sessions. The marketing department then commences work on the product roll out.

Reprinted by permission from the *U.S. Software Channel Marketing and Distribution Guide* by Linda Kazares, The Ambit Group; published by the Software Publishers Association, 1992. For information or to order, call (202) 452-1600.

CHAPTER TWENTY-ONE

The Changing European Distribution Channels

SORTING OUT THE OPTIONS

By David Smith, XPAND

David Smith, a former Apple Europe third-party channel manager and Apple world marketing manager, is the founder of XPAND, an international company that helps the Apple community bring products and solutions to international customers.

Editor's note: For reference, this article was written in 1992. As you read this, please bear in mind that the economic and business situation in the European Community continues to change, as do distribution channels there.

MANY people expected 1992 to be a watershed in the evolution toward a single European market. However, I'm convinced that, at least for the time being, the European Community (EC) is likely to remain a collection of individual, independent markets—and the most successful developers will be those who don't in the near-term try to group them together conceptually.

Developer opportunities in Europe—the Europe that is a collection of individual markets—have never been better; as Chapter 33, "International Success Stories: How Big U.S. Companies Hit It Big Abroad," points out, a host of U.S. developers, including small companies, are successfully competing in Europe. And if you think the U.S. market is large, take note that the EC as a whole in the long run will likewise be quite large.

Although a true EC single market is still years away, that's not to say there won't be near-term changes in Europe's computing industry. Apple's shift in 1991 to a high-volume, low-price strategy has already affected the third-party industry there (and almost everywhere else). Add that to the economic changes taking place in the EC, and you'll better understand the current personal computing environment in Europe.

Most notably, the distribution situation is undergoing a metamorphosis, and developers today have more distribution options to aid them in establishing European beachheads. To help you begin sorting out the options, I'll give you a snapshot of the current distribution situation in Europe, some differentiating information about each channel, and an outlook on the role each channel might play in the EC, based on XPAND's experience and studies of this market. Then, I'll give you a way to put the options into perspective, based on your product's U.S. price point.

OVERALL TRENDS AFFECTING DISTRIBUTION

Several trends are affecting the distribution picture in Europe.

Increasing Segmentation

As different kinds of customers with new kinds of needs are attracted to the Macintosh computer, developers are faced with selling their wares to an increasingly diverse audience—not unlike what the automobile industry went through as it evolved. That industry has come a long way since Henry Ford said, "You can have any color you like, as long as it's black." Over the years, Ford accommodated diverse tastes and needs by segmenting its customer base; as a result, today Ford has an extensive product line catering to a wide range of drivers.

The Apple community is going through the same segmentation process. For example, Apple Europe has been split into four customer-oriented divisions: large accounts (and government), business (small- and medium-sized businesses), education, and consumer. Of course, within each segment there are a number of subsegments. Each division pursues its own channel strategy.

Software Prices

An important trend driving the U.S. industry today is the falling price of software. However, international channels can't yet effectively distribute products that sell at low price points in the United States, without increasing their retail prices so much that high-volume sales are virtually impossible. Our European customer research found that, on average, street prices of software in Europe are double U.S. prices. One reason for high international pricing is that marketing costs in Europe are much higher than in the United States. For example, the average cost to reach a magazine reader through an advertisement in the United Kingdom is six times the cost in the United States.

Table 21-1 is a financial model of the margin and pricing structures for various European distribution channels. This information (except for CD and electronic distribution, of course) applies to hardware and software. The model is based on an imaginary product with a suggested U.S. retail price of $100.

Looking at the "cost to customer" row, you can see that a U.S. customer buying the product through mail order in the United States will pay $55; an international customer could pay $102 if buying the product through the traditional full-service distributor/dealer channel. Our European customer research indicates that this increase of 84 percent is representative within the industry.

TABLE 21-1 Cost of U.S. Software in Europe

Column	1	2	3	4	5	6	7	8	9
U.S. Retail Price	$100								
	U.S. Market		**International Market**						
	Distributor Cost	U.S. Mail Order	Sole Full-Serv. Dist.	Multiple Full-Serv. Dist.	Volume Dist.	U.S. Mail Order	Int'l. Mail Order	CD Dist.	CD Dist. w/Dealer Kickback
Dist. discount	58%		55%	55%	55%			55%	55%
Co-op marketing funds	0%		3%	0%	0%				
Dist. cost before shipping	$42		$42	$45	$45	$49	$56	$45	$45
Shipping & currency	2%		10%	10%	10%	10%	5%	2%	2%
Shipping cost	$1		$4	$5	$5	$5	$3	$1	$1
Dist. buying cost	$43		$46	$50	$50	$54	$59	$46	$46
Dist. gross margin	12%		30%	18%	12%	18%	18%	18%	18%
Cost to dealer/retailer	$49	$49	$66	$60	$56				$56
Dealer gross margin	30%	12%	35%	35%	35%				15%
Cost to customer	$70	$55	$102	$93	$87	$65	$72	$56	$66
Uplift over U.S. mail order	26%	0%	84%	68%	56%	18%	30%	1%	19%
Gray marketing likely			Yes	Yes	Yes		Yes		

European customers are not happy about paying more than a 20 percent increase (uplift) over U.S. street prices, which is a situation conducive to gray marketing (and piracy). The only channel in this model capable of delivering products in Europe with less than the 20 percent increase are CD-based distributors, who benefit from negligible shipping and inventory costs other than manuals. (Note: For simplicity we have assumed that local sales taxes are the same in all markets. All numbers are rounded.) Here is an explanation of each column in Table 21-1.

- *Column 1: U.S. dealer/distributor channel to U.S. customer.* This column shows how a product flows from the developer through the U.S. distributor and dealer to the U.S. customer. The distributor's buying cost is $43, and it sells the product to the dealer for $49 after adding its 12 percent margin. (This margin is often much lower for high-volume products.) So, walking into a U.S. dealership, a customer can expect to pay about $70 for this product.

- *Column 2: U.S. mail order to U.S. customer.* U.S. mail-order companies often purchase stock from U.S. distributors and, as with dealers, can expect to pay $49 (assuming they don't get volume discounts). However, mail-order companies sell the product for $55 because they don't have the overhead associated with running a dealership operation. This is the lowest price a U.S. customer can expect to pay for the product and the major reason why mail order is the most significant channel in the United States.

- *Column 3: Sole full-service distributor and dealer to international customer.* In international markets, the traditional first step for developers is to appoint a single full-service distributor to undertake the localization, marketing, and technical support activities that developers themselves carry out in their domestic markets. Our research found that more than half of international distributors paid higher prices than their U.S. counterparts receiving a smaller discount of 55 percent, which is counterbalanced by a cooperative marketing fund offered by that developer (say 3 percent). Of course, shipping and currency costs are significantly higher overseas, and the "landed cost" could be $46.

    In exchange for this high degree of added value, these distributors demand a margin of approximately 30 percent. (Many developers are surprised that the margin is often much higher then they expect.) Add that to the dealer margin of 35 percent, and the product hits the street at $102.

- *Column 4: Multiple full-service distributor to international customer.* Often, developers appoint two or more full-service distributors. In such a case, because distributors don't have an exclusive contract, they are unlikely to offer significant marketing or other services because the orders they create could be filled by a competitor who offers a lower cost. Thus, in this scenario it is normal to assume that distributors list the product in their catalogs but don't otherwise promote it. This means that they don't receive any cooperative marketing funds from the developer and they work on slimmer margins of 18 percent. They sell to a dealer at $60, and the product retails at $93.

- *Column 5: Volume distributor to international customer.* If a developer has a local office creating demand for a product, it may eventually ship in high volumes and become a target for a U.S.-style national volume distributor; the distributor has finely tuned box-moving operations capable of making a profit on 12 percent gross margins. It sells the product to the dealer for $56, and the customer pays $87.

- *Column 6: U.S. mail order to international customer.* Considering the street price in Europe through the previously mentioned channels ($87 to $102), it's not surprising that many international customers prefer to purchase a U.S. computer trade magazine and use a credit card to order a product directly from a U.S. mail-order company. The shipping and duty costs are higher than they are for U.S. customers, and the international buyer pays approximately $65.

- *Column 7: International mail order to international customer.* For high volume products, local (European) mail-order companies will buy a product from a national volume distributor for $56. The local mail-order company is not importing the product, so its shipping costs are low (5 percent). It sells the product to the customer at $72, a 30 percent uplift over the mail-order cost to U.S. customers.

- *Column 8: CD-based distributor to international customer.* Shipping and currency costs are low because CD-based distributors don't carry inventory other than manuals. The manuals are mailed to customers after they have paid by credit card to have the software unlocked from the CD and downloaded onto their hard disks. Through this channel, European customers can pay almost the same price as their U.S. counterparts: $56.

- *Column 9: CD-based distributor to international customer with dealer kickback.* CD-based distributors may offer dealers an incentive—usually a 15 percent kickback—to introduce customers to this new channel. This increases the customer price to $66—still below the 20 percent uplift level that leads to gray marketing and piracy.

Customer Buying Patterns

In researching how Europeans buy personal computing products, we found that more than 95 percent of large corporate customers and more than 85 percent of small business and education customers want to try software before they buy it—and less than half of all customers found it possible to get demo packages legally. Because of the lack of demo software, European customers use fewer applications than do their U.S. counterparts. The need to distribute demo software has been so strong that, after discussion with Apple, we created the *XPAND Electronic Expo*, which delivers demo versions of software, QuickTime movies, and product information on CD-ROM to customers and industry insiders worldwide.

A Distribution Explosion

In the late 1980s, there was a distribution bottleneck in Europe, but in the last few years the distribution scene has exploded. Now a variety of channels exist, and developers are no longer forced to choose only traditional European channels, which are full-service dealer/distributors. The additional channel options include such things as VARs, multiplatform dealers, AppleCentres, retailers, computer superstores, national mail-order companies, pan-European mail-order companies, U.S. mail-order companies, national volume distributors, pan-European distributors, software-only stores, CD software distributors, and electronic software distributors.

However, it's not likely that all of these channels can remain intact as the EC struggles to life. The distribution situation has started to shake itself out as distributors are forced to adapt to changes in the industry and the EC as a whole. Our studies and experiences indicate that channels such as large national mail-order companies, superstores, national volume distributors, electronic distribution, and CD-based distribution are likely to truly come into their own. Traditional dealers and full-service distributors—the more popular, well-entrenched channels of the past—will probably play a reduced role in the future. To give you a better picture of the distribution players and their positions in the European market, here is an overview of each channel and a current prognosis for its role as the EC emerges.

FULL-SERVICE DISTRIBUTORS: VULNERABLE, HIGH-END FOCUSED

In Europe, there is an overall trend away from full-service distribution and toward the U.S. national distribution model. In the United States, developers use national distributors to "move boxes" and for dealer credit control, while developers handle marketing and technical support themselves.

Editor's note: For an eye-opening overview of how one U.S. national distributor operates, see Chapter 19, "Understanding U.S. Distribution Realities: How to Approach a National Distributor."

Because most developers don't have marketing and technical support offices in overseas markets, they often engage a full-service distributor in each country, who supplies marketing, localization, and technical support services—and marks up the product to cover the cost of these activities. However, as the push toward lower-cost products and high-volume distribution grows stronger, full-service distributors may not remain as dominant a channel in Europe. There are some key reasons for this trend.

- *When volume increases, developers may choose alternative distribution options.* Full-service distributors are vulnerable in the evolving EC because, in effect, they are putting their own time and money into promoting and supporting someone else's product, hoping they'll reap the reward when sales increase. In reality, when volume increases dramatically, the developer often drops the full-service distributor in favor of a box-moving one that can increase the developer's margin. As a result, full-service houses find themselves constantly creating markets to the benefit of box-moving distributors who later supplant them and reap the rewards.

- *Full-service distribution is an expensive business.* Running an effective marketing, technical support, and localization business is expensive, and full-service distributors need reasonably high margins (around 30 percent) to support their infrastructure. This means that the products they carry reach customers at almost double the U.S. prices (after the dealer margin is taken into consideration). Our research has found that European customers learn of U.S. street prices through U.S. magazines, and they aren't happy about paying premiums in excess of 20 percent (never mind double the U.S. price!). Instead of buying through the full-service distribution channel, they sometimes enter the gray market, importing the product directly from overseas.

  As mentioned earlier, the falling price of software and hardware in the United States—and the resulting volume increase—hasn't been mirrored in international markets. Full service distributors often can't make a profit on products that have been successful in the United States because it's simply too expensive to create the necessary demand.

- *It's expensive and resource-consuming to create demand.* Assuming that developers can get their products stocked by a "box-moving" distributor in

Europe, to be successful developers must, as in the United States, take responsibility for creating international demand. A number of marketing and technical support agencies—surrogate international offices for developers—have sprung up in response to this need for local marketing and technical support. However, working with these agencies requires a great deal of a developer's time and resources. No matter how you approach it, you still must create demand whether you do it yourself or have someone do it for you.

All of these circumstances are changing the role of full-service distributors in Europe. In many cases, the role of this distributor is declining, especially for products and companies that are established in the market. These distributors are being forced to move up-market and to serve customers who are prepared to pay for added-value services. Many full-service houses are therefore focusing on areas such as high-end publishing and networking and communications products, which they can sell at high prices and achieve high margins.

Therefore, full-service distributors can continue to serve companies, including smaller ones, with high-end products that are entering the European market for the first time. They can also serve developers whose resources are so limited that this distribution arrangement is the only feasible way to penetrate the market. Full-service distributors can help these developers establish a presence in Europe; however, in the long run, developers who have been successful may need more breadth to handle increased demand and may move on to broader distribution arrangements.

DEALER/DISTRIBUTORS: GOOD IN SMALL OR VERTICAL MARKETS

To explain what appears to be happening to dealer/distributors in Europe, I'll use a parable: Apple opens a subsidiary on Mars, and the first order of business is to recruit a dealer channel. These dealers need to sell localized versions of third-party hardware and software, which is difficult when there is no established distribution infrastructure. So the Martian dealers climb into spaceships and fly to Macworld San Francisco or Boston, where they meet developers and offer to distribute their products on Mars. The developers see this as an incremental business opportunity and perceive no problem in giving the Martian distributors exclusive distribution agreements.

The dealers return to Mars with several agreements in hand and begin importing products, which they sell either to other Martian dealers or directly to their own customers. Over time the businesses grow and mature, and some of these "dealer/distributors" decide to focus exclusively on distribution and not compete with their dealer customers. The dedicated distributors approach U.S. developers, offering them a less constrained distribution channel than the existing dealer can. As the Martian market matures, the developers begin taking their products away from dealers and giving them to the dedicated distributors.

The moral of the story is that the generalist dealer/distributor is viable in a small or immature market where the economies of scale don't favor the larger specialist: The larger the market, the fewer the products being distributed by dealers. As the EC takes shape, this scenario is quite probable. Currently there are relatively few dealer/distributors in larger European markets (such as the United Kingdom and France), but they thrive in smaller markets such as Denmark and Norway.

In my opinion, dealer/distributors will survive because they'll find niches in vertical market segments. Complex, high-price, low-volume products are best distributed by these dealer/distributors, who can offer a complete computing solution to vertical market customers who need hardware, software, customization, training, and technical support. If your high-end product is destined for a vertical market in Europe, this distribution arrangement is an option for you, as may be VARs.

VARS: GOING VERTICAL

In the face of proliferating retail channels (such as computer superstores), Value Added Resellers (VARs) are finding it increasingly difficult to maintain margins on hardware and software. To survive, they therefore must reduce the number of products they carry and begin offering such things as integration or software customization services. Because their business models usually are based on margins in excess of 40 percent, VARs are moving into highly complex vertical markets, such as engineering and architecture, where hardware revenue is negligible and software is the real money maker.

NATIONAL VOLUME DISTRIBUTORS: WELL SITUATED FOR THE '90s

Most products are currently shipped to European customers through national volume distributors; they act as the local arm of companies such as Ingram or Merisel, moving boxes and handling dealer credit control. In all fairness, they offer more services to developers than do many of their U.S. counterparts: For their 12 to 20 percent margins, national distributors not only move boxes and handle dealer credit, but they also manage trade show activities, create co-op advertising campaigns, and provide limited technical support.

Their businesses have grown significantly during recent years, and they have learned how to cope with increasingly intense competition. Overall, they have responded well by becoming more efficient, and have been rewarded by growth and profits. I think national volume distributors are well situated to continue growing in the EC of the 1990s if they continue to improve their inventory and distribution systems.

PAN-EUROPEAN VOLUME DISTRIBUTORS: BEFORE THEIR TIME?

The concept of the large, pan-European distributor will work best only when Europe is truly united economically and thereby offers this kind of distributor an economy of scale. The concept of a single European warehouse supplying various markets is currently not very feasible due to problems inherent in shipping products across borders, multiple languages, and other logistical considerations.

Ingram, Merisel, and Computer 2000 (a German company) are currently the major players. Because the EC today is not conducive to true pan-European distribution, these giants are establishing themselves independently in each (currently) separate European market by buying local volume distributors. They use their U.S. predominance to convince developers to sign global distribution agreements. This enables these distributors to compete in multiple markets and forces local distributors into a bind, since they know they can't compete with the larger distributors' lower prices.

When we have achieved a united European market, pan-European distributors will surely be major players; but until that time, I don't think they will have a significant influence on distribution to individual, local markets.

MULTIPLATFORM DEALERS: SUITED TO LARGE ACCOUNTS

To survive, many dealers who were previously tied to a single platform have begun to carry products from multiple platforms. Macintosh and Microsoft Windows are obvious choices, but the workstation market can also be profitable. The concept of one-stop shopping which multiplatform dealers offer, appeals to the purchasing departments of large corporations, who usually own hardware from a variety of manufacturers. This is where the future lies for multiplatform dealers. (They currently number about 20,000 in Europe.)

RETAILERS: PROBABLY NOT BEST FOR THIRD-PARTY PRODUCTS

European retail is very similar to its U.S. counterpart; it basically offers developers floor space and order-taking facilities. Retailers' purchasing departments prefer one-stop shopping and usually deal with only a handful of the aforementioned national volume distributors. (Don't bother trying to get retailers to consider your product if it isn't sold through their established supply channels.) They are powerful and usually demand products on consignment, sale or return terms, and/or extended credit terms (often 90 days).

Because the revenue from Apple Europe's consumer business unit is defined as all income earned through the retail channel, Apple Europe has been recruiting and educating retailers at a fast pace. For Apple, the most successful retail model in Europe is FNAC in France, which probably has the most unlikely range of products. In addition to the usual cameras, stereos, TVs, and other consumer electronics items, they sell theater tickets and hold art exhibitions and presentations. The computer department offers a full range of Windows and DOS machines alongside the newly arrived Macintosh Performa models. They sell music CDs as well as a range of non-Macintosh software and a small proportion of Macintosh packages. Apple is also testing a number of retail channels in the United Kingdom.

I predict that these European retail channels will become the primary distribution mechanism for low-end Macintosh computers but won't be a significant channel for software and third-party hardware, other than products bundled with CPUs. This seems to match the mood of the market: Our research found that customers expect to buy CPU hardware and software from separate retail outlets (except computer superstores, covered later in this chapter), just as they wouldn't dream of buying their music CDs from the same store where they bought their stereo systems.

COMPUTER SUPERSTORES: ON THE RISE

When we asked small business owners about their ideal channel for purchasing personal computing products, they chose the computer superstore. They perceive that it offers a wide range of products at reasonably low prices and, most importantly, customers can see products before buying them (something not possible with mail order, a major competing channel). On the other hand, large corporations have complex purchasing processes that prevent their buyers from purchasing from superstores or other retail channels. They therefore prefer to buy from dealers who offer credit arrangements.

Computer superstores are flourishing in many parts of Europe, and new ones seem to pop up almost weekly. Their growth has been fueled by preferential pricing and extended credit facilities from the major personal computing manufacturers, who expect superstores to outsell established dealers and become their major channel in coming years.

In Europe, these stores are small and pedestrian in comparison with some U.S. superstores, and they carry only a fraction of the stock. They usually operate only one or two cash registers, compared to the 5 to 10 (and up to 30 at peak times) at some American superstores.

Who's opening these superstores? Established retailers, dealers, mail-order companies, distributors? All of them, it seems, but mostly dealers and mail-order companies who have rented a large space, hired retail sales people, and run aggressive local advertising campaigns. Tandy has established electronic superstores in Scandinavia, and it is likely to have aggressive growth plans for the rest of Europe, where it already owns chains of small retail stores. Also, some large department stores are teaming up with computer superstores. My opinion is that experienced retailers will eventually take over this quickly emerging channel.

The European computer superstore could become very significant for Apple developers if they can get their products onto the shelves. However, it will be difficult to do so in the near future; developers must begin to offer low-cost products with high retail margins on a sale or return basis—something the distribution infrastructure in Europe can't handle right now.

SOFTWARE-ONLY STORES: NOT AS VIABLE AS IN THE UNITED STATES

Although Egghead and other software-only stores have been successful in the United States, there has never been a large, successful chain of software-only stores in Europe. In large cities, small independent software stores have tried to create a niche for themselves by selling games and low-cost business software, with very little success: The cost of inventory and need to regularly write off vast quantities of obsolete stock make this business very risky.

Although the software market is growing on all platforms (Nintendo and Sega games are phenomenally successful), the growing superstores and mail-order channels will probably continue to prevent software-only stores from becoming successful in Europe.

NATIONAL MAIL ORDER: SIGNIFICANT GROWTH AHEAD

Most personal computer software in the United States is sold through mail order. However, this isn't the case in Europe where, until recently, mail order has been quite insignificant. There are at least three reasons for this difference: Most European PC mail-order suppliers have gone out of business while owing customers refunds, which has hurt the suppliers' credibility; in general, mail order has a very poor image in most parts of Europe; and Europeans don't benefit from the same "out-of-state" sales tax exemptions as do some customers in the United States.

In our research I was surprised to find that many European customers would never consider buying computer products from a European mail-order company, but they were happy to buy from large U.S. mail-order companies. After further research, we found that these customers didn't trust their local suppliers and wouldn't give them credit card details without some assurance that the suppliers were financially sound and credible.

Credibility is now improving as the large U.S. mail-order companies set up European subsidiaries. MacWarehouse has quickly established strong subsidiaries in the United Kingdom, Germany, and France, and is being followed by many of its domestic competitors. However, European customers are still a little disappointed that pricing is so much higher than in the United States; most prices are marked up 50 to 100 percent.

I believe that in the next few years, growth in the mail-order business in Europe will be the most significant distribution trend for developers selling products mainly to small business users who, unlike most large corporate users, can place orders with credit cards. Companies like MacWarehouse can distribute low cost software in the major European markets with a fraction of the energy involved in setting up a more traditional local distribution arrangement.

PAN-EUROPEAN MAIL ORDER: PROBABLY NOT YET

It is almost as time consuming and expensive to ship boxes from one European country to another as it is to ship them to Europe from the United States. Until we find ourselves in a truly united Europe, a single European mail-order facility supplying a number of countries will probably find it difficult to succeed.

However, because the European telephone infrastructure can now handle pan-European toll-free numbers, it is possible to operate a single order-processing center to serve customers throughout Europe; for example, operators fluent in a variety of languages could staff the telephone lines. If a developer were to try to recreate its U.S. mail-order (direct sales) operation in Europe, it could be done from a single country, and customers would be under the impression that they were talking to a local office. However, pan-European mail order will not be widely feasible for many years.

CD SOFTWARE DISTRIBUTION: HOT COMPETITION FOR U.S. MAIL ORDER

A single CD-ROM can be loaded with many software packages and delivered to dealers, distributors, and customers at a relatively low cost, making this distribution method quite attractive. (Of course, the software has to be protected from piracy.)

We conducted research in 1991 that revealed that European customers gave a high rating to CD-ROM as a channel through which they would buy low-cost software (less than $100). This is important, given that European software buyers want to try software packages before they buy them. On the other hand, developers were worried about potential piracy and channel conflict problems, and they didn't seem interested in exploring any form of electronic distribution that departed from the traditional shrink-wrapped disk with manual.

To date, CD-based distribution has not been used extensively in the U.S. market because its competition, mail order, is an efficient channel for low-cost, low-margin products. However, CD-based distribution clearly is an attractive international channel because it is the only way to offer U.S. pricing to overseas customers. (To better understand why this channel offers almost unbeatable prices in overseas markets, see columns 8 and 9 in Table 21-1, earlier in this chapter.) Windmill and Instant Access are the leading CD-based mail-order distributors in the international Macintosh market, and they work with developers of all kinds and sizes. They have encryption (locking) algorithms and offer their own local unlocking centers in European and Pacific markets. Other large developers are pressing their own CDs and establishing their own unlocking procedures.

The financial model for CD distribution is unbeatable today. Without shipping or warehousing costs, this channel offers European customers prices that compete with U.S. mail order. Some developers continue to resist CD distribution, but it will probably succeed, given the forecasted explosion of CD-ROM use (and Macintosh computers with built-in CD-ROM drives), and will eventually become as significant an international channel as mail order.

ELECTRONIC SOFTWARE DISTRIBUTION

Several years ago, the French government established a national on-line service called Minitel and ensured that it would succeed by giving away terminals. Terminals are now installed in almost all French homes and businesses. Commercial software is distributed through this on-line service, and France Telecom collects the money and pays the distributor. However, the process is painfully slow, for two reasons: The transfer rate of Minitel is 75 bits per second (bps) in one direction and 300 bps in the other; and because France Telecom charges by the minute instead of by the application, Minitel slows down the transmission speed of an application so that the download time corresponds to the product's price. In other words, it could take 12 hours to download a word processor or spreadsheet package.

But people *do* use Minitel to buy software, and it will become increasingly popular as transmission speed increases. (High-speed ISDN lines are widely available in France.) Europeans can also use AppleLink and other on-line services to download and place orders for software, and this trend will increase as international telecommunications bandwidths broaden. Satellite TV has become very popular in Europe, and that technology can also be used in the future to deliver software at a fast rate.

SORTING THROUGH THE OPTIONS: DOING YOUR HOMEWORK

After spending many years marriage-brokering developers with distributors, I have found that choosing a channel is a very personal and individual process; what works for one developer will probably fail for the next. Unfortunately, there's no simple "how-to" or formula that applies to everyone. However, you can make some generalizations about what your appropriate channels may be, based on the U.S. price point of your product.

Figure 21-1 (on the next page) shows the relative relationships between key factors that you should consider: the retail price of a product, channel margin and added value, channels through which a product flows, customer willingness to pay a premium for value-added services, and the potential unit market size for a product.

Here's an example to help you interpret the chart, reading downward: If your product's U.S. retail price is $100, then the channel margin for the product in the United States and Europe is low and the channel would not be likely to provide many services to you or your customers. The most effective channels for this product would probably be those that are least expensive, such as mail order, CD distribution, or electronic distribution. At this price point, the customer is usually not willing to pay a premium for added-value services; however, at such a low price the potential market size is probably large.

There will be exceptions to this scenario in individual situations, however. For example, if you aren't established in Europe, you may wish to engage a full-service distributor who offers you a higher marketing support level to help you create a presence there. The cost to you, of course, will be higher, but the long-term benefits of getting a foothold in Europe may be well worth it.

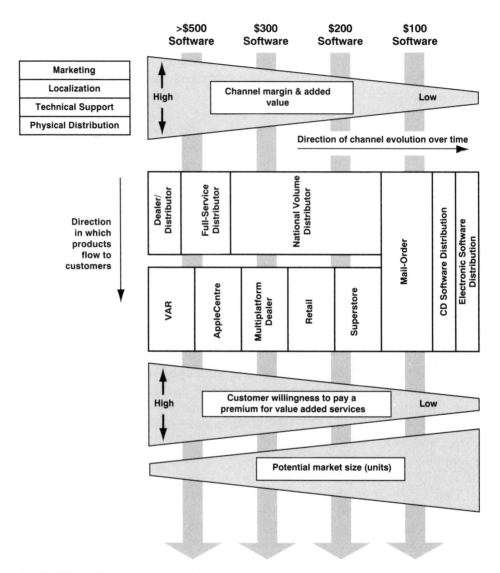

FIGURE 21-1   Relative relationships between software and channels

Here's another example: If your product's U.S. retail price is $300, your channel's margin will be higher and chances are that you may need some degree of channel services to help you sell this higher-priced product (which will cost buyers more in Europe). You could use a European national distributor, who may then sell your product to a multiplatform dealer, retailer, or computer superstore—depending on the nature of your product and the possible margins for the national distributor. At this price point, depending on the complexity of the product, customers may be willing to pay for some degree of services. Your market size will probably be smaller than that for a less expensive product.

Obviously, to be successful in international markets, you must make the effort to understand the strengths and weaknesses of various channel options—either yourself or by hiring experienced international sales and marketing representatives to assist you. Although on first inspection the proliferation of channels appears to be something of a maze, it isn't unnavigable. The time and effort you invest in doing a little bit of homework will pay off handsomely: It will increase your chances for taking advantage of the huge market potential available in Europe now—and in the EC of the future.

CHAPTER TWENTY-TWO

The Advantages of a Site License Program

SECRETS OF HOW AND WHY SITE LICENSES CAN BE EFFECTIVE

By John Shagoury, ON Technology

John Shagoury is a former vice president of sales and marketing for ON Technology, a software company based in Cambridge, Massachusetts, that specializes in workgroup applications.

ALTHOUGH there are certainly many pros and cons to the complex issue of site licensing, this marketing technique has worked well for us. ON Technology has found many situations in which the benefits are well worth the time and effort involved to institute a site license program. The bottom line: Our larger customers need alternative ways to purchase mass amounts of products.

For us, the secret to making the site license an effective sales agreement has been listening to what customers want, understanding why they want it, and then creating a win-win agreement that meets the needs of both parties. We've found that this has often meant the difference between getting the account or getting the boot.

It's never easy for a company to decide whether it should begin offering site licenses. We made the decision based on the type of products we sell, workgroup applications that run on networks. We felt that our products' success depended on our ability to get them accepted and utilized on every node within a large network and that dealing directly with larger customers was the most effective way to achieve that. I hope that this chapter will give you some ideas and define some issues to think about to help you make the right decision for your company.

I can almost guarantee that if you decide to implement a site license program, you won't be 100 percent successful the first time out. It will take some trial and error, but don't get overwhelmed or totally frustrated. Just make sure that you think about the details not only from the customers' perspective but also from your own internal viewpoint. Define the internal systems, processes, and procedures you'll need to effectively administer and maintain a site license program.

In general, whether site licenses are right for you depends on the kinds of products you offer, how flexible you can be in your distribution arrangements, and how well you understand customers' needs. Here are some of the things we've learned through our experiences.

DEFINING "SITE LICENSE"

Large corporate customers have been asking for site license programs for years, but when you're sitting across the table from them, the first thing that's important to discern is what they actually mean when they use the term site license. It has become a catchall phrase for many different implementations. For example, some large customers have instituted a centralized electronic network to distribute software to users. Their idea of a site license usually is to receive "golden disk" privileges, in which a master copy of an application is put onto a server. All the users can download the application for use on their machines. Some customers push to pay one price for unlimited enterprise-wide use; others pay for a specified number of users, with the stipulation that they'll pay extra if the total usage exceeds the agreed-upon commitment.

Regardless of a company's purchasing or administrative structure, it reaps a cost benefit by committing to a certain volume. Often, what customers really want when they ask for a site license is a Volume Purchase Agreement (VPA). Corporate customers feel that if they are willing to commit to hundreds, or thousands, of copies of your product—and to take them all in one order—there should be some price compromise on your part. This typically means offering a better price for shrink-wrapped software than even the most aggressive reseller can offer at the same volume. This option serves many companies very well because it meets their needs whether their purchasing process is highly centralized or very decentralized.

The basic difference between a site license agreement and a VPA is really the way the software is delivered. With a VPA, products are usually delivered in caseloads or in special multiuser packages with limited documentation. We've found the VPA negotiation to be somewhat easier; because the license and warranty information is already in the package; there is less need for the legal departments to get heavily involved. Most of our agreements with large corporate customers tend to be the VPA kind.

WHY CUSTOMERS ASK FOR SITE LICENSES

Before deciding what kind of site license agreement to create, you must understand what arrangement will best meet a customer's needs. There are four major reasons why large customers typically favor a site license or VPA: better prices, user standardization, uncomplicated distribution, and reduced inventory.

Price

Price always seems to be an issue when you discuss large quantities. Many IS (information systems) or user-department managers have a fixed annual budget for software. Their job is to use that limited amount of money to generate the largest possible productivity increase through the cost-effective purchase of software and services. Cost-effectiveness: That's the motivation for a customer to want a site license.

An important factor when you're entering a site license price negotiation is whether the customer's software budget is managed centrally or departmentally. Centrally managed software budgets, usually administered by the IS department, typically require that IS managers negotiate software agreements. In such a case, the IS department controls the budget and "user departments" have no budgetary responsibility for software purchases.

Centrally managed budgets usually present a much easier situation to deal with than the alternative—departmentally managed budgets. The latter usually means that site license negotiations occur with the corporate purchasing manager. This can frustrate developers because the purchasing manager typically has little idea of the value (such as enhanced productivity) your software brings to the company. Usually, the purchasing manager's focus is only on price, terms, and conditions. This person has been assigned to make the purchase on the most favorable terms possible and often doesn't truly differentiate between buying software and purchasing office supplies.

Standardization

Standardizing all users on a single application allows a company's internal support organization to do a much better job. Any time a software product is purchased in volume for company-wide distribution, there will be a large percentage of novice and intermediate users, which potentially means a large internal support burden. During the last few years, corporate support organizations have remained relatively stagnant in terms of head count and resource growth; at the same time, the user base they support has grown tremendously. Several years ago, the average ratio of support person to users was perhaps 1 in 150; today, in many companies it has increased to 1 in 400.

Standardizing on a specific application also allows IS organizations to enhance user productivity by more effectively developing and supporting customized templates and applications written around a standard piece of software. Not only can corporation-wide processes (for creating and distributing forms, planning meetings, or doing expense reports, for example) be put into place, but users can also share more information.

Distribution

Many large companies with centralized purchasing want to distribute software to users more effectively. There are various reasons for this, most of which make a site license attractive to them. One reason is that it gives the IS organization control over the implementation process. For example, with our Meeting Maker product (a meeting scheduling tool that runs over networks) or an E-mail package, it is very typical for the IS organization to install the product in one department or one server group at a time. It can add 50 or 150 users per week and effectively manage the implementation process at a rate that won't cause it, or users, confusion or frustration. Alternatively, the IS procedure may mean installing the software individually on every user's machine.

In either case, by controlling the distribution process, the IS people can make sure they get to every user, ensure that the software is installed correctly, and know that they have accurate records of which users have which software. Applying the adage "Knowledge is power," the more the IS/support organization knows about what software is being used, how, and by whom, the better it can support users and maximize their productivity.

Inventory

Another benefit corporate customers look for in site licensing is inventory reduction. Very few users need the packaging, and, as we all know, very few use the manual. (One IS manager told us about a user who requested a manual for a site-licensed product. The IS manager knew that the user subsequently never looked at the documentation because the IS manager gave the user a German manual—and the user never called back to request the English version.) Therefore, an IS manager wants to distribute software without needing a small warehouse to hold unopened or unneeded inventory. This can be accomplished by giving the customer either a master of the application that can be downloaded from a server or a set of diskettes from which the IS manager lets staff members install the application on machines around the company.

If you can pin down exactly why your customers want a site license and the specific benefits it would render to their company, then you're much more likely to create the necessary win-win situation that keeps your revenue flowing and your customers happy.

PRODUCTS THAT LEND THEMSELVES TO SITE LICENSES

Another decision is whether your product is a site license candidate. Site licenses aren't ideal for all kinds of products. Don't waste precious sales resources trying to sell site licenses if your product is an unlikely candidate. There are two basic criteria that will help you determine whether your product may be well suited for a site license or a VPA: product category and competitive position.

Certain categories lend themselves to these arrangements because of how the products are used. Often, you have a candidate if a user organization must standardize on the product for it to work effectively. Network-based products such as our Meeting Maker product come to mind. It's ideal to license because, much like E-mail, it will be installed on every machine in a department or organization; all users on a network need a copy for the product to work effectively. Also, if you develop an application in a new product category or one that fills a specific need that currently isn't being addressed, there seems to be more urgency on the part of corporate managers to get it installed in the entire user base. Utilities in a new category are particularly good candidates in this respect.

On the other hand, products in existing application categories such as spreadsheet programs or word processors are usually more difficult to site license because customers have already acquired many of these after several years of purchasing. Also, product categories such as graphics packages or databases tend to be unattractive candidates because they typically are not put on every user's machine; they are highly specialized apps that are used by fewer people.

The other determinant of whether a product may be a licensing candidate is the product's competitive position within its category. If you're up against one or two strong market leaders in a particular category and the fight for market share is tough, it may make sense to explore site licensing. The idea is that there is a certain number of large companies that tend to be much more concerned about price than anything else when making a purchase decision. A developer who knows how to successfully target such accounts can make some strong market share inroads with an aggressively priced site license or VPA program.

DEVELOPER BENEFITS

I believe that if done correctly and wisely, site licensing can have many benefits for developers. The first is competitive entrenchment. We all know that in the Macintosh market, the *MacWeek* 200 represent well over 50 percent of the installed base of machines. This "hit list" of 200 companies is easier to reach if you use an effective sales strategy. If your product can become the standard in its category in even 10 percent of these accounts, you've established yourself as a market force and have begun to build barriers for your competitors.

Developing a site license or VPA program that addresses customer needs and that is profitable for the developer will not only help prevent competitors from establishing a foothold in these companies, but will also help build a solid reputation that can smooth the way for you to other companies. If you're known to be "hot" with large Company X, then your reputation will precede you to the next level of accounts; your selling job there will be easier.

Another benefit is earning high revenue in a relatively short sales cycle, which has been particularly important to ON Technology. Although the selling cycle necessary for closing a site license or VPA deal is still a long one, overall I think that the cycle is shorter for the amount of revenue it produces. In effect, in one order, you can get what might otherwise take your sales rep a year and many customer visits to accomplish. This is particularly important because most Mac-only developers are still trying to build a stronger revenue position.

We've found that sacrificing some money on the cost-per-user side of the equation in exchange for more paid-up-front users is usually a winning situation. The one-time large purchase also tends to increase your longer-term revenue by generating more upgrade potential. These days it seems as if most developers are releasing upgrades about every 12 months. A site license program can increase the number of upgrades sold.

So if your company is still somewhat small (less than $10 million), I believe that it makes sense to go for the larger up-front order. As your product line matures and your business grows, there will always be the opportunity to increase your revenue per user; but to help you get successfully through the short-term growth spurt, I think that the overriding focus needs to be on bringing in as much revenue as possible. The site license or VPA avenue shouldn't be overlooked.

Licenses Help Build Your Installed Base

Another benefit of site license programs is that they help build a very important asset, your installed base of customers. A developer's installed base is an asset that, if nurtured effectively, can return untold dividends in the long run. An installed base of satisfied users creates a loyalty to the product that makes life difficult for the competition. The quicker you can build a large installed base (assuming that customers are satisfied with your product's performance), the stronger the barrier against the competition you have constructed. This should translate into a better chance for your company's long-term success.

Creating a large, loyal installed base leads to long-term relationships with customers, which has definite advantages. As your products permeate a customer's organization, they can become a critical part of that company's overall computing strategy. This gives you the ability to share ideas and information (prudently, of course) about your long-term strategic direction and product focus with customers so that they can do better technology planning.

When this happens, the sales effort for your next product starts at a very early stage, because this relationship usually makes these customers want to be involved in the alpha and beta testing of future products. When customers see a need for these future products and are part of your feedback loop, they are more inclined to be early adopters when the products are commercially released. It also lets users give you input earlier in the development process, which can result in your being able to deliver products with maximum customer appeal.

This relationship can also provide you with excellent customer references. Quite often, while potential customers are evaluating your product they ask questions about its large-scale performance—that is, how well it works when hundreds of connected people are using it, as is the case with Meeting Maker. If you can give prospects the names of a few very large satisfied customers, this may provide them with the impetus to close the deal. IS managers respect the opinions and advice of their counterparts at other companies much more than they trust the words of your sales reps. Having a loyal installed base to call upon as a reference is an asset that should be coveted.

Site licensing also helps reduce the potential of piracy. This is not to say that large companies knowingly make illegal copies, but a site license helps protect you against uninformed users who don't know they are doing the wrong thing.

Looking at the big picture, I believe there are many benefits that you and your customers can get from a well-planned and executed site license/VPA program. It takes careful consideration to plan the process and excruciating attention to detail to get it right in the beginning, but if you do it for the right products in the right way, it can be well worth the effort.

CHAPTER TWENTY-THREE

The Ways and Means to Fight Piracy

DEVELOPER PRACTICES—SOME THAT WORK, SOME THAT DON'T

By Karen Wickre

Karen Wickre is a marketing and publishing consultant and free-lance writer based in San Francisco, California.

Editor's note: This chapter was written in 1992. Some companies' antipiracy activities may have changed since then.

SOFTWARE is the currency of computer users. Unfortunately, some users come by their bounty through an unfair exchange—piracy, software theft, "softlifting," as it has been called. No matter the slang, the effect is the same. Developers routinely lose from unrealized sales, users experience a half-baked (or worse) version of your product, and software companies spend valuable resources trying to recoup losses.

Piracy is industrywide and pervades all platforms; it has been a tough issue to grapple with. As Aldus General Counsel Curt Blake remarks, "Other industries don't have to justify battling theft; why do we, as software vendors? Someone [who copies an Aldus program illegally] isn't paying us anything for our product, and they use it to make money—to create professional pieces for which they'll charge a lot, using our product that costs a fortune to create."

Some estimates say that piracy, in all its forms, costs the worldwide industry billions per year. Worse yet, the problem extends far beyond single-user problems to entire companies—and even to dealers and distributors who rely on and trade in unauthorized copies. To compound the problem, customers don't always know or appreciate the work and resources that are invested in software development and sometimes balk at paying full price. Sandra Boulton, who specializes in copyright protection for AutoDesk, says, "People say to me, 'I use AutoCAD only 20 percent of the time; why should I pay the full price?' I tell them that they might drive a car only 20 percent of the time, too, but automakers are going to charge 100 percent for cars, no matter how little they are used." The intensive effort some developers and trade associations must put into educating people about what's wrong with copying software is an indication of how little consumers understand about what goes into creating good software and of their lack of understanding that piracy is theft.

LEGAL MEASURES

There are legal means of protecting yourself from illegal copying; pirates can be found and prosecuted. It takes some sleuthing (or an informant) to build a case against them and commitment on your part to prosecute them.

Large developers often use legal resources to pursue corporate pirates. Litigation has been remarkably successful; but before you embark on this path, you must first weigh its potential cost—in time, legal fees, and other resources. A legal solution may work best in situations involving many copies of illegal software and when it's likely that you can embarrass the company, dealer, or distributor into coming clean and paying up.

STRENGTH IN NUMBERS

Fear of the adverse publicity that sometimes results from software raids keeps some developers from pursuing pirates on their own. Therefore, many developers support collective efforts of the SPA, the Business Software Alliance (BSA), and country-specific associations. Furthermore, the SPA Copyright Protection Fund, supported by Apple and a dozen or so of the largest software publishers, files lawsuits against companies, large organizations, dealers, educational institutions, and mail-order operations that violate the law. The group also works toward strengthening U.S. copyright legislation. The BSA is the SPA's international ally, and many companies with large international markets (such as Apple, Microsoft, Novell, Lotus, and WordPerfect) work through it as well as through the SPA itself. The BSA was established in 1988 to combat piracy outside of the United States, in countries where copyright laws are often weak or nonexistent.

Both organizations have created numerous effective campaigns and legal procedures that member companies collectively use to pursue pirates. Members can use SPA or BSA printed materials, brochures, and guidelines to spread the word to their own staffs, distributors, and customers. The SPA, with assistance from Apple, has created a software inventory program called SPAudit. It searches hard disks and creates an inventory of commercial software programs on them. This helps companies ensure that their employees comply with copyright laws. A piece of ammunition that has been widely distributed is the SPA's 12-minute videotape "It's Just Not Worth the Risk."

WordPerfect Corporation ordered 10,000 copies of the tape to help educate its international sales and marketing group. "We want to train our reps and have them inform their accounts" about the issue, says Beth McGill of WordPerfect's corporate communications department.

(Of course, there are also technical solutions to pirating, ranging from copy protection to serialized software to user-counting server applications. There are also special integrated security programs that vigilant corporate users can install to protect and control the use of applications. However, for the purposes of this chapter we'll focus on non-technology solutions only.)

CREATE YOUR OWN MIX

In addition to participating in industry groups and exploring technical fixes, you can create your own mix of legal, educational, and marketing activities to combat piracy. When deciding which fronts to fight on, consider the factors described in the following paragraphs.

Commitment of Resources

What level of internal commitment is your company willing to make to antipiracy activities? Are you willing to devote a staff person's time? Do you have the resources to run both internal and external awareness? Will you represent your company at user group and professional association meetings that address the subject?

Target Market

If your customers are primarily home users or if your product has a fairly exclusive installed base, you may have to spend more in legal costs to pursue the culprits than you will ultimately recoup. In that case, public awareness may be your most cost-effective measure. On the other hand, if you reach a broad corporate market and sell through multiple channels, you may be able to recover some losses and get publicity that will deter other customers from pirating—or at least they'll recognize that this is a problem that someone cares a lot about. As Lotus' Corporate Communications Manager Bryan Simmons says, "Where we really try to fight hard is against large-scale corporate customers who are abusing us."

Retail Price

When it comes to using pricing strategies to discourage piracy, the results seem to be mixed. Adobe Software Legal Counsel Steve Peters says, "We have prices on our products that range from a suggested retail of $99 to $15,000, with lots of price points in between; we have been surprised to see that pricing doesn't seem to make a difference in piracy. If you make something affordable, some people view it as something they shouldn't have to pay for and they pirate it. If you make it expensive, the incentive is there [to pirate] because the price is high." However, Brøderbund Vice President of Product Development Harry Wilker says, "Most of the solutions, such as special pricing deals, work with high-priced software. Our software is low-cost, so we're some of the most pirated software around."

Pricing strategies may be most effective in fighting piracy when you sell multiple or network copies. When AutoDesk released version 11 of its best-selling AutoCAD program, it created a new scheme to discourage interoffice (or cross-classroom, where CAD programs proliferate) softlifting, the practice of copying programs within organizations or for office-to-home use. That version offers a "floating license," which essentially limits network use of AutoCAD to a set number of people (as many as the buyer requests) who can log on to the program from their own computers. Only that number of users has access at any one time, although the buyer can request to change the number (and buy additional access licenses). The price is based on the number of accessible copies needed, and there is a sizable discount offered for large quantities.

Because it has a big education market, AutoDesk also offers a locked version of the prior AutoCAD release exclusively to its education dealers. The original version 10 retailed for $3,000, but the locked edition—still a useful tool for all levels of drafting students—costs just $495. "We wanted to encourage students to use AutoCAD, and a lower price helps us do that," says Sandra Boulton.

By itself, a single product's retail price may not make or break an antipiracy strategy. But as part of an overall campaign, creative discounts for group sales or network-access copies can go a long way to discourage unauthorized use. In developing a pricing strategy, you'll need to do a variety of calculations to discover how elastic your price can or should be. It's a common assumption that simply lowering a product's price will increase the customer base. However, many more factors enter that equation. You should carefully research and estimate variables such as the potential size of the customer base, the number of stand-alone or multiple workstation environments there might be for your product, what the buying patterns are for your customers and product category, and what margins are acceptable for the market. Making reasonable estimates from this kind of information will contribute to your peace of mind about creating the best possible pricing schemes. To whatever extent your prices can discourage piracy, all the better.

MARKETING AND EDUCATION METHODS

So what's the best way to hammer home the concept that piracy ultimately hurts users, hurts you, and slows industry growth in general? An AutoDesk brochure puts it this way: "Software piracy...leads to higher prices and less incentive for innovation. If software were not so frequently stolen, developers could recover their development costs more quickly and go on to fund new development efforts. Overall, the effect is to stifle variety and creativity in the market."

When 18 developers met at Apple in the autumn of 1991, they discussed many ways to fight piracy collectively and individually. The group felt strongly that education programs are among the most beneficial ones needed to build long-term financial and mind-share successes. Those who are active in the antipiracy movement favor several approaches, as described below.

User Education

Aldus has a brochure that ships in every software package. It asks, "Is it okay for my colleagues and me to copy each other's software?" After answering several questions in a candid Q&A format, the last comment, "I'll bet most of the people who copy software don't even know they're breaking the law," is followed by "Most people don't purposely break the law—they would never consider, for instance, stealing money out of someone's pocket. If you're part of an organization, see what you can do to initiate a policy statement that everyone respects. And as an individual, you can spread the word." By distributing information like this, notes Aldus' Blake, "You want to encourage people to do the right thing. And there's no [more] excuse about legalisms or small print." Likewise, Lotus puts a copy of "How to care for and use your software," an antipiracy brochure, into every box it ships.

AutoDesk's antipiracy campaign, which began in 1988, is probably the industry's oldest and most comprehensive. In addition to using education and marketing strategies, the company actively pursues pirates; it has sued or settled for full retail price on pirated copies of its products and has developed materials to distribute to end users, user groups, resellers, and schools.

Editor's note: To learn more about AutoDesk's antipiracy program see Chapter 24, "How to Discourage Piracy: How AutoDesk Makes Back Two Dollars on Every Antipiracy Dollar It Spends."

"Don't take a risk with a copied disk" is the theme (and the title) of one of AutoDesk's printed guides to preventing software piracy. The 20-page booklet includes a full explanation of AutoDesk's software license, a review of copyright law, and definitions of softlifting, counterfeiting, and hard-disk loading. AutoDesk also provides information about SPA and BSA initiatives, a list of procedures for ensuring legal use, the software code of ethics, a software registration form, and templates for an employee memo and company policy regarding software use. The campaign tag line is used in a poster that features the concept of worldwide software raids. The AutoDesk Antipiracy Department also produced an animated video about piracy, using AutoDesk multimedia products, for distribution to a general audience—with a special emphasis on students.

In addition to creating antipiracy materials, developers can raise the visibility of their companies and the piracy issue by writing about the subject for business and computer magazines and by speaking to user groups and professional associations. Aldus' Blake says, "We respond actively to requests for speeches from consulting firms, consumer-fraud groups, and business groups." One of the Big Six accounting firms in the United States has asked Aldus for information about piracy to factor into software costs, as part of its auditing and consulting services to clients (thereby raising the issue in its own industry).

Another tack is to encourage corporate executives to create policies and procedures that make purchasing software quick and easy; that way, there's less incentive or temptation to copy. The more seamless the internal process and the faster the access to a reputable dealer, the easier it is for those who buy software in bulk to stay legal.

Channel Education and Incentives

To effectively educate the channel, you must work closely with resellers, dealers, and distributors; you should also create incentives to encourage quick response. Aldus has created an antipiracy program kit especially for resellers. It emphasizes how to talk to customers about piracy, what to do if buyers appear uninterested in honoring antipiracy measures, and, as a last resort, when it's appropriate to send legal reports to Aldus. (In the case of legal action, says Curt Blake, Aldus will settle with the customer for the full list price and give a percentage to the reseller who reported the theft.) Aldus is also working to educate VARs. "If someone buys numerous machines and no software, red flags go up," says Blake.

The Asian software market is notable in this regard, says Microsoft International Antipiracy Specialist Alison Gilligan. Microsoft is testing an international program, "Work with the Original," aimed at authorized dealers. It consists of an ad, a direct-mail campaign, trade-show appearances, and press interviews. The theme is carried in a ten-page brochure and single-page "Software Piracy and the Law" fact sheets, tailored to several key Asian markets where piracy is known to be prevalent. Microsoft also launched the "Protect Yourself Against MS-DOS Counterfeiting" campaign in the summer of 1991. A brochure mailed to retailers focuses on the problem Microsoft has had with the wholesale copying of its operating system.

"Every month, tens of thousands of counterfeit copies...are distributed to unsuspecting users," says the brochure. It goes on to say, "This untested software causes serious problems for PC buyers." As a result, says the brochure to retailers, the company has taken "extraordinary steps to eliminate counterfeiting" to "protect your customers, your profit margins, and ourselves against illegal competition." It reminds dealers that "every illegal copy sold is the loss of a potential sale for you."

The "extraordinary steps" referred to in this campaign are the use of two difficult-to-pirate holograms and a distinctive die-cut that are visible on every package of the MS-DOS 5 Upgrade—a major innovation. Gilligan notes that these measures have slowed the counterfeiting cycle, which boosts legal sales of a new product or version during the critical roll-out period.

Dealers who sign the Microsoft software code of ethics and comply with the anticounterfeiting program win membership on a "corporate honor roll," meaning that they receive special Microsoft publicity and can participate in promotions and giveaways to attract and keep customers.

Self-Education

Although educating customers and the channel is an excellent antipiracy measure, you shouldn't overlook the importance of educating members of your own company. A prudent move is to take the steps necessary to ensure that your own house is "clean"; that is, make sure that everyone in your company understands and is in compliance with copyright laws. This will set the best possible example for your customers, dealers, and others in the industry.

Program Cost

No matter who the audience is, the cost of any education campaign depends on your level of commitment: how many internal resources you provide, how many existing resources (such as SPA and BSA brochures and videotapes) you use, the overall scope of your effort, the size of your audience, and your goals.

OTHER MEANS

In addition to creating marketing materials for antipiracy education and public visibility, developers are addressing piracy in several other key areas.

Concurrent Licensing

The concurrent-use license is an emerging antipiracy tactic that has been employed by several major developers. They have changed their licenses to allow for "concurrent use" of a software program by a "designated user." Lotus, Aldus, and Microsoft, among others, now permit users to legally copy their programs for home use. No one wants to "put users in technical violation," says Aldus' Blake. "We're not interested in splitting hairs but instead in [pursuing] people who really violate the spirit of the law by buying ten Macs and one copy of software—with the intent to copy."

Site Licenses

A site license gives a corporate buyer the right to have many users working from a single copy (or a specified number of copies) at designated locations for a flat fee. Originally designed for the world of mainframe-to-terminal computing, site licensing has been used in the personal computing market as an attractive sales tools and an effective way to manage large-scale upgrades. Attorney Eric Doney also notes that in some instances these licenses "are used to assure penetration and uniformity in a single large account or to legalize installations that were simply not amenable to individual license control for one reason or another. In other words, they were a recognition of, and one solution to, the reality of widespread illegal copying—before the advent of aggressive antipiracy campaigns."

However, some developers today frown on site licensing as a solution to widespread illegal copying. When it comes to piracy, Doney believes that "the attraction of the site license has diminished as user and management sophistication regarding licensing terms has grown over the last few years."

"There's some danger in using the term site license," says AutoDesk's Sandra Boulton, "because it becomes an uncontrollable issue in the marketplace. It connotes *carte blanche* use. We prefer quantity discounts and floating licenses to site licensing. In essence, what [some] people really want with a site license is a reduced price. We'd rather deal with it as a discounting procedure than as a licensing issue. That way, it gives us a measure of control."

However, many developers today do use site licensing and feel it is an effective way to fill customer purchasing needs.

Editor's note: For more information about site licensing from a company that's been there, see Chapter 22, "The Advantages of a Site License Program: Secrets of How and Why Site Licenses Can Be Effective."

Other Licensing Strategies

When the group of 18 developers mentioned earlier met to brainstorm piracy solutions, it was recognized that there is a need to achieve more consistency and clarity in license agreements—perhaps a more standard agreement. Although there would be legal ramifications to a standardized agreement, the industry is working toward making licenses more consistent and clear.

But whatever the exact wording of a particular license, attorney Doney thinks that most of the existing ones "do a pretty good job." In the majority of the 3,000-plus piracy investigations his firm has handled, "the misuse is fairly blatant, not the result of license agreement misunderstandings," he says. Continually rewriting licenses to reflect and accommodate new uses and ways of working, coupled with an ongoing education process, can help eliminate user misunderstandings that may contribute to piracy, says Doney.

To help draw users' attention to the license agreement and to help them better understand it, you might consider adding a "license quickstart" list to the agreement or to the packaging. An easy-to-read list (not "fine print") of the do's and don'ts, written in layman's terms, may attract the attention of customers who don't take time to read the fine print.

Registration Incentives

Some estimates indicate that, industrywide, only about 30 percent of software buyers actually register their legally purchased copies. If you create attractive incentives to reward customers who take the time to register—such as with ongoing or enhanced tech support, special upgrade offers and discounts, user tips, and other perks—more buyers are likely to register. Creating such incentives and actively publicizing them emphasizes the value-added benefits of legal software and encourages the purchase and registration of software.

Also, repeat-purchase incentives can be a particularly enticing alternative. If you offer registered users the opportunity to get future or additional products at a discount, you receive two benefits: More users will register and you increase the likelihood of cross-selling to your installed base.

Aldus' Blake personally advocates another registration incentive: At purchase, the developer provides only limited printed documentation with the software box and offers a more complete package when the user registers. This approach may work best with a complex product such as PageMaker or Persuasion, for which thorough documentation is desirable for taking full advantage of its features.

Another idea to encourage registration and its benefits is to make the process simpler, perhaps by instituting a short form the user can send directly to the developer via E-mail, for example, when installing a program.

Amnesty Programs

Developers have mixed reactions to amnesty programs—that is, programs of the sort libraries and local courts sometimes conduct to collect for overdue books or parking tickets. "We've talked to some current customers who've bought one of our products, and they say, 'How do we justify your excusing thieves when we paid for it?' It's hard to make a case for amnesty," says Aldus' Blake.

Although Microsoft is not inclined toward the concept of amnesty programs, it has mounted short-term campaigns in Italy, Spain, and the United Kingdom as part of a BSA effort. The Spanish program, Cease Fire, consisted of an educational promotion about piracy, a well-publicized promise not to sue offenders during the campaign, and a hotline to call about legitimate dealers and proper software management tools. Participating BSA members sold a lot of software during the three-month campaign, says Alison Gilligan. But in the end, she says, "We're concerned that [offering amnesty] punishes legitimate users more than anything else."

Upgrade Incentives

Amnesty may work best in conjunction with an aggressive upgrade program. In 1988, after Symmetry Software realized that its outliner program, Acta Advantage, was among the most pirated pieces of software in the business, the developer made a time-limited amnesty offer to users. For $50 and a copy of a screen shot, which proved that they indeed had the program, users received the latest upgrade and would from then on be considered legal. The result? Symmetry believes that it doubled its customer base, according to Marketing Coordinator Samantha Kirk.

Acta Advantage also has a large following in Japan, where its Japanese distributor, Nippon Polaroid, estimates that the number of illegal users may be 15 or 20 times as large as the number of registered ones. A product called Acta 7, released in Japan, is in line for a similar amnesty promotion, says Nippon Polaroid Marketing Manager Jaemes Shanley. He cautions other developers about the timing of such promotions. They should be held after the product is launched and registered users have been upgraded, he says, because "we are sensitive about the need to ensure that the promotion doesn't turn into a de facto endorsement of illegal copying and doesn't compromise the resellers who support Acta in this market."

The proposed campaign will be targeted to experienced Mac users (those who have been using the Mac for at least two years, says Shanley) and will run for about 60 days. The cost of receiving amnesty will be about half the list price of the product and will also require that a user do the following: turn in the disk with any earlier versions of the program; provide the name of the regular software dealer, who receives a portion of the revenue from the sale; and offer a suggestion in writing for improving Acta or extending its capabilities. In exchange, users will be registered, become entitled to support and upgrades, and receive the localized Acta 7 Japanese upgrade software and manual. "Our expectation," says Shanley, "is that we can triple the base of registered Acta users in Japan—and gain valuable insight into user needs, which can guide development of future enhancements or new products from Symmetry."

MAKING THE DIFFERENCE

"The root of the piracy problem," says attorney Eric Doney, "is that anyone with a personal computer can create an unlimited number of perfect copies of most commercial software tools. Never in the history of the marketplace has there been a comparable situation. Our challenge has been to educate the public that software duplication is not only illegal, but also is unfair and should not be condoned by anyone."

No matter which means developers use to encourage legal software use, educating buyers as well as dealers about piracy problems—and using a well-stocked arsenal of solutions—is bound to help stem the tide.

CHAPTER TWENTY-FOUR

How to Discourage Piracy

HOW AUTODESK MAKES BACK TWO DOLLARS ON EVERY ANTIPIRACY DOLLAR IT SPENDS

By Sandra Boulton, AutoDesk, Inc.

Sandra Boulton is the director of the copyright protection program at AutoDesk, Inc., a developer of computer-aided design applications, located in Sausalito, California.

SOFTWARE piracy is a problem of tremendous proportions. Even the most conservative estimates indicate that piracy costs the industry $2 to $4 billion worldwide. The United States alone accounts for $1.5 billion of that, despite tough copyright protection laws. Therefore, any antipiracy program should focus on the U.S. market as well as on markets in other countries. My company, AutoDesk, uses a program in the United States and Canada as a template for programs in other parts of the world. Unfortunately, in international markets we often have to contend with laws that are often weak, not enforced, or nonexistent. Therefore, antipiracy activities in these markets are typically more expensive and more difficult to implement.

AutoDesk, like most software companies, has a significant piracy problem. We estimate that seven to ten illegal copies of AutoCAD, our flagship product, are made for each legal copy sold. These illegal copies have such a dramatic impact on our bottom line that we can't afford *not* to try to stem the tide. Like many companies, we briefly experimented with physical copy protection, but the user community reacted with such concern that we dropped the protection from our U.S. copies in 1986 (but left it on all international versions).

At that point, we decided that illegal copying should be countered by legal action. In the United States, duplicating our products is a direct violation of the license agreement and is thus a federal crime punishable by a fine of up to $25,000 and imprisonment for up to one year. Civil law also allows us to recover losses based on the number of copies produced or to collect damages of up to $100,000 for willful copyright infringement.

Since the inception of our antipiracy program in 1988, we've investigated thousands of cases. Our financial recoveries have been substantial. Sales made directly as a result of the antipiracy program have topped $3 million. We also try to keep tabs on indirect sales that result from the program, but that can't be directly tracked; we estimate that last year alone, these incremental sales were half a million dollars. The bottom line: For each dollar spent on antipiracy activities, we've made back more than two dollars.

PROGRESS THROUGH EDUCATION

To tackle retail and corporate piracy, we've developed an aggressive program. Our approach includes independent action as well as cooperative efforts with other companies and associations that are fighting piracy. Our program focuses on user and dealer education; dealer participation; and, when necessary, legal action.

Education is also a key strategy in our war on piracy. We produce antipiracy kits that contain literature for dealers and users, conduct public-speaking tours that educate and warn of the consequences of illegal duplication, and encourage the press to recognize and openly discuss the problem. We also place advertisements in national publications. The ads focus on the benefits of buying legal versions of products—what users get with a legitimate copy and what they don't get with an illegal one. Other ads aim to educate the many people who don't even realize that copying is illegal.

Distributors and dealers with a strong commitment to increasing sales by decreasing piracy are of the utmost importance. In many parts of the world, even a 10 percent decline in piracy can result in a hundredfold increase in sales, which benefits both the manufacturer and dealer. It's very important to educate your sales and distribution channels about how important these antipiracy campaigns are—to themselves, the manufacturers, and the local economy. I often make the point that 40 to 75 percent of the money spent on legitimate software stays in the country where the sale occurs. This represents the support, training, and margin on sales provided by dealers and distributors to the local economy.

COOPERATIVE EFFORTS

Groups such as the Software Publishers Association (SPA) wage their own wars on piracy, in which we participate. We also encourage local software associations and distributors in other countries to take such action as placing antipiracy ads. For example, ANIPCO, the Mexican software association, developed an ad that focuses on educating users who don't know that copying is illegal. The text of the ad says something like "The copy-holic is the last to know." A group of distributors in Chile took a particularly interesting tack. They created an ad that tells software users to be sure they have bought original software and shows them that only original software carries a special, recognizable seal.

AutoDesk is also a founding member of the Business Software Alliance, now an arm of the SPA. This group combines the forces of leading business-software companies worldwide in an effort to educate users, prosecute offenders, and improve copyright legislation. With this group, we've conducted numerous raids of corporations and retail pirates, which have resulted in significant publicity (in such high-profile publications as *BusinessWeek* and *The Wall Street Journal*) about piracy and the penalties levied on offenders.

In a raid, we procure a court order that allows our attorneys (when operating in another country, we usually hire local attorneys) and the proper law enforcement agents to enter an establishment and search for specific things. We have them look for evidence of pirated software: manuals, diskettes, and the like. Properly done, the raids are usually a surprise to the company in question. We search the computer directories and the premises, as set forth in the court document. Of course, we first prepare for the raid by conducting an internal investigation of the suspected offender to provide the court with the proper evidence to get permission for the search.

After such raids and the ensuing publicity, legitimate sales jump tremendously. For example, during a raid on a retail operation in Hong Kong, we confiscated more than 100,000 manuals and diskettes. We followed that with a series of raids on corporate end users. After the raids, our sales boomed in that part of the world.

WHEN THE LAW IS UNCLEAR

Unfortunately, support of antipiracy activities by local law enforcement and the underlying legal structure is not strong throughout the world. Where no formal antipiracy protection exists, we work with organizations such as the SPA, but we also have to rely on our own resources. Often we depend on distributors to help plan and implement regional campaigns and to provide referrals to local attorneys.

Even low-cost but well-planned programs can be successful. For example, we did a very successful letter-writing campaign; by carefully targeting the suspected pirates and crafting a tough but diplomatic letter, we got substantial results. The letters usually outline the information we've gathered about the recipient, such as how many pirated copies they have. We also quote the local copyright laws and ask the recipients to respond to our local representative by a certain date if they don't want to hear from our attorneys. In many cases, an overseas company assumes that you won't go to the trouble to pursue their ten pirated copies. When the letters arrive, you suddenly don't seem to be quite as far away as they thought you were. Sales in some countries more than doubled after we sent these letters.

Indeed, as ambitious as our U.S. efforts are, they are nothing compared with our worldwide efforts, especially in markets where copyright protection laws are poorly defined or difficult to enforce. Even blatant piracy can be hard to battle. In Malaysia, I sought out an AutoDesk product that had been released in the United States the day before at a retail price of $300. I purchased it for $3; for an additional $10, I got a manual (complete with our copyright notification). The company gave me a receipt. It took all the major credit cards; the salesperson changed my money for me and duplicated the disk while I waited! Of course, the disk was missing some files, so the application was useless. But even if I had bought a copy that worked, I would have had to contend with various operational problems and lack of support.

FINDING THE CULPRITS

In the United States and Canada, we rely on many individuals to report piracy. About 80 percent of our reports originate from dealers; the rest come from consultants, former and current employees, and competitors of offending companies. Several people have called me and said very quietly, "I don't want my boss to hear me tell you, but we've got illegal copies here." (You may wish to consult a lawyer before taking action on such a tip.)

Our program includes dealers and distributors, because they're the closest to the customers, but it places them in a tenuous position: They want to uphold the copyright laws, but they're afraid of losing future business. As a result, a cornerstone of any program must be complete confidentiality. When we receive a report about a particular customer's possibly pirating software, we leave the dealer totally out of the investigation. We check our database and determine which serial numbers are registered to the customer. If it conflicts with the number the dealer reported to us, then our attorneys send the customer a letter requiring that the customer contact them directly and purchase a quantity of legal copies equal to the number of pirated ones—or face a lawsuit. Those purchases must be made at full retail price which further penalizes the pirate because discounted software is so readily available.

We do compensate dealers who report piracy; because a legal sale would have resulted in some profit for the dealer, we feel that a sale through the antipiracy program should also result in compensation. We also require dealers to install and support any packages sold through the antipiracy program.

MAY I SEE YOUR LICENSE, PLEASE?

We've had several impressive successes. For example, when a department of the Canadian government insisted that it had the right to copy our software across its network without paying for the copies, we tried for several months to resolve the problem directly with its representatives. When that got us nowhere, however, we were forced to take legal measures. Imagine workers' surprise when 30 armed Mounties appeared at their door and demanded that they move away from the computers. The incident got a lot of press, which focused on our approach to the problem: diplomacy first, legal action second.

We also remedied problems at a large naval architecture firm. The firm had annual sales of $37 million plus and more than 700 employees—and 43 illegal copies of our software. We recovered $150,000 from that company for the infringement.

We've also succeeded in identifying and prosecuting individuals who are duplicating and selling illegal copies. We participated in an FBI raid in which we seized bootleg manuals and diskettes and an entire customer list that gave us names, addresses, and personal information about everyone who had ever bought software illegally from this individual. We obtained a temporary restraining order and a default judgment of $100,000 plus $35,000 in attorneys' fees.

There are many reasons for embarking on a vigorous antipiracy campaign. You may not always get immediate results, but the time spent and the effort invested will usually increase sales. With the persistence and support of local distribution channels, there's great potential for making dramatic gains in world markets.

PART SIX

Supporting Customers

"If you think customers are a pain, try doing without them for 30 days." I wonder who first said that—a vendor or a customer? Good customer support lays a foundation on which you can build loyalty and get customers' tongues wagging about you; it also paves the way for selling them upgrades and new products and services. As one of our authors puts it: "A satisfied customer spreads goodwill better than any magazine article or favorable review."

Chapter 25, "The Anatomy of Good Customer Support," describes the process of and philosophy behind creating and managing an effective customer support system—based on one that has set the pace for the industry. This part of the book also ventures beyond more traditional support activities and explores intriguing, cost-effective ways to supplement your support system. For example, in Chapter 26, "Publishing a Customer Newsletter to Enhance Support," you'll read about how one company reduced the load on its telephone support lines without sacrificing support quality. Chapter 27, "Using On-line Services as a Marketing and Support Tool: How We Use the AppleLink Network," describes how one developer harnessed the power of on-line services to help cost-effectively support resellers and customers worldwide.

CHAPTER TWENTY-FIVE

The Anatomy of Good Customer Support

By Marsha Terry, WordPerfect Corporation

Marsha Terry is the Macintosh customer support team leader for WordPerfect Corporation, a developer of word processing applications located in Orem, Utah.

IT'S 7 a.m. Mountain time in the United States, and the phones have started ringing. On the other end of the lines: a secretary in Des Moines, a student in New York, a lawyer in L.A., a professional writer in Atlanta. Each is looking for a solution to a perplexing word processing problem. Thus begins a typical day in the life of WordPerfect customer support, in which we handle an average of 16,500 calls that each last an average of eight minutes. During the course of the day, almost 800 operators staff the 33 toll-free numbers with 487 incoming lines.

Reaching this level of service certainly didn't happen overnight. It was an evolution that began when cofounders Bruce Bastian and Alan Ashton chose to support WordPerfect products—from the moment the corporation opened its doors in 1979. In the early days, they were the ones taking customer S.O.S. calls. However, they soon realized that the task was so big that the existing staff could either program or do support work. So they hired five or six operators, who, with only a manual and a little training, started answering the increasing number of calls. Because networks hadn't yet been invented, operators shared information by circulating memos. Eventually these memos became entire books that filled several filing cabinets—and then networks, E-mail, and a fast text-retrieval system came to the rescue.

When sales began to skyrocket, support operators were sometimes hired at the rate of 20 per week. Phone lines were added as quickly as possible after an extraordinary onslaught of calls literally began jamming the system of toll-free phone lines throughout the state of Utah!

THE SUPPORT MISSION

Support can do much more than simply assist customers. It can also sell products. I once overheard a conversation in a local computer store. A customer asked a sales rep's opinion about which word processor to purchase. The rep's advice: "With this product, you get a word processor. With WordPerfect, you get a word processor and an 800 number."

It's not hard to guess which product the customer purchased. When a customer faces the prospect of taking home a new product, high quality toll-free support can be the mitigating factor. A satisfied customer spreads good-will better than any magazine article or favorable review—and generates revenue for you.

If you create your support department with the correct philosophy, the sky is the limit. Successful customer support springs from a way of thinking, an attitude. Just creating a support function isn't enough; actually, that's the easier part. A support department is likely to have little impact on your company's success if it isn't built on a distinctive attitude about what customer support is supposed to do for you and your customers. The foundation of a good support program is a well-defined goal or purpose that is meaningful to the company as a whole and that is well understood and articulated through-out your ranks. Once you understand conceptually what you want your support effort to accomplish, then you can plan an implementation strategy that puts your philosophy into practice.

Here's our mission statement:

"The purpose of support is to *satisfy* our customers and *improve* our products. We courteously and efficiently *teach* our customers how to use our programs effectively. We do not bluff answers, we act in a *friendly* manner to give accurate and timely solutions. We *follow through* with our customers by keep-ing our commitments."

Certain words stand out, and not by accident: satisfy, improve, teach, be friendly, and follow through. These few words sum it all up. They form the basis of our entire customer support program.

SATISFACTION—BY THE CUSTOMER'S STANDARDS

How well you satisfy customers' needs is the measure of a good support program. It's not enough to just *handle* customers; to be successful in the long run, you must truly *satisfy their needs*—which goes way beyond just taking calls and disposing of them in some manner.

Many companies I've needed support from have lacked two important things: good troubleshooting techniques and a friendly attitude. Yes, they listened to my problem. But often that was where the communication ended. It seemed as if they automatically (too quickly) knew what was wrong and offered me a "quick fix." It was very clear that the operators were just checking off a list of questions to ask (no personal touch). If my questions made them stray from the list, they became lost and unable to answer my questions (lack of troubleshooting). To put it simply, I was not satisfied.

How can you tell when a customer is satisfied? There are lots of ways. During actual support calls, one way of assuring that the customer is satisfied is to restate the question before offering a solution. This has several advantages. It saves the customer's and your time because you discern what the customer is really asking. It also reduces phone time and makes the customer realize that you care enough to find out the true nature of the difficulty. For example, three callers who ask, "How do I crop a graphic?" may really be asking three different questions. One customer may need to know how to size the graphic to fit a certain space, another may want to know how to "trim" one side of the graphic, and a third may just want to move the graphic to another location. Restating the question narrows the possibilities and helps you define what the customer really needs. Take notes during the call, restate the key points covered, and verify that you answered all the questions.

Here are some key techniques we try to use during all calls to help assure satisfaction.

- *Listen.* Focus on the customer. The most important thing at this moment should be what your customer is saying.

- *Restate.* "So your problem/question is...?" Wait for a response; if it isn't "yes," listen some more and try again.

- *Gather information.* Ask appropriate questions. Get the information needed to solve the problem. Mull over all the factors that relate to the problem.

- *Troubleshoot.* Give exact instructions. Being vague or assuming that the customer knows the computer as well as you do can increase frustration levels for both of you.

- *Use resources well.* Know which are available and how to use them.

- *Make a decision.* Don't drag out the call. When progress stops, decide what to do. It's better to research the question and call the customer back than to bluff.

- *Close the call. Make sure the problem is solved.* Check your notes to make sure all the points have been covered. End with a smile in your voice.

Another thing we do to determine if callers are satisfied is to call them back sometime after the initial contact. Perhaps a week later, we call to ask some simple open-ended questions that give customers a chance to express themselves, and whose answers are a good barometer of their satisfaction: "Were you satisfied with the service you received?" "Was your question answered?" We've gotten the most useful information by asking questions that require some thought on the customer's part.

Take notes. Reiterate what you think you've heard to verify it, and let the customers know that they are important to you. You can even finish by giving customers a tip or asking if they have any other questions. You took some of their valuable time; offer something in return.

SELF-IMPROVEMENT

Customer support is probably one of the best ways through which a company can gather information to help improve a product or how it is marketed.

Each customer has a reason for calling. The questions themselves are important, but the reasons they are asked can point to some excellent opportunities for self-improvement. By determining the real reason for the question, you can discern important things such as whether the manual is clear about how to use a certain feature or if users have difficulties using a feature the way they thought it was designed to work.

If you track this information, then, in a sense, each customer has a direct voice to a programmer. And if your tracking methods are accurate, you can use the information to tailor your products to customers' needs. We use three tracking methods, each with a specific purpose. Every customer support team creates a Common Call list to record how many customers call with the same question. If a question is popular enough, it can be placed on a Hotlist, an extension of the Common Call list that is used in more ways. For example, programmers use it as a development tool because it allows them to see exactly what users want and how many want it.

When a customer's problem can't be solved by phone or can't be duplicated, we create a Software Trouble Report (STR). It is forwarded to a specialist who becomes responsible for solving the riddle. Each specialist is assigned a specific feature or area of the application. By having specialists handle STRs, we reduce duplication of effort and can pinpoint exactly how many customers have a specific question. This may all seem a bit overwhelming, but remember —we created our department over a long period. We started with STRs and added the Common Call list and Hotlist as the department grew.

TEACHING CUSTOMERS—USING THEIR PERSPECTIVE

Teaching customers how to use your product is probably one of the best goals a quality support team can strive toward. However, doing this isn't as simple as it appears. Good technical support teaches the customer how to use your product *in the way the customer wants to use it,* not the way the manual dictates. Most users don't have the time to hack away to get a program to work. The extra minute it may take you to understand how a customer wants to use a feature—and then using that perspective to teach the customer—is well worth it. (A convert can be a convert for life and will sing your praises to anyone who will listen.)

Our way of teaching customers entails nothing special; all we do is ask questions to find out how and why they use our product and then tailor our teaching methods accordingly.

PLEASE...DON'T HANG UP!

Make the customer your friend. It doesn't take much effort, and a cheerful attitude goes a long way. The way an operator answers the phone—the attitude transmitted in the first response—can set the tone for the entire call and perhaps for that customer's entire relationship (or lack thereof) with your company. If you think your voice doesn't convey your attitude, just think about some of your own telephone habits. Have you listened to yourself lately? Do you sound like a programmed machine or like a friend? Do people wait for your beep so that they can leave a message?

Make your personal greeting cheerful, and from the very beginning let the customer know you are "alive." When you talk to your friends, don't you call them by name? Give your name during your greeting, and get the customer's name sometime during the call—and use it. Most greetings last four seconds or less. What you say in those few seconds and how you say it can make or break your relationship with the caller.

Being friendly can start even before an operator answers the phone. How many times have you called a number only to hear, "All our operators are busy. Please stay on the line, and you will be helped in the order your call was received"? After a few minutes have passed with no human response, you start to wonder if they all went to lunch and forgot to tell anyone—or if you just are number one-thousand-and-one in the queue. Maybe the hold music puts you to sleep. No matter; your time is being wasted. You are attached to this machine until someone answers or you hang up.

A little more than a year ago, we decided to make our phone system a little more friendly. We hired "hold jockeys." Instead of hearing the drone of canned music, callers who are put on hold hear live jockeys who play the latest music and give live reports about how long the current wait is to reach particular customer service groups. They also tell you about any new products or programs and give you tips about how to prepare the questions you want to ask.

FOLLOW THROUGH

In addition to getting a customer's name, get a phone number so that you can call back if you have more information. (I have hung up more than once and realized that I had forgotten to tell the customer something.) One day we were joking about doing support on a higher plane, on which you would know and be able to solve customer problems before anyone phoned. Short of being able to do that, we rely on follow-through. By calling customers back, we are in essence on the line with them before they have a question.

Because operators keep track of their calls, they choose which customers to call back. Team leaders also call customers back at random to gather information for improving our service. Remember, a callback is valid only if you ask, "Can I help you with anything now?" This is another way to add personalized service to your support.

THE MAKING OF A GOOD SUPPORT OPERATOR

To put these pieces together into a working whole, you must have the right kind of people answering the phones. Over the years, WordPerfect has found that standard hiring practices don't always work well when hiring a support operator. Not everyone can do phone support well; it's a special talent. Support operators don't deal face-to-face with customers; they must talk through a wire without the advantage of using body language, gestures, or facial expressions to help convey their meanings. All they have are their voices and vocal mannerisms. Even some of the best teachers and sales representatives would flounder in such circumstances. And a degree in computer science doesn't automatically make someone a qualified support operator. Some candidates may well be the most intelligent people who have ever crossed your doorstep; but without the ability to communicate information over the phone in a way that is meaningful to callers, they will be completely useless in a support department.

Those who have never given technical support over the phone may have a hard time understanding this. But think of it this way: Imagine putting a novice user in front of a computer and helping that person create a fully formatted ten-page document. But here's the catch: You have to give instructions from the next room.

To help gauge whether a job applicant has this special skill (it probably won't be evident on a résumé), during the interview process we often have the candidate "take a call." We give the applicant a few pages of basic support information and then simulate a customer call. The reaction to the call and the mannerisms portrayed during the conversation give us some good indicators of what an operator's behavior might be in a real situation. We listen not only to the words spoken but also to the tone, phrasing, and logic used during the call. After candidates have passed the initial interview, we test them in an eight-hour lab for basic DOS, Macintosh, and WordPerfect knowledge. If it goes well, the job may be offered.

A new hire first becomes a trainee. We give trainees three weeks of special training covering phone etiquette, phone skills, specific product information, and where to look for answers. They begin listening to calls with a "model" on the first day of training. The phone model is an experienced support operator who has the skills we would like all operators to have. The first few times in the model system, new operators only listen to calls, but by the end of the first week, they begin to trade off every other call with the phone model. The model is never the same; a trainee works with many during the training period because we like new operators to experience different working styles to help them develop their own. The trainers continually assess the abilities of each trainee and eventually send them to teams.

OUR MAGIC NUMBER IS 22

The structure of your support organization is also paramount. Our organization has changed over the years to meet our growing needs. Currently, the department is divided into teams, each with a team leader and up to 22 operators. Each team answers 11 incoming toll-free lines, so only half the team is answering phones at one time. The others can be studying, attending training classes, or calling customers back.

Why 22? There are 22 working days in an average month. With a 22-member group, a team leader can meet with one operator each day. We also conduct weekly team meetings to discuss topics that concern the entire group. Because the groups are small, team leaders know their teams well and can give each member individualized attention. The same personalized service you give your customers is important to offer your operators, too.

I urge you not to try to create a customer support department like this overnight. It takes time and a lot of effort. We started with toll-free lines, but there are other choices; a 900-number service line or other toll-line is better than no support at all. Start small. Install only enough phone lines to track customer interest. Use any new technology available. For example, automated fax machines can give customers answers to commonly asked questions. Phone systems can track each call and indicate what your peak times are. Then, as you uncover customer needs, adjust as necessary.

LIVING COLOR

Supporting your products can be a very colorful experience. We all have heard of the customer who couldn't find the "Any" key on the keyboard. ("Hit any key...") And how about the customer who wanted to know if her cat could possibly have created the new file that had "magically" appeared on her hard disk? One of my first support calls was from a customer who wanted to know where the paper came out of the computer; he didn't know he had to buy a printer.

The 800-MAC-HELP line (our first Macintosh customer support line) was the most exciting of all. Before the phone number was assigned to WordPerfect it had belonged to a personal-crisis help line. Needless to say, we changed the number after receiving a few desperate phone calls having nothing to do with computers! But overall, my favorite calls are from customers who apologize for calling. My response to them is, "I wouldn't have a job if you hadn't."

CHAPTER TWENTY-SIX

Publishing a Customer Newsletter to Enhance Support

By Maria Abreu and Doug Levy, Deneba Software

Maria Abreu is the editor of the *Deneba News*, and Doug Levy is vice president of corporate communications for Deneba Software, a software development company located in Coral Gables, Florida.

ALTHOUGH some companies view their customer newsletters as sales tools, we think of the *Deneba News* as an extension of customer support. Our quarterly user newsletter might have the effect of generating sales—for instance, an existing or prospective customer might make a purchase based on information that appears in the *Deneba News*—but that's not the publication's main goal. Instead, the newsletter serves to strengthen the relationship that began when the customer bought our product. Thus, we view it as a function of customer support.

We believe that user support is just as important as the software we develop and market. Having an ongoing relationship with our customers helps us stay on the cutting edge of software development and offer features and services our competitors haven't even thought of. We want to know how our customers use our products, what they use now, and what they're looking for in the future.

A FORUM FOR EXCHANGE

How does our newsletter fit into this philosophy? Together, the customer support department and the *Deneba News* act as a forum for the exchange and dissemination of ideas between end users and Deneba.

The newsletter was born in 1989, when we realized that many calls coming into our support lines comprised a fairly common set of questions—meaning that our support team was spending a lot of time answering the same queries over and over. It became obvious that if we had a broadcast mechanism for addressing these questions, our customers would get the information they needed and our support people would have more time to spend on the less typical inquiries.

It also meant that we didn't have to add more support people, phone lines, and so forth just to keep up with the increasing incidence of most-asked questions that results from a growing customer base. Of course, the support staff still must grow as the installed base increases, but it doesn't have to grow as much if there's a communications vehicle that sends out effective information about the most common problems. In our case, the economics are pretty simple: It costs much less to produce a newsletter that goes out to 250,000 people than it does to hire, train, insure, and equip a larger staff of support personnel.

CREATING THE NEWSLETTER

The *Deneba News* began as a four-page, black-and-white, no-frills newsletter that was written, edited, and produced by Deneba's communications director in his "spare time." It quickly became apparent, though, that the project deserved a greater resource commitment because it was creating exactly the intended effect: When the newsletter covered a particular area, the number of calls to the support lines about that area would drop significantly once the newsletter had reached the customer base.

It didn't take long to recognize the value of this communications tool and assign a full-time editor to the project. We also brought in our advertising agency to redesign the publication so that its "look and feel" was more in keeping with the overall corporate and product image Deneba was trying to convey. Since our ad agency was already responsible for creating and maintaining Deneba's corporate identity, we knew that the agency would be the perfect choice for redesigning the newsletter along those lines.

In addition to wanting the design to better tie in with our corporate look, we also had to face the issue of putting our money where our mouth was. Two of our key products—Canvas and UltraPaint—are, after all, graphics products, so we naturally wanted a design that reflected a professional graphics orientation.

These goals not withstanding, we made sure that the new look wasn't too slick—after all, the *Deneba News* isn't a sales piece. We wanted it to look like a credible, useful information source. The newsletter in its professionalized form is now eight pages in length and uses two or four colors, depending on the nature of the topics in a particular issue.

THE PLANNING PROCESS

Because we've established the *Deneba News* as a mainstay of our customer communications, we have put a process in place that ensures that it addresses the most significant issues facing our users. The process basically involves having the customer support department monitor the pulse of the registered user base and contribute the bulk of the material for the newsletter.

In all cases, the content of the newsletter ultimately originates from our users, whether it be in the form of letters or phone calls to Deneba's customer support department or through our on-line forums on AppleLink, CompuServe, and GEnie. The customer support department currently handles approximately 500 inquiries per day, 75 percent of which are technical in nature.

Each customer support representative maintains a "call log," a database that records the nature of each incoming call: which product the call is about, the specific problem or question dealt with, any user suggestions, and the length of time it took to resolve the issue. We compile the information from this database into a report and print it regularly. The reports help us monitor user needs and determine new directions for development—and they are a main source for generating the content of the newsletter.

Priorities and Pizza

Preparing for a new issue of the *Deneba News* is a team effort. All the customer support representatives submit an outline of topics and/or specific items they feel are important, based on the information in the call logs. We compile the outlines into a master list; then we discuss them in a brainstorming session that includes the editor of the *Deneba News* and representatives of the customer support staff, complete with pizza and lots of espresso. Together, we distill and prioritize the outlines and sort them into the three general categories discussed later.

In prioritizing items for the newsletter, we take several factors into account. We are especially concerned about the frequency with which an issue comes up and which items would benefit the largest number of users. We make a special effort, however, to address specialized uses of our product in occasional articles throughout the year.

Although a member of the customer support staff occasionally writes an individual article, the editor (who is the only full-time newsletter staff member) does the bulk of the writing. Once completed, the articles go to the customer support team, which double-checks them for accuracy and general content.

Content: The Big Three

In general, material included in the *Deneba News* falls into three categories: product update news, tips on how best to use the software, and frequently asked technical questions.

Product updates, as you might expect, cover upgrades and revisions. We devote as much space as necessary to telling readers about new features and benefits. Product tips generally consist of time-saving shortcuts and methods for achieving special effects. For instance, we might run a half-page article about how to deal with the seemingly unexpected appearance of low-memory messages or include a two-paragraph item on working with TIFF files. Frequently asked technical questions appear in a question-and-answer format. We break these out by product so that all the Canvas questions, for instance, are grouped together and are separate from the Spelling Coach and UltraPaint questions.

In feature-length articles, we also address complex issues such as editing pixel maps in Canvas or UltraPaint or saving Canvas files as Encapsulated PostScript (EPS) files. No matter what kind of article, we try to use as many screen shots, illustrations, and pieces of spot art as we can and still not clutter up the page. The graphics not only clarify the content but also liven things up.

Our driving theme is to give readers as much "meat" as possible. We like to think that we cut right to the chase, stick to meaningful and useful information, and avoid any kind of padding. This is in keeping with our philosophy that the newsletter isn't a sales tool but is a communication vehicle to let customers know that we're there and that we're listening.

THE PAYOFF

It really doesn't cost much to produce the *Deneba News*, relative to the savings we realize in other areas. The biggest budget hit comes from postage. Like any other newsletter publisher, we don't get the same economies of scale with postage as we do with printing costs; that is, as our print run goes up, our cost per unit for printing goes down, but there's no similar break for postage. Right now, we print 250,000 copies of the newsletter each quarter. We mail them to registered users, resellers, field salespeople, and user groups—so postage isn't a trivial issue, even at third-class bulk rates.

As mentioned earlier, though, our experience is that this method of customer communication results in a substantial decrease in the demands placed on our support lines. We've never specifically quantified the actual savings, but it's safe to say that we can see a 40 to 50 percent drop in questions on a particular topic once it's been covered in the *Deneba News*. As far as an overall return on investment goes, it's pretty clear that the newsletter saves the company significant money, although the budget for the newsletter is a straight expense. Even though our support people spend a fair amount of time researching and contributing material for the newsletter, they're spending much less time than they would answering the same questions on the phone. In short, their time is better spent and benefits a much larger base of users.

The other payoff is more direct: Customers tell us that they appreciate the newsletter, which validates the main reason for its existence. We receive lots of unsolicited tips and ideas from our readers plus general feedback that they enjoy it.

Should this be a more sales-oriented tool? Who knows how users might respond if that were the case? We suspect that they wouldn't be as enthusiastic if we treated it so. The right approach for Deneba has been to focus on the support angle. If someone sees an article and is motivated by it to buy one of our products, that's just icing on the cake.

CHAPTER TWENTY-SEVEN

Using On-Line Services As a Marketing and Support Tool

HOW WE USE THE APPLELINK NETWORK

By Liz Brooking, Radius, Inc.

Liz Brooking is a former comarketing manager with overall responsibility for the AppleLink icon for Radius, a graphics systems company located in San Jose, California, whose major markets include color publishing and digital video.

Editor's note: Radius' AppleLink bulletin board structure and any stated programs and costs may have changed since this chapter was written in early 1993.

A S global networks become more pervasive, a new breed of marketing and support tool is evolving: on-line services. To companies that, like ours, need cost-effective customer contact and support alternatives, on-line services offer a way to augment more traditional customer communication efforts.

Specifically, we participate in the AppleLink Third-Party Publishing Program. This program allows developers to publish bulletin boards, called "icons," on the AppleLink network. Because AppleLink is a crucial tool Apple uses to communicate with its enormous worldwide base of resellers, distributors, third parties, and a variety of customers—as of February 1993 there were upwards of 28,000 U.S. and 10,000 international subscribers—it offers developers a way to more easily reach their own subset of this customer community. Resellers and distributors are the primary customer group of Radius, making AppleLink an excellent choice for us.

BENEFITS OF PUBLISHING ON-LINE

Because AppleLink reaches our key customers, there are several tangible benefits of publishing an icon on the network.

- *It extends our customer service reach.* The AppleLink icon is a tremendous asset to us because it offers resellers and developers what we previously couldn't provide—Radius product information 24 hours a day, seven days a week, from virtually anywhere in the world. Instead of forcing customers with questions or problems to rely solely on telephone communication with Radius, we give them access to much of the information they need via the AppleLink network. Furthermore, sometimes it's faster for customers to find information on AppleLink than to phone us, especially if they need to do so during a peak calling hour of the business day.

Customers also are no longer constrained by the need to reach us during our normal business hours; 24-hour access to AppleLink helps overcome the problems posed by time zones and holiday and weekend schedules, which is especially important for international customers.

Although many questions and problems can't be totally addressed via an on-line service—and there's no substitute for direct customer contact— overall, publishing a bulletin board helps give resellers and developers the impression that Radius is there for them all day every day. It therefore improves customer satisfaction, which we all know is worth its weight in gold.

- *It improves technical support.* The AppleLink publishing program makes our technical support effort easier, reduces the manpower needed to solve customer or developer problems, and often reduces our related out-of-pocket costs, such as for postage. For example, a key part of our bulletin board is the Current Radius Software folder, which contains the most current versions of our system software. Often, a customer must install a more recent software version before our service representative can diagnose a problem. Instead of waiting for a postal service to deliver the software, the customer can download the software directly from our bulletin board in minutes. Then our support person's troubleshooting job is easier and quicker. (Sometimes, just having the most recent software version solves the customer's problem.)

  Many older Radius products are still in the channel, and resellers can get technical information about them from our bulletin board. For instance, some of our early products (pre-NuBus) designed for use with the Macintosh Plus and SE models require a more complex installation process with which resellers occasionally require assistance. We've therefore posted HyperCard stacks that help guide resellers through the process.

- *It enhances user satisfaction.* Improving the quality and speed of service we give resellers thereby increases the level of service resellers can offer users. If a reseller can solve a customer problem more quickly and easily, everyone wins.

- *The program is cost-effective.* Using an on-line service such as AppleLink is a cost-effective way to distribute information, software, and tools; in essence, it gives your constituents 24-hour service. Because you control the amount of time and resources dedicated to creating and maintaining the bulletin board, you can tailor your efforts to accommodate your pocketbook.

Since there no longer are startup or maintenance fees for participating in this program, the only out-of-pocket costs for us are the usual charges for the connect time needed for posting items to the bulletin board. (If you publish a read-write area, there is also connect time for retrieving customer inquiries and comments.) On average, we spend a total of 50 hours of access time per month. Specifically, our customer service area usually spends about 32 hours per month, developer services 8 hours, and marketing approximately 10 hours. However, in our experience, most of the cost involved is invested in the manpower needed for publishing the Radius board rather than in connect time.

In our opinion, the investment is a small price to pay to give customers increased service and access to Radius. And when you consider the price tag on distributing this information by alternative methods such as brochures, disks, or telemarketing, the cost of AppleLink is inconsequential—and the convenience superior.

SHOULD YOU PUBLISH ON-LINE?

Is using an on-line service such as AppleLink right for your company? To answer that question you must first decide whether you could benefit from such a program, given your particular circumstances. Does the service reach an audience that is important to you? Is reaching this audience more effectively an important goal? Are you willing to devote the resources and effort needed to make your board successful? Are you willing to make a firm commitment to this program? In our case, the answer to each question was "yes." The audience that AppleLink reaches is very important to us, and we are committed to augmenting our marketing and support efforts for this important group of customers.

However, we chose a more limited level of participation because our resources are limited; we don't take advantage of every capability offered by the program. For example, we don't currently publish a read-write area, such as a discussion folder. While this activity could be valuable, managing it would consume more time and manpower than we can afford: Someone must be assigned to make sure that customer questions posted to a read-write area are downloaded, forwarded to the appropriate people internally, and answered in a timely fashion. Likewise, to stay within our budget, we rarely take advantage of options such as the Third-Party Connection, the Multimedia Forum, or the Publishers' Forum.

However, so far this doesn't seem to have hurt the amount of traffic on our board, and we seem to be on par with similar publishers. For example, in a typical month our icon is accessed as many as 4,200 times, 5,300 documents are read, and 1,600 image files are downloaded.

DETERMINING CONTENT

Once you've decided to take the plunge, you must decide what information to publish. Our marketing and marketing communications staff are responsible for establishing this, and they have issued a clear policy about *exactly* what should be posted to our board. Getting agreement to this policy from everyone with authority to post information to your board is critical.

To decide what to publish, we asked ourselves: Who is the audience? What is our overall objective in using an on-line service? What kind of information do we need to communicate to this audience? What information do *they* need? What existing material can we use? We also took cues from other icons. In fact, I highly recommend this tack to new publishers: Examine the range of information other companies post and emulate what appears to be successful. In particular, scrutinize competitors' boards and, where appropriate, offer similar information.

Radius' resulting three general content categories are customer service, developer support, and marketing. To organize that information, first we configured the top level of folders under our icon; then we decided what items each folder would contain and solicited agreement from key individuals in each respective area of the company. There has been minimal work to *create* content because most items are reformatted versions of existing materials such as press releases, data sheets, reports, and so forth.

Examples of our customer service folders are Dealer Training, Current Radius Software, Technical Support, Service, Parts Pricing, and Information folders. Developer information can be found in the Developer Services Folder. The marketing folders include such items as the Domestic SRP, Demonstration Files, Product Information, Reseller Programs, Events, Press Releases, and Marketing Bulletins folders. The New Information folder contains pointers to all new items that are posted on our board.

Once you decide what kinds of items to post, you may want to create a prototype of your board. Visualizing it will help you find mistakes, determine if your material is organized efficiently from a user's point of view, spot any obvious omissions, and solve any other problems.

Who Has Access?

AppleLink allows you to restrict folder access as needed, so you must also determine which AppleLink subscribers will be granted access to each folder. With a few exceptions, most information on our board is available to all AppleLink customers. Sometimes we post items that only our developers should have access to, so we restrict the use of those folders to developers only. Also, discount information and incentive program details are appropriate for resellers and not developers, so we also restrict access to that information.

There are also some international business considerations that may require you to restrict folder access. For more information, see Mistake #5 in the "Board Maintenance" section of this chapter.

HEAVY TRAFFIC AREAS

While marketing-oriented information is frequently used by customers, our customer service-oriented folders are the most accessed; customer access of the Current Radius Software folder alone makes up 51 percent of our total monthly usage. The items in this folder ensure that resellers, developers, and users have the most current and compatible Radius software for their products.

We think that part of the reason our customer service folders are used so often is that service technicians may be the people in reseller organizations who use AppleLink the most. Because this kind of information has a more immediate and tangible benefit to these people, it is accessed more often. Service technicians may not see a pressing need to review other kinds of information, so they are more likely to postpone reading items in other folders until something, such as an AppleLink Extra! announcement, calls their attention to them.

Attracting Attention to Information

There are several ways to call attention to the information you post under your icon. The AppleLink Extra! is an excellent way to direct attention to specific areas of the bulletin board. It is a custom "splash" screen AppleLink subscribers see the first time they access the network on any given day. Usually, it refers to a file or folder under your icon and gives the reader the path to the file. These screens use text and simple graphics, but there are size and content limitations. (For example, you can't mention a product's suggested retail price.) An Extra! costs $500 for a half screen (although you can receive a discount for buying more than one at a time). Since only one or two are published each day, you should reserve your space well in advance.

Using an AppleLink Extra! announcement definitely increases the readership of items that we feature in it. For example, we use it to augment new product announcements by highlighting either the related press release or data sheet. We also created an AppleLink Extra! to inform resellers about our board, in addition to sending them a notification letter and putting a notice in our monthly reseller newsletter. Whenever we publish an Extra!, we get a spike of approximately several hundred accesses per day, even in a part of the bulletin board that normally is accessed less often.

Another effective way to draw attention to your icon is to publish AppleLink path information in all your communications vehicles (such as channel announcements). These "pointers" constantly remind resellers that they can get additional information from your bulletin board.

BOARD MAINTENANCE

How you manage your board will depend both on the level of support and resources you can devote to it and your priorities. Because AppleLink is an important communications component of our customer service, developer service, and marketing functions, our icon is managed by three people, one person from each function. Those people, called sysops, are responsible for maintaining their respective areas of the bulletin board. Although no single person is devoted full-time to this activity, AppleLink responsibilities are a well-defined, important priority in each sysop's job description. Our sysops are responsible for collecting information to be posted; formatting and disinfecting documents; posting documents, copyright, and patent information; and purging outdated items. Their most time-consuming tasks are disinfecting files and establishing path names.

Along the way we've learned a few "do's and don'ts" about maintaining our board. While some degree of personal preference is involved in how you manage this activity, we all share a lot of the same challenges. Here are some important mistakes we've learned to avoid during our two years as an AppleLink information publisher.

Mistake #1: Posting a Lot of Disk Files

Our experience suggests that you shouldn't use disk files (files created by applications other than AppleLink) if you can avoid it. The user must download and expand them—a cumbersome and time-consuming task at best. To avoid this, we prefer posting AppleLink-format text files whenever possible. However, this requires that you reformat disk files into the AppleLink format. As you reformat files, don't forget that AppleLink doesn't accept tabs, margins, many special characters, and type styles (bold, italics, underlines, and the like). And because readers don't get the usual visual clues that break up text in longer documents (such as boldface headlines), they can easily become lost and your information may lose its impact. Make sure that it's obvious how the text is broken up (by all-cap headlines, subheads, rows of asterisks, and so forth).

A similar mistake is using image files indiscriminately. Although some developers like to use the image file format, we tend to avoid it because it can be cumbersome for users. When I use electronic mail, enclosures or addenda such as disk or image files are usually the last things I want to open because of the effort required. If it's not clear that I need the information in the file, I may put off opening it or may totally ignore it. My experience is that bulletin board readers are no different. However, if we *must* use such files, we try to give as much information about their content as possible in the cover memo so that the reader doesn't necessarily have to download the file to understand exactly what it contains.

We learned our lesson the hard way. For example, our Marketing Bulletins folder contains a lot of information that positions our products against the competition; it previously included a variety of graphics and tutorial information in image file formats. While the information was very valuable, customers didn't access it because those files were clumsy and time-consuming to download. Because it would require expending more resources than are available to reformat this information into AppleLink documents, we now put less emphasis on that kind of information on the bulletin board (we instead mail it to customers) and focus on folders that customers access more often.

Mistake #2: Ignoring Board Usage Patterns

As an information publisher, you receive usage reports for your icon from the Apple OnLine Services (AOS) group. Review these carefully to see what is accessed frequently and what isn't, and use this data to tailor your efforts. For instance, if a particular folder isn't often used, try to understand why and use that information to modify or eliminate it. Or if a particular section of your board is heavily used, you may wish to increase the level of resources you allocate to managing it.

Mistake #3: Letting Your Information Become Outdated

It's very important to keep your content current and to constantly assess whether the information in each folder is still of value. You must keep readers' expectations up and give them a reason to browse your board frequently. If you do nothing with your board for a long period, such as several months, your inactivity will become clear to customers and they'll be less likely to bother accessing your board at all. But if you post information regularly, readers will notice that there's always something new for them and will tend to access your board more often. However, don't post items that aren't useful or germane because they'll notice that too, and it will turn them off.

The publishing program gives you the option to include a New Information folder in your top level. I highly recommend it. When you post new files to the board, the AppleLink network automatically updates your New Information folder with a reference to the new postings. (The system also recognizes any access restrictions you may have put on the folders that new files are posted to.) This folder is a real plus for users. Because they don't have to review each folder or subfolder within your icon to find newly posted information, it reduces their connect time and saves them money.

Mistake #4: Underestimating the Commitment Needed to Maintain Your Icon

Don't underestimate the resources and commitment needed to make AppleLink a useful communications tool, particularly if you publish a discussion board. If you don't regularly download user questions and comments and respond to them in a timely fashion, users may become annoyed, which undermines the effectiveness of your board.

Mistake #5: Thinking Locally, Acting Locally

If your audience is global, be sensitive to international concerns regarding your bulletin board's content. Some of the issues you may encounter include those centered around local advertising practices; for example, in some countries comparison advertising is illegal; before posting items, you should review them for that type of content.

It's equally important to be sensitive to international pricing issues; a product's price typically varies from country to country. Also, if your marketing programs vary between countries, post your material in audience-restricted folders to prevent confusing or offending resellers who are excluded from these programs. The ideal would be to create localized folders for particular countries, although that probably requires increasing the resources you allocate to your bulletin board.

BEYOND RESELLERS

AppleLink is already a valuable marketing and support alternative for reaching resellers and developers. However, Apple has made AppleLink available to everyone; as an increasing number of users subscribe, we'll be able to greatly extend our use of this tool. Reaching users directly will help ensure that they get an accurate and consistent message from Radius—and AppleLink will take on an even greater significance in our marketing mix.

PART SEVEN

Getting and Managing Repeat Business

Especially in this industry, you just can't take customer loyalty for granted. That's why making a concerted effort to drum up repeat business is so crucial. How do you turn buyers into loyal fans? To help answer that, this part of the book looks at the phenomenon of "installed-base marketing," which is jargon for selling to existing customers.

Chapter 28, "Installed-Base Marketing: Tips on How to Keep 'Em Coming Back for More," examines what it takes to make subsequent sales to your existing customers. It also offers profitable tips on how to entice customers to come back for more. One of the most obvious ways to generate repeat business is to offer upgrades. Chapter 29, "The Upgrade Black Hole: Why Some Upgrade Campaigns Get Stalled," is a study of the problems—including some you may not have dreamed of—you can encounter when conducting an upgrade campaign and how you can avoid them. It also offers sage advice about how to evaluate and hire an upgrade fulfillment firm and gives you a model of how to calculate fulfillment pricing.

CHAPTER TWENTY-EIGHT

Installed-Base Marketing

TIPS ON HOW TO KEEP 'EM COMING BACK FOR MORE

By Dee Kiamy, Open Door Communications

Dee Kiamy is president of Open Door Communications, a strategic communications consulting practice located in San Jose, California, that serves high-technology and entertainment companies. She also developed and edited this book.

CAR manufacturers are famous for it. Fast-food chains need it to survive. Even credit lenders and mutual-fund brokers rely on it, and airlines can't stay aloft without it. It's called installed-base marketing. This trendy jargon for getting repeat business evokes images of frequent fliers, Lee Iacocca, and not leaving home without it.

Now add *your* products to that list. As the computer industry grows up and becomes more segmented (read: more competitive), repeat buyers become a linchpin around which long-term profits—and survival—revolve. In this chapter, we'll look at some of the general concepts involved in installed-base marketing and some specific examples of how developers have implemented installed-base marketing strategies.

Caution! There are no pat formulas for installed-base marketing. What you do and how you do it depends on many factors: market conditions, your company's goals and structure, the resources available to you, and, of course, the nature of your hardware or software products. The options are so numerous that discussing them all would be impractical. I hope these guidelines and suggestions will strike a chord or two and become a launching pad for your own creative marketing.

REPEAT BUSINESS COSTS YOU LESS

The importance of getting repeat business may seem obvious, but on closer examination some of the ramifications are not. First, selling to an existing customer is less costly than recruiting a new one. Estimates of what it costs to create a repeat customer run the gamut, but the most reliable say that making a repeat sale costs one-third to one-half of what it costs to recruit a first-time buyer. It makes sense: Selling software or hardware to someone who already likes your products consumes less time and money. And if you do it right, you'll inevitably have more resources to invest in other efforts, such as increasing your market share.

Also, a market as volatile as this one can force you to sharpen your competitive edge. Something new and different is always beckoning to customers, and hardware and software buyers without established loyalties may find it easier to migrate to untried territory. In the Macintosh software market, this consideration is especially important. In one sense, the same asset that empowers Mac users—the consistent interface—may also exacerbate their fickleness. Users can easily experiment with alternative word-processing packages, for example, with relatively little training or time investment. It follows that a customer can switch loyalties relatively easily if the developer doesn't *actively* attempt to hold customers.

Creating and nurturing loyalty and reducing the "fickle factor" is the crux of installed-base marketing. There are no pat formulas for this marketing genre, nor is success merely an accident.

The repeat purchase is a fascinating study, but comprehending the psychological dynamics between buyer and seller is much easier said than done. Theodore Levitt expressed it well in the *Harvard Business Review*: "The buyer expects the seller to remember the purchase as having been a favor bestowed, not as something earned by the seller....The seller owes the buyer one." Therefore, Levitt says, you are forced to make the second sale from a deficit stance. Regardless of whether you agree with (or even like) those dynamics, negotiating a sale with this "psychology" in mind can help you to overcome that deficit and turn the transaction into a win-win situation.

In essence, nurturing loyalty is the key to offsetting the deficit. Books have been written about it, and it would be impractical to try to address such a broad and complex subject here. But some rules of thumb are

- put the customer first
- provide the best-possible first experience with your product and company
- create additional products of interest to the customer
- make it easy for customers to buy again
- know who your customers are and what they buy.

PUT USERS FIRST

When all is said and done, putting customers first is what helps you stay solvent. You should constantly ask yourself how your decisions will affect your customers, put yourself in their shoes, and act on it. Be sure to avoid the trap of lip service. *Every* employee must take up the challenge of customer satisfaction. Fostering this attitude from the top of your organizational chart to the bottom—including your distribution chain—is as important as any other facet of marketing. (There's an excellent discussion about this in Chapter 7, "The Practice of Customer Focus: The Importance of Driving Business Decisions with Customer and Market Data.")

Also, consider your customers' needs when structuring internal company procedures. It's far too easy to let your own bureaucracy get in the way of making money. For example, if a sales rep makes a sale, makes all the necessary promises and guarantees to the customer, and gets the commission before all the promises are met, there might be little incentive to hang in there until the current customer is satisfied—unless you've set up a system that specifically delegates after-the-sale responsibilities.

With those attitudes established, creating the optimum experience with the first application or piece of hardware is paramount. Success breeds interesting results. First, happy customers are predisposed to buy again. For example, if users are pleased with your word processor, when they're ready to invest in a spreadsheet program, they're more likely to give your product serious consideration. Second, happy customers are walking advertisements; they spread the word to friends and colleagues.

MAKE A LASTING IMPRESSION

Because first impressions often make it or break it, you must assure that customers have the best possible initial experience with your company. Make it easy for them to get information and product assistance. Make them feel important. And don't forget, as far as many customers are concerned, the reseller is your duly deputized agent; the customer gauges you, correctly or incorrectly, by the standard the reseller sets.

Creating and maintaining a long-term relationship with customers means firmly implanting your product and company image in their brains. The more you and your product become part of customers' daily life, and the more customers will rely on you to fill their needs, then the less important actual products and prices become. The ultimate results when buying from you becomes *routine.* To achieve that kind of relationship, you must communicate with customers regularly—and *listen well.* "Out to lunch" is a shingle you can't afford to hang on your door.

HELP THEM BUY WHAT THEY WANT

You can't make a repeat sale if you don't have another product or service of interest to customers. It's much easier to get people to buy what they want than to want what they buy, so to speak. A technology-driven market tempts developers to focus on creating the buyers' desire for the technology, working from the product to the market rather than the reverse. Granted, some developers have had their successes using this technique, but it usually works only if you have a really, really *hot* product.

One of the best ways to determine your products' appeal is simply to ask customers. Allow them to participate somehow in your product development or evaluation process. Some developers provide customers with toll-free numbers and carefully document customer input. Furthermore, when it's practical, getting resellers' input can also be helpful. Based on their face-to-face relationships with your customers, resellers can offer practical suggestions about what customers like, how they buy, pricing, and other important considerations.

THE BEST MOUSETRAPS ARE THE EASIEST TO GET

Make it easy for users to buy again. Even if you peddle the least expensive, best mousetrap ever built, you may lose the second-time sale if the purchasing process was painful the first time around. Often, deciding *what* to buy is as difficult for a customer as any other part of the decision-making/purchasing process. Supplying buyers with the right kind of details can help make their decisions easier; for example, offering information and demonstrations that match their needs to your benefits is surefire fickleness prevention. Many customers also respond well to incentives that force them to make up their minds quickly, such as special deals with near-term expiration dates.

Once customers have decided to buy your product, make it easy for them to get it. Try to avoid imposing special restrictions on sales. One way to do this is to allow buyers to work with their usual resellers; people are most comfortable dealing with familiar faces. At the same time, if buying disrupts normal purchasing routines, you may also lose good customers. All too often an excellent deal that propels customers into a second or subsequent purchase turns into an administrative headache for them. If you arrange a sale that makes them go outside their prescribed circle of approvals or adds to their already towering pile of paperwork, you might as well ask them to transcribe the Manhattan telephone book.

So, if at all possible, allow customers to process their paperwork in their accustomed manner. If they've bought your product through a special rebate or other incentive plan, honor the deal but still allow them to go through their usual purchasing procedures—even if you must restructure your own. (If you do offer an incentive or other promotional item, fulfill it as quickly as you can.)

Next, we'll explore some techniques and strategies that specific companies have used to put installed-base marketing into practice. We'll look at how to determine who comprises your installed base, how to organize that information and put it to work, how to communicate with customers, and how to encourage them to buy additional products.

HELLO—IS ANYBODY OUT THERE?

No recommendation about how to encourage customer loyalty will be useful if you don't know who your customers are and what they buy. Therefore, creating and constructively using a database is a prerequisite to targeting your installed base. Without it, pinpointing existing customers is like netting a particular fish in the ocean, an often frustrating process that costs a bundle. But with the right database, you essentially reduce your territory—and scale down the costs—to the size of an aquarium.

The first step in marketing to existing customers is as easy as learning who they are and what they've bought. Sounds simple, right? Not quite. Product registration cards have traditionally been the way most marketers harvest that information, but only a fraction of buyers actually complete and send in the cards. So not only must you devise attractive incentives that offer customers a bonus for letting you know who they are, but you must also make it easy for them to do so. Although you want to be practical in choosing incentives, the secret is to offer something of perceived value or something that isn't easy to get elsewhere. People love to know exactly how good a deal they're getting. If at all possible, point out the item's value, whether it be monetary, aesthetic—whatever. Remember, the higher the perceived value, the stronger the incentive to return the card. On the other hand, take pains not to misrepresent (even unintentionally) or distort an offering's value, which could potentially disappoint and disillusion customers.

The most common incentives are premiums such as T-shirts or coffee mugs imprinted with a product or company name (people can't seem to get enough of these). Alternatively, you can offer a product somehow related to the one purchased (for example, XTree once offered a free disk optimizer for the return of a XTree Mac card) or even a special book or how-to manual related to the application (Aldus, for instance, has offered a *Guide to Basic Design*, a handy and useful incentive for PageMaker users).

Regardless of how attractive your goodie is, you must also make it easy for buyers to send in the registration card. If you make them find and address an envelope, insert the card, buy a stamp, and find the letter carrier, you've lost them. Self-mailing postage-paid cards eliminate a lot of the hassle and result in a substantially higher return rate.

Another key is making sure users actually see the incentive offer. People who usually ignore registration cards will never see your offer unless you put it somewhere that it just can't be missed. Although it can be printed on or somehow attached to the registration card itself, a more successful tactic may be to promote it separately, such as in a special flyer enclosed with or wrapped around disks.

Dealing with the "Unauthorized" Customer

When considering who your customers are, don't neglect the pirates—those who've "somehow stumbled" onto your product. Unless your software company is unusually fortunate, in reality your installed base probably includes multitudes of users computing with unauthorized copies (some customers are aware of it, some aren't). Getting the most accurate handle on your installed base means finding out who these folks are. Market research can provide this information, but it's costly. And so is hiring an attorney to chase these people down to find out who they are.

Some developers have chosen to offer such users a kind of amnesty. For example, developers have offered "unauthorized" users a "no questions asked" opportunity to get the benefits of legal use of an application without threat of penalty for previous copyright violation; for example, the developer may ask these users to send in some proof of having used the program (such as a screen dump) and perhaps also a nominal fee. In return, they receive the latest version of the application with a serial number, user's manual, a registration card, and support.

Editor's note: There's more about amnesty programs in Chapter 23, "The Ways and Means to Fight Piracy: Developer Practices—Some That Work, Some That Don't."

HARNESSING THE INFORMATION

Once you've obtained this hard-earned information, you must harness it, consolidate and organize it, and put it to work for you. A well-planned and managed database helps you target the very best customers: those who have bought once and are the most likely to buy again.

Creating this pool of customer information is but part of the quest. The other is to constructively use it. When appropriately devised, a database of your customers is a veritable gold mine. By cleverly interpreting these nuggets of information, you can deduce ways to attract the customer a second time. Studying the information also forces you to dispel some of the myths you've been carrying around about who your customers are and who they aren't.

Planning a database is counterintuitive; you must back into it in order to move forward. A natural urge is to define the organization and format first; but, on the contrary, that should be the last step. Experts agree that the most prudent first step is determining how you will use the information and the actions you'll take based on what you've learned. Ask yourself questions such as "Will I use the information as input to help create new products? Will I plan mailings to special portions of the database? Will I use it to decide which promotion strategy or message to use? To help determine buying patterns? To help reallocate sales territories and resources? To make decisions about resellers?"

Another pitfall to avoid is basing the structure of the database solely on what you need today or to get you through a crucial sales period, rather than anticipating how the market and your customers may change in the foreseeable future.

Thoughtful, intuitive planning also helps determine which important tidbits you should elicit in the limited space available on the registration card, in user surveys, or through other marketing research. Determining exactly which questions to ask is a highly individual matter—it's important to consider not only what kind of information your company needs but also what you plan to do with it. If you do a good job envisioning how you'll use the information, the database's organization and format will fall neatly into place. Veteran database planners suggest starting simply. They recommend that you start with a basic database that is less interactional and interrelational. As you move forward, you can then see relationships form and then decide how to interconnect the information.

Unless you're adequately prepared for the task, setting up and maintaining a database can produce gargantuan administrative headaches. You might consider consulting with a professional database company or even hiring one to manage your list from soup to nuts—but it can cost. On the other hand, manpower, computer time, and other necessary resources can quickly devour the budgets of the less experienced who opt to go it alone. One alternative is to share the database and the outlay of cash with another (carefully chosen) company.

LET THEM KNOW YOU'RE THERE

First, you find out who they are and what they buy, and keep careful records of this information. Then you get into what most people regard as installed-base marketing: regular communication with customers. Based on a company's individual needs, there are infinite combinations of telemarketing, advertising, direct-mail, public-relations, and other techniques that can fill the bill. But one popular and particularly cost-effective channel is the user newsletter.

Mailed on a prescribed schedule (monthly, quarterly, and so forth), newsletters can contain all kinds of useful information: tips on using your products more effectively, articles about how your products stack up against the competition, announcements about upgrades and new products, and instructions about how to navigate user-oriented resources in your company. Depending on the kind of information published in the newsletter, you may also get a bonus: If you give customers the right kind of information, you may reduce some of the load on your telephone technical support department.

Editor's note: For an example of how Deneba Software does this, see Chapter 26, "Publishing a Customer Newsletter to Enhance Support."

When considering a newsletter, bear in mind that its effectiveness is directly proportional to your commitment—how regularly you provide it, how timely and reliable the information is, and how appealing you make it. If customers can't depend on it, if they consistently get the information first from another source, or if the information isn't clearly presented, you might as well stand in your parking lot and tear up hundred-dollar bills.

Local and national user groups are two other good channels for communicating with your installed base. Teaming up with local groups for a product-demonstration night can be a win-win affair. Many developers have been pleasantly surprised by the turnout when they've mailed invitations to such meetings jointly to their own local installed base and the user-group list. This assumes, however, that you devise and adequately promote a program that delivers a one-two punch that appeals to your customers. Not only do you get a shot at your installed base, but the user group also gets exposure to potential new members.

Editor's note: For a discussion about what it takes to create a user group contact program, see Chapter 32, "Creating a User Group Marketing Program That Pays for Itself."

If the resources are available, another way to meet customers face to face is to sponsor your own ad hoc user groups. For example, Aldus made a 12-city tour; in each city, it sponsored several customer events, including a Macintosh computer night. Invitations were mailed to the installed base in each city. The evening consisted of product demonstrations, a talk by a key Aldus executive, and a drawing for free products. According to Aldus executives, attendance in each city ranged from 175 to more than 400 people.

MAKE THEM AN OFFER THEY CAN'T RESIST

Once customers are satisfied with a product, a natural next step is to offer them a discounted upgrade (remember the incentive rule?). Again, make the offer as irresistible and the process as uncomplicated and hassle-free as possible for the customers. Some developers feel that allowing resellers to help in the upgrade process works well for everyone; it allows customers to deal directly with their usual reseller, and it helps resellers cement their relationships with customers.

But when it comes to the size of the discount, opinions vary. One faction says that customer loyalty should be rewarded and that good-faith relationships can be cemented through discounts. History is on their side; upgrade discounts have become *de rigueur* as the industry's evolved, and customers have come to expect them. However, discounting policies are being carefully scrutinized by some developers who want to break with what they feel is an outmoded tradition. They point out that the concept of the upgrade has changed, dictating a need to rethink pricing strategies and exercise extreme caution in determining them.

One development executive points out, "Software upgrade policies originated when the industry was young and immature. Back then, upgrades basically fixed problems in the original software version, and there was a tendency to offer low prices. But now that some products are more mature and more reliable, upgrades not only fix any remaining problems but also extend, sometimes greatly, the functionality of the application. In that case, for the upgrade price, the user essentially gets an enhanced set of features, new documentation, in essence a completely new product—a fantastic deal."

No matter which side of the fence you're on, when you set out to determine if and how to offer discounts to your installed base, you'll want to weigh what it costs you to develop, produce, and market the product and its perceived value against the potential to cement customer loyalty.

MOVING THE CUSTOMER TO THE NEXT BIG BUY

Another strategy in marketing to the installed base is to sell customers additional and sometimes totally different products from the one they first bought.

One technique that works well for recruiting first-time buyers often works even better on those who have already purchased from you: demo versions of your products. For little (or preferably no) investment, potential users can see for themselves how the product works. Although we tend to think of product samples as being only for food or mouthwash manufacturers, it works wonders in the computer world as well.

Several companies have turned first-time buyers into repeat customers by offering a software sampler—crippled or minimal versions of products that are adequate for trial use. A bonus: Trials allow users to discover features and benefits important to them that haven't been advertised or otherwise highlighted in product promotions or demos—features that often propel them into the sale. When you hear a trial user say, "You didn't tell me your product could do that!" you should prick up your ears. Such proclamations can clue you in on ways to change or better target, demonstrate, and promote your product.

An obstacle to getting customers to take the plunge is the difficult-to-pinpoint learning curve anxiety. The anticipation of having to invest valuable time and effort in learning new and seemingly difficult techniques can be scary; fear can overwhelm customers whose checkbook is otherwise open and waiting. Your challenge is to anticipate this problem and plan your demos and promotions to diminish its effects on potential buyers. A proven technique to help customers overcome these fears is to demonstrate how the new product is similar to the one they already own. If you can make them realize how much of what they already know is useful, the fears more easily melt away.

There are no secret formulas for getting your customers to love you, to buy from you again and again. There are no substitutes for knowing your market, working hard, persisting in tough times, and being creative. But if you actively pursue loyalty, get to know your customers, help them to know you, and purposely plan toward those goals, you'll less often be watching—with regret—as they switch to a competitor's products.

CHAPTER TWENTY-NINE

The Upgrade Black Hole

WHY SOME UPGRADE CAMPAIGNS GET STALLED

By Jordan Levy, Upgrade Corporation of America

Jordan Levy is president of Upgrade Corporation of America, a Buffalo, New York, company that specializes in software upgrade marketing.

FIRST, the good news: Upgrades usually can generate a flood of money from a company's installed base. In 1990, the software industry generated more than five percent of its revenues through selling upgrades—$1 billion, according to the Software Publishers Association. Projections indicate that by 1992 this number will rise to $2 billion, making the upgrade business virtually an industry unto itself. (These numbers include "predatory" or "sidegrade" sales, which are sales made to a competitor's installed base.)

Now the for the bad news. The opportunities are alluring, but there's another side of the coin: The same hoped-for influx of orders can crash your phone system, bring chaos to the shipping department, and antagonize and alienate thousands of your once-loyal customers.

THE CHALLENGE OF UPGRADE SELLING

Selling upgrades entails a special kind of marketing that is at the same time easier and more difficult than selling the previous version of a product. You've got the advantage of selling to someone who has used the product, so you have a ready-made audience for your pitch. However, it will be difficult to sell the upgrade to any customers who didn't like the product.

Even if their experience with the product was satisfying, users may still decide that they don't need the upgrade. In that case, you have a real job to convince them that they need the added features; if you can show that you're truly adding value to the product, you'll get a better overall response. (I've been very interested to note that, at least in my experience, Macintosh customers generally seem to upgrade at higher rates than do DOS users.)

In addition, in many instances the channel was involved in selling the original product; the reseller(s) took a piece of the pie. Upgrades, on the other hand, can be sold directly to customers. Therein lies the rub: Many developers who successfully market initial versions of a product find themselves in a quandary when it comes to selling upgrades. If you don't understand the process and the resources it can consume—and if you don't have a well-planned, well-executed upgrade campaign plan based on the resources at your disposal—you risk wreaking havoc on your organization and your customers.

Successful upgrade sales depend on your knowing how to avoid several obstacles that often get such campaigns into trouble. One key decision is whether to do the campaigns yourself or to hire an outside firm to handle part or all of the job. (For more information, see "How to Hire an Upgrade Campaign Manager," in this chapter.) Here are some potential problem areas to troubleshoot if you opt to do it yourself.

ABANDONED CALLS

An upgrade offer usually results in a surge of calls that can overwhelm a company's phone system. Typically, half of the response to your campaign will come via your toll-free phone lines. If the volume of calls exceeds the system's capacity, you'll aggravate a lot of people. Moreover, roughly 15 percent of people who get blocked or abandoned the first time never call back, and those sales are lost forever. You must also make sure that you have enough people staffing the phones. Callers generally won't wait more than 30 seconds to talk with a sales representative.

As an aside, I'd like to point out the importance of giving customers a toll-free telephone number. Making customers pay for a call (or for a postage stamp, for that matter) is an excellent sales prevention tactic; it dramatically reduces the response rate. If you don't have a toll-free number, chances are that you'll lose much more money in sales than you would ever have spent on postage and phone calls.

Having the appropriate telephone equipment, the right number of incoming lines, and the right kind and number of people staffing them can help avoid this problem. However, the real key lies in prevention—through planning. Often, when companies are planning upgrade campaigns, the drive or desire to "just get the revenue flowing" is so strong that it gets in the way of managing the campaign the right way. You have to put the horse in front of the cart; you can't get the revenue if you can't handle the traffic.

Thus, you should do some creative and resourceful planning. For instance, if you have 10,000 customers on your upgrade list (thus 10,000 upgrade offers to make), you can stage the mailings instead of sending them out all at once (and suffering the resulting phone jam). Instead, mail 1,000 each week for ten weeks or 2,000 a week for five weeks—whatever will help match your resources to the potential volume of incoming orders. This will stagger the response and make fulfillment much more manageable. Understanding how the response cycle ebbs and flows is also useful in avoiding abandoned calls and phone jams.

In addition, bear in mind that the response rate of up to 13 to 18 percent that we've seen as being typical to upgrade campaigns is higher than the average response to other direct marketing offers (which run from half a percent to three percent). If your company is already doing other direct marketing business, an upgrade campaign will cause a major spike in activity during that time.

ORDER ENTRY MISTAKES

Entry mistakes are expensive and time-consuming to correct. For example, if you incorrectly enter even a single digit of a credit card number, correcting that error costs dearly in labor, bank charges, customer callbacks, and customer ill-will and loss of confidence.

Conducting telephone order entry therefore requires a specific skill: typing without looking at the keyboard. People who must do otherwise are the single largest cause of order-entry mistakes. If you must look at the keyboard, it's very difficult to type an order correctly while carrying on an intelligent conversation with a customer; it's important that order takers have this special skill. And of course, because these people also answer the phones, they must be articulate and well informed, understand and use good phone etiquette, express themselves well on the phone, and so forth.

INFORMATION REQUESTS

Only 50 to 60 percent of people actually place an order the first time they call. Many of these nonbuyers want more detailed information such as spec sheets, demo disks, and answers to technical questions. Closing these sales depends on how well you are able to supply that information. You must hire and train people who are capable of answering questions as well as taking orders, and you should be ready to fulfill information requests immediately. This means keeping at hand a well-replenished stock of whatever literature is appropriate and having a system in place to quickly send all needed information to a caller.

You may opt to have the same operators who take orders also answer questions, or you can plan a strategy for forwarding the caller to an appropriate designated support person. In any case, the process should be effortless and as transparent as possible to the caller.

CREDIT CARD AND CHECK PROCESSING

The majority of customers—60 to 80 percent—pay for upgrades with a credit card. Here the bottleneck is getting the card approved, which can be a very time-consuming process that can be complicated by invalid accounts and errors in recording the card number and expiration date.

Handling hundreds of small checks is another unbelievably people-intensive process because of the sheer volume and attention to detail required. As many as 5 to 10 percent of checks bounce, which can create serious problems for a developer. Another thing that can clog the pipes is the process of matching checks to the original orders. Often, a check comes from a different office than the one the user listed, and it sometimes carries another company name. If an order number isn't noted on a customer's check, the matching process can be a showstopper. Anticipating this problem and putting procedures in place to handle the flow of checks and credit cards will help avoid this potential jam.

Open Orders

When customers offer purchase orders or checks to pay for upgrades, most developers put the order on hold until the money actually arrives. As many as 35 percent of these payments will never show up without prodding, even though the customer was really prepared to pay. To capture the enormous amount of money left on the table, open orders should be pursued aggressively with invoices and follow-up calls.

SINGLE-COPY FULFILLMENT, ORDER TRACKING

Most software companies are accustomed to shipping pallets or truckloads of products to a handful of large accounts. It's suddenly very different when you have to ship tens of thousands of "onesies." An inefficient shipping system can make fulfillment costs skyrocket; in addition, upgrade customers tend to judge software companies by their turnaround time. People don't want to wait three or four weeks for your product, when another company ships its goods immediately. Setting up shipping procedures to handle this influx of small orders goes a long way toward being able to fill customer orders in a timely fashion.

Order Tracking

Especially when shipping is delayed, a lot of customers—about 30 percent—call back to find out what happened to their orders. From their point of view, you're just waiting for their calls and are prepared to ship the product the moment you hang up the phone. You need to be able to give the customer an acceptable response. For instance, are you still waiting for the customer's purchase order or check? Is the customer located in a shipping zone that takes five days for delivery, and you shipped the product only two days ago? Did the product actually ship?

If you don't have an automated order tracking system, you're going to spend a lot of time and money making those customers happy. Customer service in general and, in particular, your ability to give customers answers is probably the Number 1 determinant of whether they will do business with you in the future.

RETURNS

As many as five percent of upgrade customers will take advantage of a money-back guarantee (or will discover that they ordered the wrong disk format or have a similar problem). It's amazing how many people will call to complain that they didn't get what they wanted.

Getting prompt refunds to these customers is important, in part because credit card companies may impose as much as a $12 fee on you for charge-backs that involve a customer complaint. A refund process that isn't simple and quick (for you and the customers) can be a real bottleneck in your campaign and can stall your relationship with those customers forever.

HOW TO HIRE AN UPGRADE CAMPAIGN MANAGER

If the prospect of handling an upgrade campaign on your own is daunting, you might consider hiring an outside firm to do part or all of the job. When evaluating companies, here are some things you should look for.

Scope of Services

Whether you need a full-blown, turnkey operation with the entire range of services or a company to handle a smaller piece of the action, you should match your needs to the services offered. For example, can the company do only inbound order taking or can it also do outbound telemarketing? Can it warehouse and send literature? Can it follow up with a customer after sending the literature? To what extent does it get involved in customer service?

To help evaluate this, it might be useful to create a "shopping list" of services you might need. Make it as explicit and complete as possible. Then use that list—along with what you've learned from talking to those companies and to other developers who have experience with upgrade fulfillment companies—

to find the right match of your needs to fulfillment options. (You may also hire an experienced professional to help you define your needs.)

Industry Knowledge

Does the company have experience and expertise in the software industry? This can be particularly important because people who buy software naturally have different information needs than people who buy kitchen knives or music. Software customers who call for information don't just want to differentiate between the serrated-edge blade and the smooth one or between buying the cassette or the CD; they have more sophisticated information needs such as whether a package will run on a particular configuration or network. The quality of the answers they get can have a direct impact on whether they buy your product.

Credentials and References

References are very important. Getting an endorsement (or a warning) from a colleague who has used a particular company will help you gauge whether what that company says about itself is actually true. It can also help you better understand a company's strengths and weaknesses from a developer's point of view. Also, if you can tap colleagues for information that will help you avoid pitfalls or define your needs, all the better. You'd be surprised how helpful people can be who have been down a road before you.

Pricing

Getting a handle on pricing is one of the most difficult aspects of evaluating a fulfillment company. It is sometimes very hard to determine up front exactly how much a fulfillment project will cost. One of the best ways to compare pricing among companies is to combine your list of needed services with your best estimate of the volume of business, and give it to each company you are evaluating. Since fulfillment companies each have their own way of packaging and pricing "basic" services and pricing individual ones, it may still be difficult to compare the cost estimates you get—but this exercise will be helpful.

You should know up front that everything, *everything* a fulfillment company does carries a price tag; make sure that you understand the company's pricing strategy, learn exactly what is included in the pricing, and make sure that every activity you might need is defined and that a price is affixed to it.

Two things that often influence pricing are the volume of your business and the longevity of the contract. Generally speaking, a one-time project of 600 units (a small volume) will cost significantly more per unit handled than a longer-term contract with a higher volume of work. There are companies that specialize in smaller-volume jobs; if your volume is low or you are "piecing out" only a part of the fulfillment process and don't need a more complete turnkey operation, smaller fulfillment companies may be good choices.

As you examine pricing, it's important to note that out-of-pocket items should be similarly priced from vendor to vendor. Here are examples of several (somewhat) standard costs.

Editor's note: This article was written in 1992, so the following pricing information is based on shipping, telephone, materials, and tax costs in that year.

- *Credit card fees.* This is the percentage a credit card company charges a merchant for each transaction. Fees run the gamut, but the average in the United States is 3.6 percent.

- *Cost of shipping the product, literature, and so forth.* No matter which shipping service you use, the cost for that service is set by the supplier and is consistent for all users of that service. To give you an idea of what shipping can cost, a four-pound package costs about $3.36 to ship via UPS; that figure is based on the average cost of shipping that package to and from all UPS zones.

- *Cost of the phone call needed to take orders.* Again, those rates are set by the supplier and should vary only by which supplier a fulfillment company uses. The average cost is 20 cents per minute, and the average inbound call to place an order lasts four minutes.

A Pricing Strategy

To give you an idea of how fulfillment pricing is built, here's an example.

Step 1: Start with your four-pound product that sells for $100 plus a $10 shipping-and-handling fee. That makes your price $110. Now add sales tax. If you average the sales taxes from two states (your state plus the one in which the fulfillment company is located), you'll find that it averages approximately 2 percent ($110 × .02 = $2.20) across the United States. Add that to your product cost, which makes $112.20.

Now start adding fulfillment costs.

Step 2: For simplicity's sake, let's assume that you don't accept purchase orders. Eighty percent of orders will be paid by credit card, and the credit card fees will average 3.6 percent ($112.20 × .036 × .8 = $3.23) of the order.

Step 3: The average UPS charge for a four-pound package shipped by ground is $3.36.

Step 4: The cost of the average phone call (four minutes long) to place an order is 80 cents.

Step 5: You'll need a shipping container to protect the product en route. A plain brown corrugated shipping box will probably cost at least 25 cents (this cost is quantity sensitive). If your box is fancier, it will be more expensive.

At this point, fulfillment has already cost you $7.64 (add the costs incurred in steps 2 through 5), the out-of-pocket expenses—and we haven't yet calculated labor, service, and a reasonable profit for the fulfillment company. What if you had to ship a piece of literature to a prospective customer? There's the four-minute average phone call at 80 cents; plus the salary of the person taking the order; plus the envelope or box; plus postage, warehousing, profit for the fulfillment company, and so forth....

Handling the upgrade process correctly is not easy, but it certainly is essential to the long-term viability of your business. How you address this business segment and what level of importance you assign to it in your sales and marketing plans will have a direct bearing on the future of your company. And, as we often tell our clients, "If you don't put your users into the latest technology, someone else will!"

Portions of this chapter were reprinted with permission from the Sept. 4, 1991 issue of *Soft•Letter*, Watertown, Massachusetts.

PART EIGHT

Leveraging For Maximum Impact

Sometimes, going it alone just won't get you to where you need to be. Many companies are finding that leveraging, that is, teaming up with others—even with customers and old competitors—is a great way to boost the impact they get from a limited marketing budget. Here are three case histories containing ideas about how to bundle, comarket, and capitalize on the tremendous potential of user groups. These chapters describe how smaller companies have made a "little" bit go a long way—with help from their "friends."

Something not to miss for people who have considered marketing to user groups but haven't yet taken the plunge: While Chapter 32 is an interesting study in leveraging, it also describes how one company created a user group marketing program that pays for itself.

CHAPTER THIRTY

The Making of a Bundle

HOW T/MAKER BUNDLES FOR SUCCESS

By Diane Kreyenhagen, T/Maker Company

Diane Kreyenhagen is vice-president of OEM and direct sales for T/Maker Company, a content and multimedia content software developer located in Mountain View, California.

OVER a period of several years, bundles have significantly contributed to T/Maker's bottom line. Bundling our products with those of other companies has been an effective way to increase our market penetration and marketing clout, take advantage more quickly of hot market opportunities, and offer customers increased value for their software dollar.

Our strategy evolved from a need to penetrate today's ultracompetitive market: When customers walk into reseller stores or open mail-order catalogs, they encounter several software titles that offer similar functionality. A customer interested in a word processor, for example, must choose between at least seven products with a wide range of prices. Faced with this plethora of competitive products (some of which are produced by giant, resource-rich companies), T/Maker, which developed the WriteNow word processor and ClickArt ready-to-use graphics, had to resort to using creative tactics to attract customers. Bundling was our solution.

BUNDLING BENEFITS

Bundling can be an effective marketing tactic because it creates a winning situation for you, your "partners," resellers, and customers, in the following ways.

- *A bundle helps differentiate your product and therefore draws increased customer attention.* Bundling is a good way to differentiate your product within its own category and make it stand out in today's more competitive market. A well-thought-out bundle offers customers more of a "whole product solution"; for example, instead of receiving only your word processor, customers also get additional programs and tools that greatly increase the effectiveness or extend the use of your product. This more complete offering will therefore help differentiate your product from competitive ones that stand alone, and may also attract more customer attention than your stand-alone product might otherwise receive.

Bundles also can help you reach new or novice computing customers. For example, in the home computing market, novices often aren't sure what individual package to buy and may hesitate to plunk down several hundred dollars for a product that meets only a single need. But if your bundle offers customers a range of attractive products that fills multiple needs at a reasonable price, you may close the sale.

- *Bundles can help extend your marketing clout.* Many smaller companies have terrific products—but small marketing budgets and little or no distribution networks with which to reach resellers and mass merchants. By bundling with a better-known product or company, a smaller company in essence can use its larger partners' marketing clout and distribution contacts to promote the bundle and help establish its own product in a channel. And if the bundle is a hit, the reseller may be more open to stocking the individual products.

- *Bundling can help you take advantage of a hot market opportunity more quickly.* To explain what I mean, I'll recount how T/Maker first entered the bundling business. Several years ago, we saw a market need for integrated packages (and at that time Microsoft Works was just about the only package available). We knew other companies were hurrying to bring their integrated packages to market, and we were faced with a decision: How to quickly seize this opportunity?

  The alternatives boiled down to either pouring resources into developing our own integrated package (which, being a smaller company then, meant diverting precious resources from other key initiatives) or finding another way to fill the needs of customers who wanted several-products-in-one. Our solution was to create a bundle with existing packages: The SmartBundle, which included WriteNow, Aldus SuperPaint, Ashton-Tate Full Impact, and Software Discovery RecordHolder Plus was born. This bundle allowed us to nab sales in the integrated package market more quickly and less expensively than we could have by developing a totally new integrated product. Similar opportunities may also await you; the key is to recognize a market trend and position yourself to act quickly on it.

- *Bundling can help reduce marketing risks.* Depending on how the deal is structured, a bundle can spread the marketing risks and investment among the participating companies. A smaller company can dramatically reduce its risk if it chooses the right partner. For example, in some cases T/Maker, as the larger partner in a bundling deal, may assume much of the responsibility for marketing the bundle, such as through direct mail; we often pay most costs, such as for the design, production, printing, and mailing of the campaign. (We ask participating developers to supply sales text, product photos, screen shots, and their company logos.) In return for its larger share of the risk and expense, T/Maker takes a larger portion of the revenues.

- *Bundling can help a multiplatform developer strengthen its case for increased or continued Macintosh development.* For example, if the Macintosh is not your company's "first" platform, by bundling with other Macintosh developers you may be able to boost the sales and market presence of your Macintosh product. Internally, this can help solidify the case that your Macintosh product is an important part of your offering—and thereby boost management interest in your company's Macintosh development efforts.

- *Bundling can increase a reseller's profits.* Resellers can also profit from bundles. In our experience, resellers are very receptive to bundles because bundles help them differentiate their inventory from the guy's across the street. Also, as resellers' CPU margins shrink, bundles are a good way to add profit to a sale. By offering a bundle to the CPU buyer, the reseller both provides the customer with great product value and increases its own margin. We usually pitch two or three bundle ideas to various resellers each quarter and frequently modify bundles to make them dovetail with resellers' promotions.

- *Bundles can offer customers increased value.* If you've assembled a good bundle, customers win because they get not only a more complete computing solution, but also a package of tremendous value. The most successful bundles are aggressively priced, and users get a group of products for much less money than if they had bought the products separately.

THE ANATOMY OF A BUNDLE

We've found that a bundle is more successful if it focuses on the needs of a particular customer group, instead of being just a bunch of products sold together. We've tried both strategies and have experienced much greater success with focused groups of products.

One example of a focused bundle is the T/Maker PowerBundle, targeted at Macintosh PowerBook buyers. We felt that PowerBook buyers, like most other customers, would want more of a whole-product solution that would help make the most of their PowerBook purchase. From a myriad of possible products, we chose those that we felt would be naturals for the "user on the go": A word processor (T/Maker WriteNow), an address book product (PowerUp Address Book Plus), an expense report application (ChipSoft Business Expense

Reports), a communications product (America OnLine), 40 fax cover sheet templates (ClickArt FaxMania) for users with a portable fax modem, and a carrying case for the PowerBook itself. We have also created bundles for SOHO (small office/home office) that included WriteNow, Address Book Plus, and Intuit Quicken.

BUNDLE SHELF LIFE

Choosing the right channels and "shelf-life" for your bundles is as important as choosing what products to include. For instance, we currently have two types of bundles: long-term and short-term. We sell long-term bundles through retail and catalog (mail order) channels and short-term bundles directly to customers through direct-mail efforts. We also offer exclusive bundles to particular reseller chains.

Long-Term Bundles

As a company, we make a strong, long-term commitment to the success of retail and mail-order bundles. We create long-term bundles with the intention that they'll remain in our product line for an extended period, usually more than a year. Examples are the PowerBundle, SmartBundle (both previously mentioned), and the WriteNow WorkShop Bundle (WriteNow, Reference Software Grammatik Mac, and WordStar American Heritage Dictionary and Correct Quotes).

Because of their strategic significance, we allocate the commensurate marketing and advertising funds to support these bundles and produce special packaging for them. In addition, our sales force devotes as much time and effort into marketing these bundles as they do our individual, unbundled products.

Short-Term Bundles

Direct mail is a very important part of T/Maker's overall sales strategy. Throughout the year, we assemble a variety of short-term bundles and market them directly to customers through direct-mail campaigns. Last year T/Maker offered more than 12 different product bundles to its installed base and prospects by direct mail. Some bundles included only one other developer's product, and others bundled as many as four. This year we plan to offer well over 20 different product combinations through various direct-mail projects.

Direct mail plays both a tactical and strategic role in our bundling strategy. While direct mail is a marketing tactic that's an end in itself (direct sales), it's also a strategy for testing which bundles are most popular; once we find a combination that works, it becomes a long-term bundle candidate. Direct mail is a complex, sophisticated science, and experimenting with it can be expensive (and frustrating) for a small company. Companies therefore are often interested in learning more about the dynamics of direct mail and want the revenues it could yield—but they don't have the resources to risk a first try themselves.

By bundling with a more experienced direct mailer such as T/Maker, they can experiment without the up-front cash risk. If the mailing is successful, they then feel more comfortable trying their own program. There's another benefit that direct-mail bundling partners receive: a mailing list of campaign respondents. Partners can use this information to conduct their own direct-mail campaigns that, for example, promote new products or offer upgrades.

DOING THE BUNDLE THING

Putting together your first bundle won't be a piece of cake, but the experience you gain will probably make subsequent efforts easier and more streamlined. The first steps you should take are deciding which of your products to build the bundle around (based on marketing goals and opportunities), identifying potential customers and what they need, and determining the channel in which to market the bundle. Once you've nailed these things down, it is much easier to decide what other products would make sense in the bundle.

When it comes to choosing other companies' products, I should point out that the bundling business works in both directions: We constantly look for partners to participate in bundles that T/Maker initiates, but we also troll for opportunities to become someone else's "third party." The latter opportunities can be hiding anywhere—not only in the third-party development community.

For example, we were approached by PaperDirect, a company that supplies papers and related presentation products to personal computer customers for use with laser and ink jet printers. They presented us with a unique bundling opportunity targeted to small businesses that want to print their own stationery, documents, presentations, and other marketing materials using desktop publishing and word-processing software. PaperDirect sells a variety of preprinted stationery, including a series of coordinated letterheads, envelopes, brochure mailers, and other items. It also sells software templates (compatible with several word-processing and desktop publishing applications) that allow users to more easily lay out their own text and graphics on PaperDirect's preprinted papers. T/Maker's ClickArt is bundled with the templates, which offers users an even more complete solution. This has been a tremendous, successful opportunity for us—with a partner outside the third-party development community.

Bundling Caveats

Here are some general guidelines that should help you ease into bundling.

- *Start simply.* If you are new to bundling, it's much easier to work with only one other company or product. The more products and companies involved, the more complicated the process becomes. If you have too many variables to juggle the first time through, you'll quickly become overwhelmed and frustrated.

  We learned this lesson the hard way. Our first bundle, the SmartBundle mentioned earlier, was a trial by fire. Not only did we have to negotiate contracts with three companies (each having, of course, its own agenda and issues), but we also had to contend with creating special packaging, putting together a complicated SKU, formulating a price that would not undermine any of our partners' channels, and handling a variety of other situations that were compounded by the number of companies involved. The successful end product was worth it, but we recommend cutting your teeth on a less complicated deal, especially if you're a small, resource-limited company.

- *Put adequate resources behind the bundle.* If you plan to launch your bundle (which you should treat as a product unto itself) into retail and mail-order channels, make sure you allocate enough advertising money, sales staff, and other support to make it a success. Bundles are a major component of our lifeblood; therefore, we treat them as we would any other major product and give them their due when it comes to resources.

- *Don't overlook international partners, and find partners with international know-how.* Don't limit yourself to only the domestic market: There often are opportunities to sell your product in other markets. Furthermore, a partner that already is established in another country can provide you with a good launching pad into that market, much in the same way that a larger, more experienced domestic partner can help you take better advantage of your home market with its presence and know-how.

  T/Maker frequently seeks partners and channels outside the United States. We have been particularly successful in Australia, the United Kingdom, and New Zealand; these markets are easier and less expensive for us to infiltrate with a bundle because they are English-language countries. If a bundle offers customers good value, is well priced, and contains strong products, the U.S. versions sometimes will do quite well in these countries. We make it a point to start investigating international possibilities at the beginning of every bundle negotiation. If a company we are considering has a U.K. or other localized version of its product, we try to arrange an international bundle when we negotiate the U.S. one.

- *Create solid contracts.* I can't emphasize enough how important it is to negotiate solid, realistic contracts with all parties involved in the bundle. Although there are too many facets of a contract to cover in this chapter, there are some key considerations to keep in mind as you begin negotiating. For instance, bundling contracts are as critical as contracts with any other business partner. They should be specific and should clearly spell out the terms of every facet of the deal. We constantly clarify issues in and add sections to our contracts, based on what we've learned from previous bundling deals.

  One warning: You should have a signed contract in hand before spending any marketing and sales money. Like any other business deal, the bundle could fall apart at the last minute for almost any reason. Also, it's important to treat bundling partners as you would any important contributor to your business. We enter contract negotiations with the attitude that our partners are a key factor in our long-term marketing and product strategy—and long-term success. We try to go the extra mile to ensure everyone is satisfied with the bundle and that all parties concerned are kept well informed during the negotiation process.

  Once negotiations are concluded and the contract is signed, communication shouldn't stop. It's important to get your partners' feedback on the marketing pieces you produce, keep them involved in the campaign's progress, and share sales results with them. Because we know there will be more opportunities to work with these companies in the future, we work at building strong partnerships now.

- *Make it clear to customers which company supports what product.* You should tell customers exactly where to turn for help with each product in the bundle. If you don't, customers may assume that *your* toll-free number is the one to call with questions about your partners' products. Furthermore, if customers call you and you then ask them to call yet another number, they'll feel as though they've been "shuffled off" and may perceive your company to be incompetent, uncaring, or both.

POTENTIAL PITFALLS

While bundling can be a winning marketing strategy, that's not to say there aren't several potential "gotchas" to avoid. Here are some of the important risks we've encountered.

- *Low pricing can create channel conflict.* Bundling can cause channel conflict and pricing confusion. How you price the bundle compared to the price of each individual product is important. For the bundle to sell well, customers must perceive they're getting a good deal on the package. However, the price shouldn't be so low that the bundle cannibalizes a reseller's sales of your individual products. Also, if the bundle and individual product price are too similar, this also causes confusion in the channel and can cause both your individual product and bundle to fail.

One way to help avoid this problem is to speak with resellers and mail-order companies before you set the bundle price. This has worked well for us; the discussion helps clue us in to what the channel's pain threshold is regarding price and gives us an opportunity to clearly explain what we're doing, why, and address channel concerns.

- *You may get "stuck" with a large inventory of another company's product.* On several occasions, T/Maker has had to purchase a large quantity of another developer's product at once to receive a lower original equipment manufacturer's (OEM) price. In most cases, these units must be specially produced (for example, no product box, only disks and documentation shrink-wrapped together), and the other company won't allow us to return any unsold products to them. If the bundle doesn't sell, we're left holding a sizable inventory of other companies' products.

  It also pays to plan ahead for disaster: Keep some creative ideas waiting in the wings. For example, if you're left with a large inventory of another company's products, you may try to sell a previously retail-only bundle through direct mail. Or, you might rework the bundle to include different products and try again.

- *Sometimes contracts expire during a hot selling streak.* Another problem arises when you've created a blockbuster bundle—and your contract with the other developer runs out. If others don't wish to renew the contract (for whatever reasons), you must drop this revenue generator from your product line—a frustrating situation at best. In these cases, we try to renegotiate the contract. (We've renewed some contracts as many as four or five times.) However, if we can't renew the deal, we try to take a positive attitude, knowing that there are always new bundles to be created.

- *Putting inadequate resources behind a bundle will kill it.* Before committing to a bundle, you should think about the considerable level of resources and energy needed to effectively promote and sell the product. If you don't put adequate resources behind a bundle, of course it won't do well. It's important to ask yourself if you are willing to put the time, marketing money, and personnel resources into a product that may not be in your lineup for more than six months or a year. This is especially important, as we all are operating in a recession economy and with limited resources and staff.

- *Bundling entails complicated logistics.* There are many logistic issues that can make bundling complicated. It's important to think through the entire process of creating, producing and shipping a bundle, and the implications to all areas of your company. For example, you'll need to add a new SKU to your product line (which is often tricky because of the large number of products in a bundle). You also must clearly inform distributors and other direct customers about this new product offering, and make sure they understand how it will affect them.

  Another consideration is whether to purchase a product from the other company or instead pay a royalty—and duplicate the disks and print the documentation yourself. If you plan to keep the bundle in your product line for several months and expect to sell a large number of units, you may want to consider doing the production yourself. Depending on the royalty agreement established in the contract, this alternative may be less expensive for you.

There are benefits as well as pitfalls to bundling, but it has been well worth the effort and risk for us. By combining our products and resources with those of other companies, we've boosted our bottom line and reached new customers. Our experience is that if you enter the process with your eyes wide open, you'll be in a good position to take advantage of the bundling opportunities on the horizon this year and beyond.

Bundle, anyone?

Editor's note: This chapter was written in early 1993.

CHAPTER THIRTY-ONE

Make a Bigger Splash—
Through Comarketing

HOW TEAMING UP CAN INCREASE YOUR CLOUT

By Steve Blank, SuperMac Technology, Inc.

Steve Blank is the former vice-president of marketing for SuperMac Technology, Inc., a Sunnyvale, California, company that develops hardware graphics products.

WHEN Apple introduced QuickTime last December, SuperMac was ready with the VideoSpigot digital video capture card to help lead the mad dash to success. To the outside world, it may have appeared that SuperMac was extremely fortunate to have introduced a product for the digital video revolution at precisely the right time. But as you might surmise from your own experience, SuperMac had been working closely with Apple and other developers on the product and its launch for more than a year.

The fact that this was a cooperative marketing effort was critical to our success. Although timing was very important—having the right product ready at the right time—the real coup was being able to harness the resources of multiple key players to launch and market the technology. We realized early on that going it alone would be a big mistake, considering the scope of the task. Joining forces with other developers—getting other players onto the QuickTime bandwagon—helped prevent the revolution from becoming an evolution.

Why was this a revolution? This was not just the launch of a new group of products; it was the birth of a new technology, a totally new way of doing things. The ramifications: Before, video manipulation belonged almost solely in the domain of professional production companies and post-production houses. With this new technology, everyday people could experiment with their camcorders and Macintosh computers and produce extraordinary video results. But would users understand the potential of this new technology? Would they be willing to use it? Would it seem approachable?

THE COMARKETING APPROACH

It became apparent that a team approach to marketing this new technology would most effectively address these questions. To get a new technology or product adopted by the mainstream market, you must offer not a lone technology, but an entire solution, a package that helps users grasp the proposition your product or technology makes and achieve satisfaction from it. *[Editor's note: This concept has been dubbed the "whole product" concept. For more information about it, see Chapter 3, "Breaking into the Mainstream: How to Move from Early Success to Mainstream Market Leadership."]* By joining forces with Apple and other developers, not only did we collectively offer users more of a "whole product" solution, but we were also able to augment our resources by leveraging other companies' efforts.

Forming the Team

We began discussions with Adobe Systems, WordPerfect Corporation, and other developers to get them committed to team-marketing the QuickTime technology breakthrough. Here's how it happened: SuperMac had developed a video-editing application to test VideoSpigot. We considered marketing it ourselves but decided against it after taking a hard look at the situation. We saw that SuperMac would be better off and farther ahead in the long run if we sold the program to another software developer, and then worked together to build the new market. We felt we could make more of an impact and sell many more VideoSpigots if another credible company marketed the software and continued its development.

SuperMac is a hardware company, and from a previous foray into software publishing, we know that it takes a dedicated, concerted focus to evangelize a new category of software—and significant marketing money and muscle. Being a hardware company, our focus and the resulting allocation of resources isn't conducive to the effort needed to market and subsequently revise a software product. After discussions with several companies, we sold the editing product to Adobe Systems, which named it Premiere.

We chose Adobe for several reasons, most importantly because of its track record of evangelizing PostScript, completely new system software that ultimately changed the face of the computer industry. We then struck a deal with Adobe to bundle our product with Premiere, and in the first three months, 20,000 copies of the bundle—VideoSpigot or VideoSpigot Pro, and Premiere—were sold. Since then, we have renewed our agreement with Adobe to indefinitely bundle Premiere with VideoSpigot and VideoSpigot Pro. With the bundle, users receive a more complete solution than they would with the individual products.

Furthermore, we felt we had to work with existing application-category leaders to effectively help users grasp the implications of QuickTime technology and our product. We contacted leading providers of word-processing, multimedia, and other software. We enlisted such companies as WordPerfect, MacroMind•Paracomp (now known as MacroMedia), and several others. A key WordPerfect person worked closely with us so that at the QuickTime introduction they could show a QuickTime movie—captured with VideoSpigot and edited with Premiere—in a WordPerfect document. MacroMedia showed Director and Action! presentations that incorporated QuickTime movies. Other companies used the technology in their products and demonstrations, as well.

Seize the Opportunity

The point I'm trying to make is that whenever a technology breakthrough is around the corner, seize the opportunity. If you can lock onto a product idea that supports the new technology concept, go for it. Resist the temptation to keep everything close to the vest and go it alone. Especially if your company is smaller and more resource-limited, find like-minded companies and do something together. Ultimately, you'll make a bigger splash and offer users a more complete package than you could offer by yourself.

PREPARING THE MARKETPLACE

The comarketing effort didn't end with persuading other developers to use the technology in their products. Because of the scope and magnitude of the QuickTime concept and the introduction activities, we also had to create very special promotional materials.

The first step was creating a white paper explaining why analog-based video had failed to become a mainstream computer operation and why digital video was the answer. During the nine months before the official QuickTime launch, the paper was widely distributed to industry influencers, the press, video enthusiasts, and anyone who showed an interest in the technology.

Next, we needed user testimonials. We instituted an aggressive beta program with industry analysts, users, and other developers. From this group, we culled several compelling examples and created both printed and video testimonials that highlighted real-world uses of Adobe Premiere, WordPerfect, and VideoSpigot. The print testimonials were easy to distribute and very exciting. (It's great to see pioneers become emotional about a technological breakthrough.) The video samples created by these testimonial subjects were impressive and highly professional in content. They demonstrated the wildly diverse uses of QuickTime/VideoSpigot that were possible with today's equipment (everything from a corporate sales presentation, to a commentary on the starkness of New York City, to an educational video about eye surgery).

We also created a "Spigot CD" that included all of SuperMac's digital video marketing collateral, testimonials, sample movies, and other QuickTime-related materials. We even modified our VideoSpigot advertisement to include quotes from these testimonials. We used the testimonials as widely as possible and included them in trade show handouts, placed them in pertinent publications, and sent them to customers who inquired about our products.

It was critical to properly educate reviewers in the computer, business, and video press who had never experienced anything like QuickTime. It was also important to make sure they understood the limitations—as well as the potential—of this fledgling technology. To get the information across, we created a nuts-and-bolts reviewers kit and guide for our product. The kit included performance benchmarks from an independent laboratory, comparisons with competitive products, educational materials about digital video, and facts about the product. We also worked closely with our partners to make sure that every reviewer had products from and contacts inside our partners' companies (including Apple). In short, we all pulled together to make the review effort stronger and more effective.

THE INTRODUCTION AND AFTERMATH

To achieve the most dramatic, high-profile launch, we introduced VideoSpigot in SuperMac's and Apple's Macworld booths in January. In addition to showing a variety of software running with VideoSpigot, we also demonstrated planned enhancements to our current system-level software, including compression and CD-ROM technology, at Apple's QuickTime room off the show floor. This demo met the objective of showing people not only the current product, but also a glimpse of the future. Our partners also talked about and demonstrated our product, along with their own, in the many Macworld panel discussions in which they participated.

Next, we had to demonstrate how this new technology would work in real-life situations. Demo '92 and TED3 were excellent venues. At Demo '92, we equipped a kiosk with a Macintosh Quadra, a large-screen SuperMac monitor and graphics card, HyperCard, VideoSpigot, and Premiere. We used those products to show attendees some highlights of the conference and other events by means of QuickTime movies that were edited and produced only hours after the events happened. A camera operator shot footage, and an editing room equipped with Macintosh Quadras, videotape decks, VideoSpigot, and Premiere created the movies on-site.

At TED3, the semiannual industry event for creative leaders in education, entertainment, technology, and design, we created an interactive "electronic newspaper." Conference guests could view articles and movies in this "video newspaper," which highlighted the previous day's events.

PUBLIC EDUCATION

These events were excellent for attracting the interest of industry insiders, but a real challenge was inciting people to buy products from our partners and us. To do that, we needed to educate the public directly. With our partners, we decided to offer seminars and hands-on classes throughout the United States and Europe. One of the easiest solutions was to fit ourselves into existing courses. For QuickTime and our products, the American Film Institute (AFI) was a natural; AFI had a ready-made cadre of interested professional users as students. We sent product managers to train these classes in a room fully equipped to make QuickTime movies.

The results were spectacular. The students ate up the technology, and their regular teachers were sold to the point that they became "evangelists" for the products. Now AFI was a partner in the process, too.

Combining the resources of Adobe, MacroMedia, Apple, and others, we traveled across the country holding a series of one-hour classes to teach people how to make QuickTime movies. To get the maximum impact from this investment, we also invited regional press people to not only cover the story, but also to learn how to make movies themselves. We also captured the mindshare of dealers by including them in these seminars with groups of potential buyers.

This three-month road show was an effective public relations/evangelism/education/sales/marketing tool. But it was by working with our partners that we were able to keep interest and enthusiasm high in two ways: By directly touching our customers, we got the best market impact possible; and by positively influencing the editorial community, we achieved favorable product reviews and technology trend articles.

CREATE YOUR OWN REVOLUTION

Yes, this is a wonderful, heartwarming success story, and I'll bet at this point you're muttering, "That's great for SuperMac, but we're just a small company. How could we do all that?" Based on our experience, here's what I think can make the difference for any company. (Think of Aldus at the birth of desktop publishing and MacroMind before multimedia became in vogue.)

- *Keep your ear to the ground.* Watch the industry and other developers—and Apple—carefully for signs of the next big innovation. Apple has described its future technology plans for system software; somewhere in there lies a tremendous opportunity. Kaleida and Taligent will also provide major opportunities for innovation and fresh approaches to problem solving.

- *When you've got something hot: focus, focus, focus.* Don't try to dilute your marketing and development efforts by working on several things at once. If your idea is hot, you'll know it. Focus on that idea/product, and you've got half the job done.

- *Start working on your solution—your products—as early as possible.* Before a new technology is fully introduced and exploited, this may seem risky. However, the payoff can be really big if you get in on the ground floor with an innovative, exciting product idea.

- *Scrap the not-invented-here syndrome.* Find other companies whose products can take advantage of the new technology and your products. Work together to create a more complete package to offer users when the technology is unveiled. You'll be able to combine the ideas, resources, and manpower of several companies, and together you'll make a bigger splash than any one company could make alone. Also, take advantage of the various comarketing activities that Apple offers.

- *Put your efforts where you can win.* Try to put your efforts and resources into a venture in which you can become a significant player, preferably Number One. If you can't, then consider not playing or finding another venture. Put your efforts into products and markets from which you can profit the most.

- *Show 'em you've got sex appeal.* Entice the media, analysts, other developers, and potential customers with well-planned and executed promotions, demonstrations, and training. Shoot for maximum impact (which doesn't always have to mean maximum investment).

- *Keep mining the vein.* Product introductions are only the beginning. As for SuperMac, we're not about to stop mining the QuickTime vein. We will continue to develop partnerships with innovative software companies and are looking for more opportunities to leverage the Apple effort. And it goes without saying—we are continuing to make our video products as innovative and desirable as possible.

See you at the movies!

CHAPTER THIRTY-TWO

Creating a User Group Marketing Program That Pays for Itself

By Terry Fleming, Timeworks, Inc.

Terry Fleming is the director of user group services and public relations for Timeworks, Inc., a developer of desktop publishing products, based in Northbrook, Illinois.

"YOU should market to user groups." You've probably heard it before (over and over again). Indeed, there have been numerous pitches urging developers to do so. If you aren't convinced or you don't know how to get started, this chapter is for you. I'll explain why Timeworks made the investment in a user group program, how it pays for itself, pitfalls we've faced, and some tips about getting started.

WHY A USER GROUP PROGRAM?

For several years, Timeworks has devoted money, time, and other resources to this activity—for several reasons. Every survey ever done indicates that people base purchase decisions primarily on word-of-mouth referrals. A user group is a collection of people who enjoy using computers and helping others use them. They enjoy sharing information with each other (and with you, if you ask). By gaining their support, you get the mind share of the largest collection of purchase influencers in the industry.

The flip side is that you could receive a negative reaction if user group members don't like what they see. But in my experience, most groups will be so darned glad you took a personal interest in them that they'll love you to pieces. (That translates to: They'll be more likely to purchase your product or service.)

There's another bonus to working with user groups: The average group contains a sampling of all the various hardware and software combinations imaginable. Members cover the entire spectrum of skill levels and groups are run, by and large, by volunteers. This is a "buffet" of willing beta test candidates who can tie your product into knots, and many of these users have a very broad feel for what the market wants. They are very outspoken and will gladly tell you how they perceive your product, company, policies, your new necktie—anything you might want to know (and some things you might not).

A PROGRAM THAT PAYS FOR ITSELF

Influencing future purchases is a long-term goal of a developer's user group program. In many cases, developers may hesitate to launch a program because it requires an investment that results in a seemingly intangible, unmeasurable long-term payback. However, our program gives us long-term benefits but also pays for itself immediately *in a tangible way.* Timeworks offsets the cost of its program by selling products directly to user groups, an approach formulated when we started the program (circa 1990). We analyzed the fixed costs to visit a user group in person (travel, meals, equipment rental, and so forth) and decided to offset that by selling products at the meetings.

But beware: There are a host of caveats that accompany this strategy. First, user groups are all too aware of current retail channel prices—especially mail order prices. If you decide to sell direct, you *must* beat the best price they can get anywhere else, or don't even bother. After all, you are approaching these people because they are special customers. Everything you do should reinforce that. If you can't (or would rather not) offer a discount, so be it. But at least don't offer your product at $10 higher than the going street price; this has a tendency to irritate group members. If you're going to offer a special price, make sure that it *is* special.

Avoiding Channel Conflict

Adjusting your selling price for the user group seems simple enough, but what happens when the local dealer gets wind of it? You're selling your products to the group for less than a dealer can buy them, a valid concern on the dealer's part. At Timeworks we continue to be sensitive to this potential channel conflict, although we haven't experienced a problem. When we present a product to a user group, we generally offer it at about 50 percent off the suggested retail price. We diminish potential channel conflict by restricting the special price to that presentation only. Also, just as in direct-mail marketing, many members will patronize their favorite dealer to buy the product anyway, which is fine. Our primary goal is to build awareness while providing a low-cost opportunity for user group members to try our product.

This way, we get both the ongoing, more intangible return on investment (influencing future purchasing decisions and getting users to tell their friends) *and* an immediate, tangible, and measurable payback that helps defer the cost of the user-group program.

GETTING STARTED

To help you decide if marketing to user groups is right for you, here are some things to consider—and some of the pitfalls you'll face—when launching a user-group program.

- *Make the commitment.* In our experience, to realize a return on your invest-ment you must take user groups seriously. Allocate your resources accord-ing to the level of commitment you desire and to a level that you *can support.* For example, it's easy to make a user-group mailing with the best intentions and make a host of promises you *intend* to fulfill. Resist! (Remember the old saying about the road to hell being paved....) Take it slowly and increase your efforts with a degree of control. Think of it this way: If you open a restaurant that can seat 100 people and you invite 1200, it doesn't matter how good the food is when more than 100 customers show up.

- *Choose the right people.* To succeed, you need a person (or staff) devoted solely to the necessary activities. Timeworks has devoted several full-time people and the resources needed to support them to work solely with user groups. The most effective people for these positions are those who can play multiple roles. They must be able to simultaneously position the product in the minds of user group members as "something they need" (marketing director), handle questions about the features and benefits they'll realize by owning your product and close the sale (sales manager), fluently compare and contrast the competition at any level (technical guru), and convey the enthusiasm of a child at Christmas (little kid). User groups have a variety of expectations that this person (and your program) must fill. (For more infor-mation, see "Meeting User Group Expectations" in this chapter.)

  Support this individual (or individuals) with administrative back-ups who are organized and who follow through well, and you'll make a major impact. Try to do all of these things with existing, non-dedicated resources on a part-time basis, and you'll also make a major impact—the wrong kind.

- *Allocate adequate resources.* Allocate the proper equipment and processes needed to keep track of user groups and all related information. Managing the data is an ongoing task. User-group presidents and contacts change from year to year, as do their addresses and phone numbers. So do factors such as group size, focus, number of special interest groups, and so forth.

We use a custom-designed data base that automates the process of organizing and tracking more than 1000 user groups worldwide. Although you won't need anything this elaborate to get started, consider future needs as well as today's while doing your planning. You'll quickly accumulate data once you start.

- *Plan for demo equipment.* When planning your resources and budget, don't forget demo equipment. Have you heard that most user groups will provide equipment for demos—free of charge—and all you have to do is show up? This is often true, but it isn't always a benefit. For example, the equipment requirements to demonstrate a database product will be totally different from those needed to demonstrate a 24-bit color image-processing program. If you want to show a QuickTime movie and all they have is an old black-and-white overhead display panel, you'll need to bring (or rent) your own equipment. In this case, factor the equipment cost into the overall cost of visiting the group, plug it into your cost/benefit formula, and see if meeting with this group still makes sense for you. If it doesn't, it may be better to avoid visiting this group for now.

- *Use outside resources as much as possible.* One excellent potential source of help is Apple. The Apple User Group Connection is a group that is dedicated to working with Apple's user groups and various professional associations. It maintains a database of hundreds of groups across the country who participate in the program.

- *Select target groups and design programs accordingly.* Groups come in a variety of flavors. They have horizontal interests (community groups, for example) and vertical interests (corporate, education, government, and so forth). Some are small, some are very large, and you should tailor your efforts accordingly.

Working with Small Groups

Because we learned early on that it wasn't economically feasible to visit all smaller groups in person, we developed the Timeworks' Ambassador Program, which maintains relationships with more than 1000 Macintosh and DOS user groups. We enlist a volunteer in each small group to be our ongoing contact. We send that person a copy of our product (which will belong to the group), literature and support needed for him or her to make a presentation about it, and order forms to give to group members (who send orders directly to Timeworks). As an incentive for the ambassador, we're testing a new approach: After we receive the first order from a group member, the ambassador receives a free personal copy of our product. The Timeworks' Ambassador Program has changed as we learn from our experiences. One thing stays the same, however: The program entails a tremendous amount of administrative time and overhead.

Working with Larger Groups

We do visit larger groups personally because they represent the greater opportunity; we reach more people per presentation and have full control over how the information is presented. However, they also present the most problems. The first is scheduling. Because every developer wants to visit them, you may have to schedule with the larger groups months in advance. These arrangements can be especially important if you are launching a new product; you'll want to schedule as many user group visits as possible during the first few months after the intro. If you wait too long, user group members will have already seen and heard about your product, and your presentation won't seem as "special."

However, scheduling is one of the more time-consuming, nightmarish administrative tasks. Getting onto a user group's agenda isn't as easy as it sounds. Here's why: Most user groups meet once a month. Some meet even less when a regular meeting day falls on a holiday. Some don't meet during the summer, since meeting attendance can drop dramatically due to vacations and an occasional conflicting tee time. There are only 12 "second-Wednesdays-of-the-month " in a year, so you only have 12 opportunities to visit a given group each year. Add to this the fact that the "second Wednesday" may be the meeting day for several important groups you want to visit, and the scheduling difficulty increases. Finally, the more established, large, and influential the group, the more likely it will book speakers eight to ten months in advance. Commit to the group's first available date; it's worth it.

Also, when you're trying to schedule a presentation, you'll sometimes find that you must share the "spotlight" with another speaker. Don't let that intimidate or stop you—it can be a blessing in disguise. Sharing with someone else serves only to broaden the overall appeal of the meeting and will draw more people to it. It costs you just as much to talk to 50 people as it does to talk to 150, so look at this as an opportunity instead of a curse. (A major exception would be when you're asked to speak alongside a direct competitor. In this case, politely offer the entire spotlight to your competitor because that's just the kind of person you are.)

Since most user groups meet in the evening, you can optimize the use of your travel dollars, too. You can combine other day-business you have in a given city with an evening appointment with a user group. In most cases, you'll have to arrange the user group meeting first, and then back-fill your other business around it.

Another problem with visiting large groups: The equipment necessary to demo your product for 500 people is usually more sophisticated and demanding than that needed to present to a group of 50.

Finally, while big groups are more cost effective to visit in most cases, I'll add a caveat to what I said earlier about visiting small groups: Don't underestimate the sales potential of reaching them. We did one presentation for a local community user group; one member was the director of facilities and systems for a major national fast-food chain. As a result of our presentation, this person became a very valuable corporate contact. You never know who you'll run into when you go to a user group meeting.

MEETING USER GROUP EXPECTATIONS

Meeting a group's expectations is paramount to a successful user-group marketing program. What do user groups expect from a developer? They expect fairness, free product, honesty, free product, inside information, free product. Did I mention free product? Don't get me wrong; they don't demand free product, but they do expect it—much in the same way that people expect you to dress up for a wedding: You really don't have to, but it's considered disrespectful if you don't.

Be prepared to donate at least one unit of your product to a group. Obviously, if you're demonstrating a $20,000 color printer, of course you probably can't afford to donate one; but if you're showing a $79 software package, be prepared to give away more than one. The group will raffle your generous donation at the end of the meeting, and maybe one winner will review it for the group's newsletter. If the winner won't be reviewing it, consider donating yet another copy to the group for review purposes.

User groups also expect you to give a mediocre presentation. What??! I didn't say they *wanted* one, just that they've come to expect it. One way to really distinguish your product and company is to deliver a dynamite presentation. Here are some helpful do's and don'ts for making your pitch.

- *Don't give them an "annual report" on your company.* When you present to a user group, the only person in the room who cares about your company's fiscal status or marketing position is you. Leave it out of your presentation. Let your competitors make this mistake and bore the audience to tears.

- *Don't take user groups lightly.* These people are on the cutting edge of the industry. Individually, they may be a notch or two below your best techno-experts, but as a group they possess more depth of knowledge than you might imagine. Not only are they knowledgeable about your product—they also often know your competition and how your product compares as well as or better than you do (not in the same marketing/positioning sense as you'd like them to have, but in the real-world "is-it-really-better" sense). If you try to buffalo them, they'll eat you alive.

You have three options: Know what you're talking about; send someone who does; or at least be humble enough to admit your limitations to them before getting too far out on a limb. Besides, it's far better for you to humble yourself than for them to humble you—which they can.

- *Do know your product inside and out.* User groups expect this, and you can't pull the wool over their eyes. Many presenters seem to know more about their companies than about the products they present, so you'll be well served to understand the basics about your product. While you'll be forgiven if you don't know about some of its more complex capabilities, if you don't know whether it is compatible with a group member's favorite word processor (for example), you can kiss your credibility goodbye. Anticipate that audience members have seen your literature and have read the current reviews (why else would they invite you to speak?). Read them yourself and be prepared to discuss anything and everything—good and bad—that you've read.

- *Don't show them products they can't buy right now (or at least very soon).* User groups expect to see the newest, hottest things, but you should resist the temptation to show them something that won't be available for ten more months. Sure, they'll gobble it up, but they'll also be disappointed when they have to wait to buy and use it. However, if you want to solicit input about a new or upcoming product, go ahead and knock their socks off with it (but make its availability or lack thereof clear). Otherwise, leave it in the car.

ARE YOU READY?

In short, if you can answer these questions, you're probably ready to go: Do you understand your cost/benefit ratio? Is it at an acceptable level? Will you be doing in-person presentations or establishing some type of remote "liaison" program such as Timeworks' Ambassador Program, or both? Will you sell your product directly to the group? At what price? Are you willing to give away product to create excitement at a presentation and help seed your market?

At Timeworks, after two years of putting the pieces in place, our user-group program is ready for a major expansion. Our user-group department is both a marketing/sales vehicle and a successful profit center. Was it worth the investment? Absolutely. We can now launch a new or updated product directly—and affordably—to the most influential segment of our customer base.

Can *you* afford to market to user groups? Can you afford *not* to?

PART NINE

Going Native with Global Marketing

Ever considered "going native"? Not in the sense of put-on-a-grass-skirt-and-roast-a-pig, but rather in the sense of adopting a point of view from outside your own borders. Here, going native equates with going global—selling a product outside your home turf.

Going global isn't necessarily the right thing for every company. Sometimes it's tough enough just to stay afloat at home. But it's important for companies, even smaller ones, to at least consider the potential advantages of competing outside their home markets. To show you why, the following chapters describe the experiences of 11 developers, most of them smaller companies, who do "the international thing." This part also includes insights from two consulting firms who help companies make the transition into international business.

The first two chapters are case studies of development companies and their common—and not so common—experiences in competing in the global marketplace. Chapter 33, "International Success Stories: How Small U.S. Companies Hit It Big Abroad," is about small U. S. companies who compete in other countries. But for a company based outside U.S. borders, going global means breaking *into* the United States (among other places). The companies profiled in Chapter 34, "Cracking the Tough Nut: Adventures in Breaking into the U.S. Market," come from that perspective.

By the way, even if you operate only in the United States, you may not want to overlook Chapter 34. I urge you to read it, especially if you're entering a niche for the first time or are doing new market development in the United States. Why? You face many similar marketing challenges at home that off-shore companies do when trying to break into the U.S. market; their perspectives and advice may give you some extra insight. (It's also fascinating to see the U.S. market as it is perceived by others and what "going native" means to *them*.)

If you're considering European distribution, you should also check out Chapter 21, "The Changing European Distribution Channels: Sorting Out the Options," in Part V of the book. It's packed with information about the nature of European channels and what channels may be best for certain kinds of products. It also includes a model that can help you determine what channels may be right for you.

A final note about the developer stories: Things, as they say, keep on keeping on. So while the key players in these companies—and the companies' international activities—may have changed since these pieces were originally written, the advice they share about going native still holds water.

CHAPTER THIRTY-THREE

International Success Stories

HOW SMALL U.S. COMPANIES HIT IT BIG ABROAD

By David Gleason

David Gleason is a free-lance writer and former localization manager for Apple Computer Europe. He is located in Palo Alto, California.

ALTHOUGH most large, multinational software developers have long been active in the world market, many smaller- and medium-sized U.S. companies still haven't stepped into the global arena. The words "global" and "worldwide" can be intimidating to smaller, resource-limited developers who understandably are hesitant to cross borders—because of the pressures of maintaining a successful business in today's market climate. However, many small development companies are successfully competing in the international marketplace. You don't have to be the size of companies such as Lotus, Microsoft, or Symantec to compete in the world market, but you should understand what is involved before making the commitment.

We spoke with some smaller developers and asked them what they thought made their international forays successful. It was clear from their experiences that it would be difficult to create a step-by-step how-to formula that would work for everyone. But they had a plethora of valuable insight and advice to offer about such important considerations as how they decided to enter markets outside of the United States; evaluated the opportunities; prepared products for foreign markets; planned a strategy for entering the world marketplace; and made contacts with international distributors. We hope that some of their experiences will pleasantly surprise you and prompt you at least to seriously consider if going global is right for you.

The companies profiled here vary widely in size, product line, and marketing and product development strategy. Their experiences illustrate that even a very small firm can be resourceful enough to create and sell products to international markets. They also show that although not all products are right for foreign markets, many kinds of products—such as personal productivity software, screen savers, optical character recognition software, educational products, electronic mail modules, and others—do have international appeal.

EACH IN ITS OWN WAY

Each company successfully found its own path into the larger and more complex world market. Here are their stories.

PASTEL Development Corporation

In 1991, PASTEL Development of New York City created DayMaker, a personal information management product. It was initially designed only for the U.S. market. Some of DayMaker's source code had to be rewritten to meet localization requirements.

PASTEL also searched for a way to use its projected international sales to boost its overall market share and expand product awareness at home. Because entering foreign markets one at a time wouldn't yield the needed revenue quickly enough, PASTEL opted to take a more global approach. PASTEL International Sales Manager Dale Scoggin says, "I don't believe in going piecemeal into one country at a time. Although initially there were a lot of marketing expenses entailed in a global product launch, they were minimal compared to the potential return. I feel that international markets can generate enough working capital to cover the operational costs and finance the steps you must take to generate more and more domestic sales."

From its sales office in Foster City, California, PASTEL followed its domestic release of the updated version of DayMaker with a comprehensive, well-planned worldwide launch; it immediately distributed an English-language version in 12 countries. Scoggin says, "We timed the international launch to coincide with the Macintosh PowerBook introduction and positioned DayMaker as the perfect product to use with the PowerBook to get your life organized." By releasing the English-language version of DayMaker in 12 major world markets, PASTEL quickly captured a significant portion of the Macintosh market share for personal information management software.

Since its global launch, PASTEL has steadily introduced localized versions of DayMaker in all the major markets of Europe, as well as Australia and Japan. It also plans to enter additional countries.

Berkeley Systems, Inc

This Berkeley, California, company is best known for the After Dark screen savers. It entered the U.S. market in 1986 with computer access software for the partially sighted. Its first product was inLARGE, a screen magnifier (later licensed to Apple and included in every Macintosh computer as Closeview). At the time, it was a small firm composed of only six people.

Berkeley Systems Public Relations Manager Monica Granados explains, "The development of our disability products was funded by grants. With government funding generally being cut, we realized that if we wanted to keep producing products for the disability market we had to also get into the mainstream market. So we started the personal products division and created Stepping Out: The Software Big Screen."

With the positive reception of Stepping Out, the commercial possibilities became evident, and in 1989 Berkeley Systems introduced After Dark. Within a year, the product's large domestic sales allowed Berkeley Systems to expand in a way that would have been unthinkable with its smaller, specialized product line. "We sort of backed into international business," Granados says. "Following the After Dark launch in the United States, we got inquiries from dealers, international and domestic distributors, and the press. We had always wanted to get into international marketing, but we felt we were too small to finance it."

The success of After Dark made international expansion too tempting to ignore. Berkeley Systems International Sales Manager Ann Crampton was then hired to expand the international program. She explains: "We had arrangements with distributors to sell Stepping Out II in Australia, Japan, and the U.K., and they picked up After Dark. With all the press coverage we received for the domestic product, all our distributors wanted to carry the product. So we just added it to our existing contracts."

Since releasing the English-language version, Berkeley Systems has localized After Dark into several languages, including Japanese. It works with distributors in Canada, Japan, Mexico, Australia, and nine European countries, including the United Kingdom, Germany, and France.

After Dark has been very successful at home and overseas. The company attributes a good part of that success to the built-in appeal of the product, its affordable price, and the introduction of low-cost color Macintosh computers. "As a screen saver, After Dark is useful, but it's also a product that users can just enjoy," says Crampton. As a low-cost product, After Dark offers too low a margin for some international dealers to sell, but the new trend to "superstores" that sell many products has increased distribution in the United States, Europe, and Japan. International sales of After Dark through distributors now accounts for approximately 15 percent of the company's total business—and the company has since grown to more than 70 employees.

Key Curriculum Press

This education developer, located in Berkeley, California, is a 25-person company that publishes mathematics materials for use in schools. It produces a wide range of education-related materials, including textbooks, workbooks, and video products; software represents about 20 percent of the product line. Key Curriculum's Macintosh product, The Geometer's Sketchpad, is a product that helps students visualize complex mathematical principles.

President Steve Rasmussen found that his motivation for expanding beyond the United States had more to do with his overall philosophy and long-term goals as an educational products publisher than with the compelling forces of the marketplace. He says, "In the long run, we think that strong international contacts will allow us to strengthen our products and keep us aware of international trends that we could use in developing products for the United States. So, our number one goal in establishing international distribution was to create some international educational ties, to take part in an international education idea exchange. Goal two was to generate moderate income from international sales that would not require a large amount of additional work, in terms of human resources, on our part."

Key Curriculum chose markets that were appropriate for its goals. "We sell most of our product line in Australia, because in the area of mathematics materials there is a growing exchange between educators in Australia and the United States. We have also established a distribution and localization arrangement in Japan. We've identified ideas and materials that we want to import from those countries during the next couple of years. In turn, our presence and contacts there will allow us to move into more extensive kinds of business relationships that will potentially allow us to export more products and grow our business," says Rasmussen.

Attain Corporation

Located in Somerville, Massachusetts, Attain is the maker of In Control, a to-do list manager. (The founders of Attain created the original version of FileMaker, which it sold to Claris Corporation.) Attain has five employees and is approaching $1 million in annual revenue from In Control. The company is targeting approximately 40 percent of its total revenue to come from international sales.

Vice President of Sales Jeff Hulton says, "Based on my 11-years' experience in international software distribution, I am convinced that a company like ours can no longer succeed without international sales." Although Hulton knew that Attain had to pursue international markets, the issue was determining the best approach. "Our process for selecting markets was opportunity driven, as is the case for many small companies. We did not have the luxury of sitting back and deciding, in a completely orderly fashion, which market to enter first. We started in the United Kingdom and Australia because there the cost of entry was lowest, and we were approached earlier by distributors. Then came Germany because we found the right distribution partner there," says Hulton.

Caere Corporation

This Los Gatos, California, company produces a number of software products, including the optical character recognition (OCR) products, OmniPage and OmniPage Professional. From the start, Caere's approach has been to build products that could easily be modified for international markets. (For more information about this kind of approach, see "Developing An International Product—From the Start" later in this chapter.) Caere began its international efforts by introducing an internationalized English version, and it later released localized versions into each country. Because OCR software reads characters that are scanned into a computer file, Caere decided that the OmniPage product could easily work with other languages that use the same Latin-based alphabet, such as French, German, and Spanish.

Caere Distribution Manager Matt Miller explains: "Right from the start, we wanted a product that was suitable for the international market. So we made sure that it supported 13 European languages. In OCR, that is very, very important." With its standard OmniPage package, Caere provides filters that allow a user to scan and read text in any of those languages. Having European language support already built in to the OmniPage product was a big asset when Caere began to create localized versions, because all of the OCR capability for that language was already in the product.

Europe was the obvious first choice market into which the company could expand. Caere Director of International Markets Larry Lunetta says, "Western Europe is an excellent first market to attack. Distributors there understand how most United States companies do business. And in Europe, because of the proximity of the markets, you can visit and work with a lot of them more efficiently, whereas in the Far East, you must travel thousands of miles between Australia, Hong Kong, Singapore, and Japan. Plus, right now there is a much larger Macintosh population in Europe than there is anywhere outside the United States."

This doesn't mean that Caere has avoided the Far East. Currently, full OCR capability on personal computers is unavailable for the Japanese market. Such technology requires far more processing power than is currently cost effective because of the enormous number and complexity of characters in Asian languages. (For more about Japan, see "[Just a Few Words About] Cracking the Japanese Market" later in this chapter.) Instead, Caere found a niche market in Japan for English-based software. "The Japanese obviously do a lot of business in English, so I think there's a growing market: Japanese companies who need

English-based tools, such as OCR, and also U.S. companies who are doing business in Japan," Lunetta says. "Caere products have been selling quite successfully in Japan, in conjunction with another company's product that translates Roman characters into Kanji."

As of 1991, Caere's international sales had grown to 39 percent of total revenues. The company is adding new countries in Latin America and is investigating opportunities in Eastern Europe, including those countries that speak Cyrillic-based languages such as Russian, Ukrainian, and Bulgarian.

CE Software

This West Des Moines, Iowa, developer currently derives about a quarter of its revenues from international sales. It manufactures a range of products, such as QuicKeys, DiskTop, CalendarMaker, and Alarming Events, but its best-selling product is QuickMail.

CE Software was convinced to begin international expansion with a 1988 trip to Europe sponsored by the United States Department of Commerce (DOC). (For more information about how you can take advantage of the DOC's help, see "The Commerce Connection" later in this chapter.) A local DOC representative advised CE Software to participate in a trip to London via a "matchmaker program" that was designed to introduce American companies to European distributors. CE Software International Product Manager Paul Miller explains, "We said to him, 'We have seven people in our company, and you want two of us to go to Europe for two weeks? We can't keep up with demand in the United States, so why should we consider international business?' His response to us was, 'The United States isn't always going to be your strongest market. If you start doing international business now, it will be much, much easier as you continue to grow.'"

Also, CE Software has many corporate accounts, and it discovered that many of its U.S-based customers wanted CE Software products, services, and support at corporate sites around the world—a discovery that helped CE Software accomplish international expansion.

On that first European trip, CE Software met with people who would later become its distributors for France and the United Kingdom. It now has distributors in Japan, 14 European countries, Australia, and Mexico.

Each of the just described companies has successfully introduced products in foreign markets. Although they've all experienced problems and unexpected roadblocks, each has found its own, often innovative, path into the world market. But they all had two things in common: an incentive to go international, driven by an awareness that the marketplace favors those who do so, and the right product to sell abroad.

ENTERING THE WORLD MARKET: INCENTIVE AND IMPERATIVE

Truly, national market boundaries have grown increasingly penetrable. "Trade borders" are dissolving, markets are expanding, and buyers are demanding more and more diversified products. The EC market, the enormous Japanese market with its seemingly endless appetite for software, the quickly expanding economies of the Far East, and the recovering economies of Latin America all offer opportunities for sales and expansion that very few U.S. companies can afford to ignore.

Furthermore, in recent years as the recession has taken a toll in the United States, many businesses have found that overseas sales have helped keep them afloat. Some experts speculate that the United States and international markets tend to expand and contract in somewhat staggered cycles. Therefore, some businesses have found that a slowing domestic demand for their products can be offset by increased international demand, thereby allowing their companies to survive and even to grow during hard times at home.

Today, almost half of Apple's total revenues come from outside of the United States. Several things are contributing to Apple's global penetration. There is a large number of localized versions of the Macintosh system software currently available. Furthermore, System 7 includes built-in globalization features such as TextEdit and the Script Manager that make localization into non-Roman languages possible. Also, the WorldScript system software, first incorporated into System 7.1, provides for a single version of the Macintosh operating system to support multiple (and double-byte) languages, including Japanese, Chinese, and Korean. In fact, System 7.1 was the first version of Macintosh system software that could be universally used by Macintosh computers in every country.

Apple also has a business services person assigned to seven regions around the world to assist developers in entering foreign markets. Apple will continue to provide products and services to encourage and assist you in the localization and distribution of software globally. Therefore, the incentive for developers to at least consider going international is there: The huge, developing world marketplace is far from saturated with many kinds of products—and the Macintosh installed base and its international features are in place to support your products. The imperative is also there: Companies that don't go global may be left behind by competitors that do.

MAKING THE BIG DECISION

The process of moving into global markets has been different for each developer. But they all started with the same first step: making the big decision to go international. As PASTEL's Dale Scoggin states, "It can be a tough decision.

Going global changes a business entirely. The whole organization has to change—the company structure, organization, everything." Not every company wants the change, some don't have the resources to handle a global expansion, and not every product has international appeal. You should take a long, hard look at your goals, products, and resources to decide if going international is right for you.

It's particularly important to evaluate your product's international appeal. Is it exclusively U.S.-focused? Does it make assumptions about language, currency, customs, or behavior that are exclusively American (or Western)? Are foreign markets already flooded with similar products that are locally produced and thus less expensive to manufacture and market? Also, because the international marketplace is constantly changing, consider what your product's appeal might be several years from now: Will it still meet users' needs, or will it be rendered obsolete by new developments in software design, marketing, or changing consumer tastes?

Even if you have the right products, there are other key considerations. For example, unless your home office is well managed and your product development is on course, your company will face even more pronounced crises and difficulties if you decide to expand. Therefore, it's important to take a candid look at your company and make certain that you are not jeopardizing domestic operations by expanding internationally.

If you determine that you can support international expansion and that your product is right for non-U.S. markets, the next step is to make the commitment and create a plan to do it right. Your overall business plan must be altered to include international operations. It should forecast for several years, and thus should include plans to periodically reevaluate and, if needed, restructure your foreign operations.

Experienced developers also warn against the natural inclination to initially focus on sales quotas. Your international effort should focus on business/market development. To be successful in the long run, first you must focus on establishing and building the market for your products.

Furthermore, veteran international developers suggest that you assign a person to perform the international function. Don't make it a part-time job for someone who has other responsibilities; if you do, you'll set yourself up for failure right from the start because the effort needed to establish, develop, and nurture international business is tremendous.

ORGANIZING YOUR APPROACH

As you can surmise from the experiences of the companies mentioned earlier, there are many ways to enter a foreign market. The two main strategies are to launch products concurrently in several markets—the global approach—or to enter markets one at a time as opportunities present themselves. In either case, success depends on having an open mind about and awareness of the opportunities for international expansion; you must also be poised to capitalize on them when they appear, that is, be ready for and responsive to opportunities.

The Global Launch

Conducting a global product launch allows you to implement your strategy in an orderly fashion and at a pace that you, not the market, dictate. Although you may be able to launch globally with both localized and English-language products, most often companies entering new markets first release an English language version in a number of major markets, perhaps a dozen or so. Gradually, these companies prepare localized versions for each major market; they then create versions for additional markets as they generate revenue. Often, a convenient time to launch globally is a few months before a major trade show, such as Macworld. This gives you a chance to meet distributors from all over the world, demo your product, and set up further distribution contacts.

PASTEL created a product release plan to leverage two closely timed events that would help promote DayMaker: Macworld in San Francisco and the Macintosh PowerBook introduction. PASTEL launched the English-language international version simultaneously in the United States, ten European countries, Australia, and Japan. Since then, it has released localized versions in all those countries and is steadily adding others, including Mexico, parts of Latin America, and the Middle East.

"The global launch process," says PASTEL's Scoggin, "was relatively straightforward. First, we set up meetings at Macworld with potential distributors. Then, to develop interest we showed them demos and explained how well our product was doing domestically. This allowed distributors to visualize their being able to sell the product in their own markets." It also gave PASTEL a chance to hold a large number of face-to-face meetings in a short time span, which accelerated the process of setting up distribution partnerships in many countries. In addition to finding distributors at Macworld, PASTEL evangelized DayMaker to Apple personnel. "Right after Macworld, every third-party marketing manager at Apple got a copy of DayMaker, a promotional brochure, and a letter of introduction from us. Creating advocates at Apple really helped to spread the word," says Scoggin.

PASTEL's success would not be easy to duplicate. Not every product release can be timed with Macworld or a similar event, and not every company can move into several markets so quickly. However, the PASTEL model is a good example of the method, scope, and timing of a global product launch. And as you can see, a global launch is within reach for even a small company.

Editor's note: For a discussion about the dynamics of conducting a global product launch, see Chapter 35, "How to Approach a Global Product Launch."

One Market At a Time

While a global launch strategy can work for a smaller company, many developers prefer to approach markets one at a time. This might mean targeting large, mature English-language markets such as the United Kingdom, Australia, and Canada. (However, don't forget that although those countries speak the same language, there are subtle nuances in the use of the language and also vast cultural differences to consider when preparing your advertising, promotion, and other marketing materials.) These markets also have software distribution systems that combine characteristics of European and U.S. ones, making your search for distributors who understand your needs and expectations relatively easier than in other parts of the world.

Key Curriculum chose this approach. "Because our product is in English, the first thing we did was identify places where we could market it with the least additional effort. Australia and New Zealand were the first markets for which we found distributors, and we also made contacts in the United Kingdom and Canada," says President Rasmussen.

DEVELOPING AN INTERNATIONAL PRODUCT—FROM THE START

How you approach markets is important, as is having the right product for international markets. But that's just the beginning. Most companies have to make at least some product changes to move into foreign markets. However, if you plan your product for global distribution from its initial design, you'll greatly increase your chances of success and reduce revision costs and time when you enter new markets. (Even if you don't at first anticipate going international with a product, things do change, and you'll probably be doing yourself a big favor if you at least consider potential international markets during product design.)

An excellent first step is to study the *Guide to Macintosh Software Localization*, available from APDA or your local bookseller. By following Apple's guidelines for localization, you can avoid time- and resource-consuming changes to source code. Putting text strings in resources, allowing room for double-byte characters in menus and dialog boxes, and using international resources for date, time, and currency are basics that you should follow, even in the prototype stage.

Localization can be expensive, especially when the costs are multiplied by the number of markets you enter. Every hard-coded text string can either cause an error or require recoding for each market. It's better to do it right the first time, then you don't have to worry about the multiplication factor. Caere Distribution Manager Matt Miller suggests, "Make sure that your product can be easily translated. That will affect how you develop source code and also how you write your product manual. The manual must be well written and concise because translation is not inexpensive."

Also, when launching a product, your attention is focused on getting the product out the door. But the little time and effort it takes to follow the Apple coding guidelines can yield marketing benefits that you may not foresee. For example, while doing a QuickMail demo in Europe, CE Software learned exactly what its programmers had done right. CE Software International Product Manager Paul Miller explains, "At a trade show in the Netherlands, a gentleman asked, 'Will QuickMail run in Arabic?' We had no idea. He told us he had the Arabic Macintosh system software with him and asked us to try it. Our president, Richard Skeie, and I went into the exhibit hall after hours, loaded the Arabic system, and our product worked! We were using part of the Script Manager support, but basically, we used TextEdit."

Even if you plan to market only the English-language version of your software in other countries, avoid the temptation during early design to neglect features that will let your product accommodate multiple languages. If you do so, you may have to pass up a promising market opportunity later on—or spend a lot of money revamping your product.

FINDING THE RIGHT DISTRIBUTOR

Finding a distributor for your products is probably one of the biggest challenges you'll face when launching a product in other countries. You must find a distributor located in the target country who knows the market, has a dealer channel for distributing products and, if needed, can provide service and support. There are many ways to meet distributors, such as attending trade shows, hiring specialized consultants, and using resources such as the Software Publishers Association. All but one of the companies interviewed here said they relied heavily on trade shows for making contacts with the key distributors in various markets.

The Trade Show Connection

Trade shows are an excellent, cost-effective place to make contact with potential distributors. At the major computer trade shows, distributor attendance is high; with a relatively low investment you can meet with many of them face-to-face, demo your product, and discuss your goals and intentions and learn theirs. At that time, you can also discuss follow-up visits to their home offices and to dealers in their home countries. This will allow you to learn the market and understand distributors' concerns, problems, and advantages before you sign a contract.

PASTEL Development Corporation was able to capitalize on the large turnout of distributors at Macworld, where it launched the international version of DayMaker. The constant flow of meetings also allowed PASTEL to meet many potential distributors at once and compare them to each other. That way, PASTEL was able to add distributors during the course of the conference—a critical component of their plan for a rapid, worldwide product launch. Otherwise, they would have been compelled to travel widely to meet distributors in their home countries, and the signup process would have stretched over a period of months. "At Macworld we were booked solid," explains PASTEL's Dale Scoggin. "And as word spread, our meetings were constantly being interrupted by people wanting to schedule more meetings."

Also, distributors who are present at trade shows can see the excitement your product generates among the software-savvy public. That can convince them to carry and push sales for your product. For example, everyone at Berkeley Systems hoped that After Dark would be a runaway hit in non-U.S. markets, but unique modules such as Fish! and Flying Toasters have to be seen in action to be appreciated. "One thing that helped us," explains Berkeley Systems' Ann Crampton, "was attending the foreign trade shows. We even exhibited at CeBit in Hannover, Germany, which was attended by 650,000 people. When they see our booth, the big distributors at first say something like, 'Oh, a little screen saver, isn't that cute?' Initially, they are unable to conceive the volume business that they could do with a product like this. And then they stop and say, 'Wait a minute, you're exhibiting at CeBit? With a screen saver?!' Then the potential of what we've got to offer dawns on them."

The Perfect Distributor?

It isn't a trivial task to find the "perfect" distributor in any market. Indeed, there may be no such thing. Distributors' range of services and expertise vary widely by country, market, and the distributor itself. Obviously, there are many, many considerations when it comes to choosing the right distributor and deciding what you want in one. However, the most important points to take away from this are the need to enter the relationship knowing exactly what you want and to treat your distributor as a partner in your success. For example, Scoggin of PASTEL says, "A key element I look for in a distributor is that it add value, instead of being only a box mover." For PASTEL, the distributor must play an aggressive and intelligent role in generating business in the overseas market.

Key Curriculum's Rasmussen agrees saying, "A perfect distributor for us is one who minimizes the impact on our company in terms of developing business abroad. As a small company, we have our hands full addressing U.S. product demand. If we can find partners who are experts in their own markets, who can minimize the overhead for us to enter those markets, then that's an ideal partner for us."

CE Software values having a solid relationship with a distributor, so it spends time coming to an understanding and mutual distribution agreement. CE Software International Product Manager Paul Miller says, "It's not only the distributor working for us, but we work for him, as well. With one of our distributors, we actually sat and talked about the philosophy of distribution. It turned out that this company had the same philosophy we did, so it was a nice match. And this is important because, obviously, European philosophies can be different than American ones. And in the Pacific, you also run into differences such as in business structures. If you can start with somewhat the same philosophy, you've got a groundwork that you can build on."

Indeed, most companies mentioned in this chapter felt that the essence of a successful relationship is obtaining the distributor's "mind share" so that it is able to concentrate efforts on promoting your product. According to CE Software Executive Vice President Ford Goodman, "A key is to have a distributor who bases a fair amount of its business on the success of your product line. If I'm one percent of somebody's business, then it's pretty unlikely that I'm going to be an important partner to him. If it's 10 or 15 percent, then it's a different ball game. That's not to say that it's the only factor; certainly, we have distributors that are bigger, and they do a great job for us. But it is a key factor, particularly when you are developing a true partnership."

WORKING WITH DISTRIBUTORS

Maintaining good, mutually profitable terms with distributors can often be the most difficult part of the process—one where small, inexperienced companies get into trouble. It would require a separate chapter (at least) to cover all the issues. The companies mentioned in this chapter offer two key pieces of advice: Keep costs down when localizing, and give your distributor an incentive to market for you.

Keep Costs Down

A U.S.-based product is always at a disadvantage to any locally produced product overseas due to costs of localization, transportation, communication with local dealers, and so forth. If you don't localize, your English-language version will almost always have less appeal to local customers; in fact, in France, many products cannot be sold unless they are localized into French.

When you do localize, someone inevitably incurs additional expense that is then passed on to either the distributor or consumer. "You must find a way to pay for the development cost up front so that your partner is not motivated to spend time and effort recouping those expenses," advises Attain's Jeff Hulton. "Make sure that distributors are motivated to achieve market share for you. Get the cost of translation covered up front, and then get it out of the way."

Give Distributors an Incentive

Any distributor, no matter how large or small, veteran or just starting out, needs an incentive to sell and market your product aggressively. Everyone whose product it carries will want full-time attention. You can help provide an incentive to push your product by thoroughly educating distributors about your product's advantages. They will understand this best if they know your product well. Remember, the distributor will have to convince not only customers but also dealers of your product's value. So the education must start with your teaching the distributor.

Attain's Jeff Hulton says, "The history of the personal computer business is littered with relationships that were created just to get a foreign language product out the door, with little attention paid to how that partner would achieve sales for you. The result is a relationship where your partner recoups costs by increasing the product's price by 20 to 30 percent." Often, a promising deal later goes sour because of unforeseen costs. "The result," says Hulton, "is that you end up buying them out two or three years later just to regain control—after the market for your product is destroyed."

Caere decided to find a way to keep its costs down and still offer an incentive to distributors. "We said, 'We'll sell you OmniPage at the U.S. suggested retail price and let you set the retail price for your country. You pay all the marketing and translation costs, but we maintain ownership.' So we both invested a lot into the process, and the distributor in turn felt it had a strong interest, a strong ownership," says Caere's Matt Miller. "And we also told them that because the semi-exclusive relationship was probably going to last at least two or three years, it would give them a window of opportunity to create the market. Almost all of our distributors recognized the opportunity and right away translated the product and our ads and ran them in their market's publications."

Similarly, PASTEL worked out a plan to generate demand for its product with the English version; the plan provided an incentive for distributors to sell the English version and subsequently generate demand for the future localized versions. Dale Scoggin says, "Because there weren't that many localized personal information management products in international markets, I saw that if we 'packed the channel' with the English-language product—got it into distributors' hands—we'd create enough demand to then move the localized product as well—and become a leader in the international personal information management market. So we promised distributors a possible upgrade from the English to the localized version, based on an individual discount plan for each distributor.

"We also worked it out so that the distributor contracted the localization out to a translation company in its own country, so we didn't have to pay for it directly. That was important for us as a small company that can't afford the capital outlay. We gave the distributor a discount on an order of international product. So, for example, the first time the distributor orders the German product, we give a discount to help offset localization costs. It's a good deal for all of us." He admits that such a plan reduces the developer's control over the localization process and requires a strong and reliable distributor to do the job right.

In any case, when working with overseas distributors or even on your own, don't forget to get expert legal advice about import/export requirements, trademark and copyright protection, and other such important matters, which can vary from country to country.

USE AVAILABLE RESOURCES

There are a variety of resources developers can tap into to move to global markets. The developers mentioned in this chapter urge other developers not to overlook one obvious source: Apple. With business services managers in every region, in many circumstances Apple can help provide marketing resources, market data, and most important, key contacts with international distributors, dealers, and other developers. Apple can assist by helping you do such things as sort out the good from the less desirable distributors. If you've worked closely with Apple before, you may also be able to use Apple people for references during the process of finding and working with a distributor. In any case, the earlier you can get Apple involved, the more it can help you.

On-line services, such as AppleLink, can be excellent resources for getting information about international opportunities. We strongly recommend that before you contact Apple you review the international information available on AppleLink. Apple also publishes a variety of articles, brochures, and other materials about a variety of markets.

The Commerce Connection

Another important resource is the United States Department of Commerce (DOC). A good example of what this resource can offer developers is CE Software's experience. That company took advantage of an offer by the local office of the United States Department of Commerce (DOC) to attend a trade seminar in Europe. It was part of a "matchmaker" program, one of an ongoing series that brings together American manufacturers and non-U.S. distributors.

A DOC officer located in Iowa, home of CE Software, strongly suggested that CE Software participate in the program to start doing business in the United Kingdom. Despite concerns that it was spreading resources too thin by sending two people to Europe for two weeks, CE Software conceded. It was rewarded for taking what it had perceived as a risk.

According to CE Software's International Product Manager Paul Miller, the matchmaker program was "basically a consulting relationship, where the DOC advised us on how to get started overseas. It ingrained in us very strongly what our expectations should be. For example, they said, 'Don't plan on setting up partners your first week in the United Kingdom; in some cases, you'll have to make a couple of trips and just initially meet with the distributors.' They taught us that the European and Japanese business culture requires making friends first, before you actually do business. You're on their turf, so you learn to do business the way their culture does it. For example, in Spain or Italy, you don't do business at two o'clock in the afternoon."

Miller recounts his European experience: "We ended up with 60 or 70 meetings during that one week. The first day we were in London, after the meetings were over Richard Skeie, our company president, said, 'If nothing else, we've had enough meetings now to already have paid for the trip, in knowledge gained.' The third day, our comment was, 'Now we've had so many meetings that we're totally confused.'"

Despite CE Software's initial concern, the trip was so valuable that Miller says, "Any domestic company that is not utilizing the capabilities of the U.S. Department of Commerce ought to be. If nothing else, you get tremendous information about foreign copyright policies, export requirements, and legal issues; we also get continuous reports from the DOC." And, the shove from the DOC into the international sphere was what CE Software needed to get started.

CE Software is not the only developer to be approached by Commerce for such a program. According to Caere Distribution Manager Matt Miller, "The

U.S. Department of Commerce contacted me about two years ago; it had been contacted by the Ministry of Trade in Japan, as part of the effort to help rectify the balance of trade between the United States and Japan. They wanted to bring 30 or so U.S. software manufacturers into the Japanese market. The DOC told us, 'We want to have a small, table-top trade show and bring in key Japanese distributors, corporate accounts, and resellers; we'll have you meet them and help match you with the right partners.'" Caere participated in the trip, and Miller says, "We went over there and had six fully packed days with business dinners at night, hosted by the Japanese Ministry of Trade. Our cost was $2,000 plus travel expenses."

Caere Director of International Markets Larry Lunetta adds, "If you say to the Department of Commerce, 'I don't have a distributor in this particular country,' it will package your marketing material and, for a nominal fee, will send it to the person who runs the trade desk in the U.S. embassy in that country. His or her job is to make your material available to potential distributors and see if one of them is interested in picking up your product."

The U.S. Department of Commerce will not take the place of your international sales and marketing staff, but with the right contacts and opportunities, it can help you get started in foreign markets by applying the enormous resources of the United States government. For more information about the expert assistance available from a variety of federal agencies and the Department of Commerce, call (800)USA-TRADE.

(JUST A FEW WORDS ABOUT) CRACKING THE JAPANESE MARKET

Finally, no discussion about going international would be complete without saying a few words about the Japanese market. The western image of Japan is often one of a closed society, hostile to foreign trade and controlled by a closely knit association of the Ministry of International Trade and Industry (MITI), the huge Japanese banks, and the industrial cartels. This common anxiety is compounded by the fact that distributors in Japan tend to be very large organizations, often subsidiaries of the huge Japanese global corporations. Doing business with them can be both confusing and intimidating.

In fact, books have been written on the subject. But even small developers can crack the Japanese market, as evidenced by the experiences of the companies mentioned in this chapter. Indeed, experiences at Macworld Tokyo and other meetings have shown developers that the Japanese market is hungry for software.

But the thought of doing business in Japan can be intimidating, at first. At the very least, say developers mentioned in this chapter, many American companies are made uneasy by the cultural and linguistic differences between the United States and countries such as Japan. But by learning the cultural expectations of your potential Japanese partners, carefully considering the Japanese market's needs, and then examining your product's distinguishing characteristics, you can often find unexpected opportunities.

Key Curriculum President Steve Rasmussen explains how Apple Computer worked with him to get established in the Japanese educational software market: "Through Apple, I established a relationship with a Japanese distributor who was focusing on the education market. These contacts started with correspondence and an AppleLink discussion; then at some point, we established personal contact. "In Japan, personal contact is very, very important in establishing a relationship. We spent some time meeting with distributors who were here from Japan; that personal relationship and understanding, I think, were important in establishing the dialog that lead to the localization of our product."

As with distributors anywhere, in Japan it is important to negotiate specific, mutually acceptable terms that include all the localization steps and other necessary tasks that prepare your product for the competitive Japanese market. "If you sit down and work out the details, you can create really good guidelines as to who does what," says CE Software International Product Manager Paul Miller. "Our distributor in Japan actually sent a programmer to our offices to assist us. The main area we had trouble with was printing capabilities. As we worked with Kanji and its two-byte characters—our QuickMail product didn't initially provide for that—they had to come in and modify some code."

In considering the Japanese market, CE Software identified and exploited an unexpected sales opportunity. Executive Vice President Ford Goodman says, "We had an advantage because Apple released the Japanese version of the system (Kanji) in the United States and Canada, where there are large Japanese-speaking populations. So we do have additional sales of Japanese versions in these locations." By selling Japanese versions of their products through U.S. and Canadian distributors, CE Software was able to increase its overall sales of these products and help recover localization costs.

A common advantage for Macintosh developers is the consistency of Macintosh system software, which offers benefits for the Japanese market where many players are contending with a wide range of operating systems. "The PC side of the house is very fragmented," says Caere Director of International Markets Larry Lunetta. "There are multiple platforms, multiple operating systems, and various environments to develop in. Furthermore, you can have multiple types of operating systems running on a single system, such as a

NEC machine. And even for Windows, there's a Windows for NEC, a Windows for Fujitsu. Apple is nicely homogeneous there."

YOUR FUTURE MAY BE AT STAKE

Despite the risks and potential difficulties, the motivation for even small companies to at least consider going international has never been greater. In fact, some feel it is more than important; it is imperative. Attain's Jeff Hulton sums it up: "Start today. Get going before your competitor does. And remember what an Apple executive once said—you should reinvent your future before someone else does it for you!"

CHAPTER THIRTY-FOUR

Cracking the Tough Nut

ADVENTURES IN BREAKING INTO THE U.S. MARKET

By Dee Kiamy, Open Door Communications

Dee Kiamy is president of Open Door Communications, a strategic communications consulting practice located in San Jose, California, that serves high-technology and entertainment companies. She also developed and edited this book.

THE U.S. market. *Hmmm.* It's a tough nut to crack, as they say in America. It would be misleading to tell you that breaking into the U.S. market is simple or straightforward, or that it's like anything else you've ever tried. *It's not.* The country is large, the competition fierce, the number and kind of local products vast, and the distribution channels complex.

However, it may be a mistake to summarily discount the notion of cracking the U.S. market. Bear in mind that because the overall market is so large, it may be worth the perceived risk if you can become even moderately successful there. Furthermore, some companies feel that doing business in America helps boost their home-country credibility; these developers say they are perceived at home as being more profitable and stable if they are successfully doing business in a country as large as the United States.

Several non-U.S. developers (even very small companies) are witness to the fact that breaking into this market isn't out of the question if you do your homework, take time to understand the cultural and business dynamics of the country and its market—and adapt yourself accordingly. To help you weigh the issues and better understand what it takes to be successful in the United States, I spoke with four companies—ACI, InterOptica, Logal, and Blyth Software—about their experiences in cracking this nut. First, I'll cite a brief history of each company's efforts to break into the U.S. market, and then describe some of the advice they offered.

COMPANIES THAT HAVE MADE IT IN THE UNITED STATES

Here are the stories of four companies, each of which has overcome its own set of odds and challenges to crack the U.S. market.

Logal/Israel

Logal is an education software developer that successfully entered the U.S. Macintosh market in late 1990. Today, the 30-employee firm sells a lineup of more than 20 products in the United States, including such titles as the Explorer series (including Physics Explorer, Biology Explorer, and Geometry Inventor) and the What's the Story? series. Currently, about 40 percent of Logal's total revenues come from sales to U.S. customers.

Getting started in the United States was a long process for Logal that began in 1987 when a group from the Boston Science Museum visited Israel. After seeing demonstrations of Logal's PC-compatible education products, the museum invited the developer to make a presentation in the United States to a select group of Boston-area publishers and university professors. Despite its efforts at that time, Logal was unsuccessful at establishing a U.S. publishing and distribution arrangement for Step (an early incarnation of the Explorer series). However, two years later, the Cambridge, Massachusetts-based research and development specialist BBN—which had experience in the U.S. education market—pointed out that Logal had a "great idea, great product—wrong machine" and suggested that the developer rewrite the application for the Macintosh.

Being a small company with limited resources, Logal was forced to find creative ways to fund porting its product to the Macintosh. It applied for and received a design and development grant from the Bird Foundation, an industrial research and development foundation that funds up to 50 percent of qualified joint projects between Israeli and U.S. companies. By 1989, the Macintosh product was ready to ship, and Logal and BBN signed an agreement with Sunburst, an American firm that would publish the product in the United States. BBN acted as consultant and codeveloper, and Sunburst as the U.S. publisher.

Sunburst provided Logal with guidelines for localizing the product for the United States. In late 1990, Sunburst began marketing this product as Physics Explorer–Gravity under its Wings For Learning name. The product has been sold mostly by Sunburst through mail-order catalogs. But now, Logal is considering expanding its U.S. distribution.

ACI/France

ACI, the French company that produces the well-known 4D database application, began its U.S. success story in 1987, just two-and-a-half years after becoming established in France. Prior to that, says CEO Marylène Delbourg-Delphis, there had been no successful database application for the Macintosh and no U.S. distributor interested in such a product.

However, in 1987 the Macintosh market expanded and market interest in a variety of Macintosh products, including databases, began to grow. Because Apple showed a strong interest in 4D (and after a U.S. firm offered to purchase it), ACI felt the product's market potential was large enough to justify entering the U.S. market on its own. The company subsequently opened a subsidiary in Cupertino, California, in the heart of Silicon Valley (and on Apple's doorstep). The business has grown steadily, and today ACI has offices in seven other U.S. cities—and has plans for more.

ACI, known at that time in the United States as ACIUS, began its U.S. distribution through Apple's traditional retail channels—computer dealers—one of the channels in which ACI still distributes its products. However, the company also aggressively marketed itself directly to customers and to the "fourth-party" development community. (These developers design and market custom applications that help make 4D even more attractive and useful to users.) One-third of ACI's total revenues now come from the United States, where the company lays claim to approximately 65 percent of the database application market share.

InterOptica/Hong Kong

InterOptica is a privately held Hong Kong-based publisher of CD-ROM travel titles such as *Great Cities of the World* and *Great Wonders of the World*. Having created products from scratch, especially for the U.S. market, InterOptica earns 99 percent of its revenues from U.S. customers. The company was founded in early 1990 by Catherine and Simon Winchester. Catherine, a programmer, and husband Simon, a travel writer, decided to combine their talents to develop and publish CD-ROM titles.

The company first broke into the market in 1991 by bundling its discs with hardware sold by original equipment manufacturers (OEMs) such as NEC and Sony. Winchester originally thought the titles market would first explode in Japan where most of the discs and drives were manufactured. However, she soon discovered that the installed base was developing much faster in the United States. At the same time, OEMs such as NEC encouraged her to do business with their U.S. subsidiaries.

InterOptica hired an agent in the United States to negotiate agreements with OEMs and to provide customer technical support. Even though the company had only five or six major OEM customers, it essentially had thousands of end users who required support for its CD title. To handle that support locally and give customers the attention InterOptica felt was needed, it quickly opened a U.S. branch office.

In 1992, after a series of successful bundle deals with U.S. subsidiaries of non-U.S. OEM companies—and with the installed base of CD-ROM drives growing at a much swifter rate—InterOptica began capitalizing on the mass appeal of its titles. (Because the titles were originally intended for bundling, InterOptica had created them to appeal to as broad an audience as possible.) The company began selling its titles in U.S. retail channels such as CompUSA, Radio Shack, and others. Because selling through multiple retail channels entailed a much more complex series of negotiations and reached more customers who would require support, InterOptica's decision to open a U.S. branch office paid off.

Currently, retail sales yield approximately 25 percent of InterOptica's U.S. business, and that number is expected to grow. To help increase its U.S. exposure, InterOptica also does "work for hire," developing CD titles for such large U.S. publishers as Random House and Macmillan New Media.

Blyth Software/United Kingdom

Blyth Software is the developer of the Omnis Seven client-server application development environment. The company started life in the United Kingdom but has since shifted its headquarters to the United States. After becoming successful in the United Kingdom, Blyth first attempted to break into the U.S. market in 1985 with a personal database product and applications. Because at that time industry interest in a Macintosh database product had not yet developed, Blyth made the decision to develop across platforms and created a Windows version of Omnis to increase sales. That product was sold in U.S. retail channels and enjoyed only a modest degree of success.

Blyth moved its company headquarters to the United States in 1987 to better position itself to compete in the larger U.S. market. In 1991, Blyth was struggling somewhat to compete with both a Windows and Macintosh version of its product in the cutthroat retail channels against competitors that sold in the $400-$500 range. It was making headway, says CEO Michael Minor, but not achieving the volume that its competitors enjoyed.

The breakthrough came in 1992 when Blyth repositioned the product (and company) to attract corporate customers instead of individuals, small businesses, and department work groups. The company also repositioned its product from being a stand-alone database application to a client-server product that could take advantage of the corporate multiplatform environment. Repositioning entailed making a number of changes, including pulling out of retail channels and selling directly to corporate customers, which Blyth now does with a 16-person North American and U.K. sales force. The company has also aggressively pursued its relationship with fourth-party developers and industry vendors such as Apple Computer and IBM.

Those decisions set the company on its current course. Today, approximately 70 percent of Blyth's revenues come from U.S. sales.

A FEW KEY PIECES OF ADVICE

Each of these companies chose a different path into the U.S. market. But while their early beginnings differ, their advice about what it takes to succeed in the United States is strikingly uniform, with only a few exceptions. Unfortunately, their anecdotes and suggestions are too extensive to include in this chapter, so here are a few of the key considerations they feel are important for developers trying to crack the U.S. market.

Don't Make Qualitative Comparisons; Instead, Look at the Differences

Mindset is critical when you approach a market as vast and complex as the United States. When examining the U.S. market, it's tempting (and natural) to make qualitative comparisons between it and your home market. But *how* you look at the differences is critical. You'll make a big mistake, say developers who have succeeded in the United States, if you predispose yourself to harboring a "good/bad" or "right/wrong" mindset. Instead, look at this challenge from the perspective of "What are the *differences* between my market and the American one? How can I adapt and adjust the way I do business to accommodate those differences?" That, these developers say, will put you in the right frame of mind to create a successful plan of attack.

Also, if you probe for and try to understand the differences, you'll be less likely to take them for granted. "You can't take *anything* for granted when you approach the U.S. market," says ACI CEO Marylène Delbourg-Delphis. "Everything is different there. If you're receptive to that fact, you'll be much more successful in the United States." (Although much of the advice in this chapter may seem to underscore the obvious, embodied in it are often-overlooked details that are easy to take for granted.)

Learn As Much As Possible About American Business Practices

The business environment and practices in the United States are likely to be very different from those in your local market. To succeed, you'll probably have to forfeit many of your basic assumptions about the way you do business and, as much as it may at first rub you the wrong way, adopt patterns and habits that are more "American."

"America is such a huge country that it doesn't need to look outside itself for products and resources to the same degree that Asian and European countries do," says InterOptica Managing Director Catherine Winchester. "Therefore, Americans are accustomed overall to doing business mostly with Americans. They feel comfortable with that, and for them to feel comfortable doing business with *you*, it's important that you do things the American way," she says.

A variety of practices differ, but here are two key items that Winchester identified.

- *Working hours and days.* Americans work different hours and days of the week than do businesses in some other countries. For example, Winchester points out, in Hong Kong many offices are open on Saturday mornings, and in some countries such as China, companies operate a full six days each week. But most U.S. corporations (large and small) conduct business from Monday to Friday, usually for eight to nine hours a day between 8 A.M. and 5 P.M. While individual workers or the occasional company may choose to work weekend hours, the norm is Monday through Friday. "For that reason," says Winchester, "on the whole it would be unrealistic to expect American companies to be responsive to your requests on the weekends."

- *Pace.* The business pace in the United States often tends to be more frenetic than in other countries. Because many U.S. companies make extensive use of such tools as electronic mail, voice mail, and toll-free telephone numbers, they usually expect to be able to move quickly on almost any issue. "Americans live in a culture that breeds instant gratification. They want to pick up the phone and get things done—not sit down, write a letter, fax it, and then wait for the response," says Winchester. They also don't expect a business phone to go unanswered; they expect a line to be picked up at least by an answering machine or voice mail.

  Therefore, electronic mail services such as AppleLink—which can be accessed from an increasing number of other on-line services such as Internet, MCI Mail, CompuServe, and others—are effective, quick-response tools for doing business with U.S. companies and customers.

Business pace also affects how you'd structure customer service operations. In the United States, customers often expect to be given toll-free telephone numbers for making product inquiries and obtaining technical support. These phone lines sometimes are staffed 24 hours a day, seven days a week. So it might be unrealistic to ask customers to pay for a long-distance telephone call to get technical support or order products, as it would it be to expect them to stay awake until midnight in their local time zones to reach you in your offices.

"Likewise," adds Winchester, "faxes are viewed differently in the United States than in some other countries. In the States, people don't send faxes when they want to get information fast. Instead, they pick up the telephone and call the person they want to do business with. My experience says that I could send a hundred faxes to the United States and it would accomplish far, far less than it would here in Asia. Americans just don't view the fax machine as a quick-response tool. But in Asia, we rely very heavily on faxes. When I'm sitting in Hong Kong trying to do business with the United States via fax, I can't accomplish anywhere near as much as our U.S.-based office can."

Be Adaptable

As you can see, the American marketplace operates very differently than most other markets. Understanding those differences is the first step; adapting to them is the next critical challenge.

Being flexible and patient is a step in the right direction, says Logal President Yoel Givol. "To get the attention of U.S. companies, you must be very flexible and willing to listen, which is often difficult," he says. "After a while we realized that we couldn't just call the shots in the huge U.S. market, especially because we come from such a small country as Israel. Furthermore, saying things like, 'Well, it works this way in Israel' won't get you anywhere because Americans do business their own way. You have to listen and learn how the market works there, immerse yourself in the system.

"If you want to work with a publisher or distributor, you really must prove yourself over a long period because it is much easier for American companies to find someone to do business with next door. You also must be patient, because it takes time for U.S. companies to become confident in developers from other countries who do things differently and who may be 6,000 miles away. From the U.S. point of view, it's very risky for a publisher or distributor to contract with a company that is far away, perhaps even in a country they've never visited," says Givol.

That is why Logal entered the U.S. market in two stages. "First we worked with a research center and a codeveloper, each of which had experience in the U.S. market; their experience helped us understand how to demonstrate that our product would work in the American market," says Givol. Armed with that insight, Givol was better positioned to pursue a business relationship with a U.S. republisher/distributor.

Don't Underestimate U.S. Geography and Diversity; Segment Accordingly

It's ironic that the same thing that makes the U.S. market seem so daunting is also the factor that makes it an immensely appealing proposition for businesses—it's sheer size, in terms of geography and number of customers. The country encompasses five time zones, tropical and arctic climates, and an incredibly diverse—and large—number of potential customers. That's reflected in the quantity of Macintosh computers sold in the country: Currently, industry estimates indicate there are upwards of six million units in the installed base, a number that is expected to grow substantially in the next few years.

"Europeans get dizzy when they think about the size of the U.S. market," says ACI's Delbourg-Delphis. "When we first decided to enter this market, it occurred to me that there were more Macintosh computers in California alone than in all of France. I decided that if we could be successful with our product in California, then we could survive in the United States."

The lesson here is to ignore the natural inclination to view the United States as a single market. It actually is composed of a plethora of market segments, a variety of buying patterns, and a large number of opinion leaders and buying influencers. Each geographic area of the United States has its own peculiarities, mini-cultures, and customer attitudes. Although Americans share many things in common, remember that demographic traits such as the average income and education level and general degree of computer literacy can vary widely from region to region. For example, the average degree of computer literacy in northern California is heavily influenced by the presence of Silicon Valley. People in the heartland of Iowa, however, where a major industry is farming and food production, may have a totally different outlook on purchasing computer technology.

It's important to carefully choose exactly which segments to target and which ones to ignore. If you target wisely, then what is otherwise an almost impenetrable giant becomes an approachable entity.

Be Realistic About the Nature of U.S. Competition

The sheer size and diversity of the United States breeds fierce competition. American customers have an amazingly large and diverse array of locally produced products to choose from. (To really get an appreciation for this, visit a U.S. computer superstore or browse through one of the many mail-order catalogs.) ACI's Delbourg-Delphis says, "People in the United States aren't just sitting and waiting for European products to come to them. They have so many resources at their disposal, and the United States is pretty much self-sufficient, considering the size of the country." If you have a realistic understanding of the scope and ferocity of competition in that country, you'll be more likely to make sound decisions.

To be adequately prepared to move into any U.S. market segment, you therefore must conduct a thorough assessment of your U.S. competition: the audience it reaches, pricing, distribution, marketing strategies, and other important aspects. Armed with this information—and a solid, technically excellent product—you can make a more realistic decision about whether and how to break into the market.

You *Must* Localize for the United States

Applications that succeed in the United States are, almost without exception, English-language products. Therefore, a product and its documentation sold into this market should be thoroughly localized for culture and language, paying particular attention to the use of American English.

"It's my perception that, on the whole, American consumers are intolerant of products that aren't totally localized," says Blyth Software President and CEO Michael Minor. "They aren't like Europeans who are willing to accept the English-language or quasi-localized versions because in the United States it's very competitive; customers have such a wide range of products to choose from."

However, localizing your product for the United States also means localizing your own mindset. "There are many cultural differences between the United States and other countries, and setting up business in the United States requires a significant change in one's life and mindset," says ACI's Delbourg-Delphis. "You can't project your own cultural habits onto Americans. You have to get rid of your bias, forget what you've heard people in your country say about what they think the United States is all about, and look at the United States—how the people live, how they think—with a fresh eye. And to understand the U.S. cultural prototype requires complete immersion in that culture. I don't think it's the kind of thing that can be totally explained to you. It has to enter through your skin, so to speak, and you must be receptive to the differences.

"This includes everything from the way you look at images to the way you position your software. For example, in the European database market you generally focus first on a product's technical capabilities. In the U.S. database market you must of course sell a technically excellent product—but focus on the interface. That is just one example of how you must change your point of view," she says.

Developers interviewed for this chapter seemed to feel strongly that localizing a product *in* the United States is important. Seemingly subtle details can make your product scream "I'm not American!" Making a simple mistake such as using the British word *colour* (instead of the American *color*), or using metric units of measurement and degrees Celsius instead of feet, inches, and Fahrenheit can be deadly. Localizing a product in the United States helps avoid such oversights. And if you can get U.S. customers to give you input or participate in that process, all the better.

Do Everything Possible to Create a Local Presence

Being perceived as a local company, at least one that does business locally, is without a doubt an important component of success in the United States, especially given the heated competition in that country. Depending on your particular situation, there are steps to take beyond localization that can help create the impression that you're a local player.

Logal has successfully entered the U.S. market by developing a relationship with a publisher there. That publisher handled Logal's manufacturing, distribution, and technical support—everything needed to get the product off the ground and selling in America.

When you're far away from customers and business partners, how well you communicate with these constituencies and handle such things as time differences can have a major impact on whether you're perceived as being a local player. The effort needed to stay in touch with the market and cultivate partner and customer relationships can be proportionate to your distance from the United States. "We have the largest AppleLink bill in Israel," jokes Logal's Givol, who adds that he couldn't do business in the United States without it.

"We do almost everything by electronic mail, including shipping our code to our U.S. publisher. However, we've made the 10-hour time difference work to our advantage. In essence, we work with the publisher 24 hours a day: During our work day, we create things and ship them via AppleLink to California at the end of our day—just as our U.S. partners are starting theirs. Then, while we sleep they work; when we come into the office the next morning, the cycle repeats itself," says Givol. Working from afar also means frequent visits to the United States and extensive travel within the country.

On the other hand, ACI, Blyth Software, and InterOptica chose to open subsidiaries or branch offices to handle their business in the United States. Whether to open an office in the United States is a difficult (and sometimes downright scary) decision. It's a big step for any developer and one that shouldn't be taken lightly. However, it would be a mistake to automatically discount the possibility of opening a U.S. office just because your gut feeling is that it might be too costly and difficult. Even smaller companies have successfully opened and maintained branch offices in the United States. (For a discussion about things to consider when setting up a subsidiary, see Chapter 37, "Setting Up a Subsidiary: How to Transition Away from a Distributor and Set Up Your Own Office," written by a developer with experience in this area.)

To give you an idea of what's involved, here's InterOptica's story. Based in Hong Kong, InterOptica opened a U.S. office (in San Francisco, California) for several reasons. "We had to support a large number of users who had received our product bundled with the hardware they bought. And as we moved into retail channels, we realized that it would be too much to expect that key people such as buyers, distributors, and manufacturers' representatives stay up until midnight to phone us. Let's face it: There are so many local companies located right there in their own time zones that they can buy from, and we had to remove any barriers to doing business with us," says Managing Director Catherine Winchester.

"Based on our experience, my advice would be for a foreign company to open a U.S. office as soon as it can possibly afford it," says Winchester. "Otherwise, it may land in a chicken-and-egg situation: The company may never be able to afford a U.S. office if it doesn't get the necessary volume of sales, and it may not get the volume if it doesn't sell from a local base."

The U.S. branch office serves several purposes for InterOptica. "On the technical side, the office provides support to U.S. customers. It also offers valuable information to our development teams in Hong Kong and China because virtually every hardware and software tool we use is from a U.S. company," says Winchester. "The heart of the multimedia world is in the United States, and we need to have immediate access to industry changes and developments. That's particularly important for us because it usually takes new hardware and software many months to arrive here, and we would rarely see early or beta versions of products if we didn't have a U.S. office. We need to be on the seed list for beta versions, and our San Francisco office acts as a liaison for gathering this information," she explains.

InterOptica's U.S. office also manages the manufacturing, which is done in the United States. A main reason: "The language barrier can present some interesting problems," Winchester says. "I make my discs in the United States because we make a large number of shipments to U.S. customers. If anything gets lost in the translation when we issue manufacturing or shipping instructions, we're dead in the water—and we can't afford that. Basically I feel it's safer if, when we need to ship discs to Idaho, the shipper knows where Idaho is," says Winchester.

Another major responsibility of the branch office is sales and marketing. Although most of the strategy is planned in Hong Kong with input from the U.S. office, says Winchester, it's up to the U.S. employees to implement the strategies. They also do such things as organize and work the major U.S. trade shows (eight major ones in 1992!)—a gargantuan task that would be all but impossible to manage from Hong Kong alone, Winchester says.

The logistics of opening a branch office—finding office space, arranging for utilities, and the like—were fairly straightforward, Winchester says. However, finding the people to staff the office was more difficult.

Winchester explains: "Finding the right people to run your U.S. office is essential. Since you, as the manager, are far away and out of sight, you need people you can trust, people who are reliable, hardworking, and ambitious. You don't want a branch office 5,000 miles away being run by people who feel they can get away with working short hours and coming and going as they please. So, hiring people who really know what they are doing and who really care about the company and want it to succeed is crucial. And we've been lucky; we found those people."

She also says that hiring local talent is a must. If you don't hire Americans to work in your U.S. office, people who know their ways around in the everyday U.S. business environment, you may defeat some of the benefit you hoped to gain from opening a U.S. office.

The branch office, located in downtown San Francisco, costs InterOptica approximately $20,000 a month to operate, including salaries, rent, phone and other services, travel, and so forth. "It may sound like a lot of money, but the cost of trying to do business in the United States from Hong Kong would probably be even higher, in that we wouldn't be able to get the sales we need to be successful in the U.S," says Winchester. "We could try to do business from our Asian base, but we feel we couldn't properly represent ourselves from way over here in Hong Kong."

A caution: If you do opt to open a U.S. office, it's important to be realistic about how much it will cost to do business in America. The size of the U.S. market, the degree of competition, and the number of opinion leaders all lead to one question: What must you spend to achieve the presence you need?

Of course, there's no single answer. When assessing this important factor, bear in mind the necessity of traveling extensively in a very large country, attending a variety of major trade shows, advertising and public relations costs, meeting with channel representatives (who may be spread across the country), and other important budget eaters. (For a discussion of how to set up a subsidiary, see Chapter 37, "Setting Up a Subsidiary: How to Transition Away from a Distributor and Set Up Your Own Office.")

Learn U.S. Channels

If you opt to open a U.S. office and work the distribution channels yourself, you should first become well versed in the nature and scope of those channels. Distribution in the United States is markedly different than in other countries; there are a wide variety of channels, and again, competition can be fierce. Dealing with a U.S. distributor is also likely to be more costly than working with your local one. For example, in many countries, distributors are responsible for creating market demand for the products they carry and often foot the bill for the necessary activities (sometimes including product packaging and manu-facturing). In America, on the other hand, distributors often expect developers themselves to create the demand that will draw customers into stores to buy products—an undertaking that can sport a high price tag. (For a detailed description of how one national U.S. distributor operates, see Chapter 19, "Understanding U.S. Distribution Realities: How to Approach a National Distributor.")

However, if you opt to partner with a U.S. publisher—who may include packaging, marketing, and local manufacturing in the deal—your partner then may shoulder much or all of the responsibility for working in U.S. channels.

Get Good Legal Advice

In addition, the legal aspects of doing business in the United States are cer-tainly different from those in your home country. Trademark and copyright protection laws differ between countries, as do other key practices such as those regarding contracts, patents, and other such items.

In the United States, some commerce and tax practices are governed not only by the federal government but also by individual states. Getting solid legal advice regarding doing business in the United States can help you avoid potential problems that you may otherwise be unaware of and will help you get off to a good start.

Get Close to U.S. Customers

Developers who have succeeded in the United States invariably emphasize the importance of getting to know the mindset and motivations of customers in that country, and developers go to great lengths to foster strong relationships with customers. A key, say these developers, is to shed your tendency toward an inner-company focus and look outward into the customer community.

Blyth Software President and CEO Michael Minor calls it "partnering with customers." "It's especially difficult to get close to customers if you distribute products through an intermediary such as dealers and distributors, who generally are more at arm's length from users," says Minor. Therefore, the burden falls on the developer to keep a finger on the pulse of the user community.

He adds: "Lots of people think that the key to success is creative marketing. But today, with technology changing so rapidly and new competitors continuously entering the ring, the only true safety net is being very close to your customers. Because of this, we proactively canvas customers. Of course, we try to address customer technical problems when they call us, but we also solicit customer input about our products and services and visit them as much as possible. Furthermore, our engineering teams meet with customers regularly to get their input about market requirements for future products. In that sense, we are partnering with customers."

Staying close to customers has other important benefits. In the long run, to be successful in the United States where technology plunges rapidly forward, it's particularly important to have a long-term vision of where your technology and market and competition are going and to manage your business accordingly. "That's very difficult," says Minor, "but one thing that helps is staying close to your customers and making sure you understand their needs. Then you must take steps to assure that those needs are met by your current and future products."

Many developers who have been successful in the United States spend a great deal of time traveling there and meeting with customers in various venues. Meeting with user groups, for example, was a key entrée into the U.S. customer base for ACI. "If you think you're selling to 'a market,' you're off track," says ACI CEO Delbourg-Delphis. "The reality is that *individual people* are your customers, and they are the ones you should be trying to reach. User groups are composed of these individuals; in many cases they are Macintosh fanatics—a very valuable audience. Overall, we really care about getting feedback from individuals."

She also says that many developers are under the mistaken impression that user groups are made up mostly of home users. "Not true," she says. "These groups are made of people from large corporations as well as small businesses, and everything in between."

Indeed, user group members have proven to be strong buying influencers for many products. These "fanatics" often are quite vocal about their product preferences, and they are frequently called on to recommend products to friends and colleagues. They also act as impromptu training and technical support people for other group members, family, and friends. These customers are so important that Apple Computer devotes significant resources to fostering and supporting user groups and often helps developers take advantage of its relationship with this constituency.

Another example of getting close to U.S. customers comes from Logal, who with its U.S. partner, Sunburst, also works with education constituencies such as the National Science Teachers Association. They sponsor booths at exhibitions and offer workshops at their conferences.

Yet another way to get closer to customers from afar is to use U.S. on-line services. They can provide excellent feedback from users at a relatively low cost. For example, you can start a discussion or forum on CompuServe or America Online that allows you to "converse" electronically with customers regardless of distance or time zone. Likewise, you may opt to publish your own bulletin board on the AppleLink network. By posting such things as pricing information, parts lists, data sheets, and technical information to your bulletin board, you can give customers and channels increased access to your company—virtually 24 hours a day. (For information about how one developer uses AppleLink this way, see Chapter 27, "Using On-line Services as a Marketing and Support Tool: How We Use the AppleLink Network.")

Partner Wherever You Can

Taking on the U.S. market on your own can seem a gargantuan task. However, if you partner with other companies who have experience in the United States, you'll in essence create allies who can help you negotiate the complex maze of opportunities and challenges. You'll also increase the clout you get with your limited resources, and you'll receive input that will help you position a product and decide what other offerings would be good candidates for the market.

Logal is a good example of partnering; earlier in this chapter, you read how that company joined forces with a U.S. firm and a research foundation, each of which had U.S. experience. This was critical to Logal's ability to establish a business relationship in the United States. "We also try to take advantage of Apple's comarketing opportunities," says Logal President Givol. When Apple introduces a major new product, it offers developers who have a new product that showcases the Apple product or technology an opportunity to participate in a variety of activities. They include such things as participation in press briefings and introduction events. "We participated in the introductions of both the Macintosh LC and System 7," says Givol. "For example, Biology Explorer–Genetics was one product Apple used to demonstrate System 7." (However, as you might expect, these highly sought opportunities are limited.)

"I think customers are also good partners," says Blyth Software's Michael Minor. "Developers sometimes view customers only as buyers of technology, people who write checks. However, they can be partners who help you position your current technology and create new products. We therefore spend a lot of time thinking about how our U.S. customers can help us. This is especially important with a product such as our database, which sells to corporations: Customers incorporate our technology into theirs and can therefore give us valuable insight and feedback about what works well and what they'd like to see in future products." Blyth also participates in activities sponsored by U.S. industry associations, such as MacIS (a large group that focuses on technology needs in corporations), who have their fingers on the pulse of Blyth's target market.

Another example is InterOptica, which joined the Multimedia Publishers Group in the United States, a consortium of companies with similar interests that pool resources to buy such things as advertising space. "Because we're a small company, it's been more effective to combine our resources with those of other companies that have similar target markets. For example, as a group we can buy a full-page magazine ad for multiple products, instead of each having to buy a tiny ad by ourselves," says Winchester.

That company also hired a public relations firm in the United States for eight months to get additional exposure. "They got us airtime on CNN twice during that time, as well as exposure in the *New York Times* and many trade and user publications. We learned a lot from working with that company and now do most of our public relations in house," says Winchester.

Put the Squeeze on Pressure Points

The fast pace of technological change and the swift technology adoption rate in the United States often make it difficult for buyers to choose products. Therefore, they turn to sources of authority that they trust. These sources are the industry "opinion leaders" (sometimes called "pressure points") and include a select group of industry analysts, editors, and other experts.

The U.S. computer industry's opinion leaders have a tremendous following both within and outside the industry, and they wield strong influence over buying choices in the United States. In essence, by reaching the opinion leaders, you reach large numbers of customers. If you make these people your allies, you'll have made major strides in influencing the decision-making process of a large number of customers.

"In the United States there seems to be more of these industry pressure points than in most other countries, and they are often a fragmented bunch who are spread throughout the country. This may make the job of getting your message to them and differentiating yourself more difficult in the United States than it is in your home country," says Blyth Software's Minor.

However, in the United States there are hundreds (maybe thousands) of public relations and other kinds of communications companies that specialize in helping developers reach these opinion leaders. Money spent on well-thought-out opinion leaders and product review campaigns can lead to increased market awareness of your product and company, and increased sales. (If you missed it earlier, you may want to have a look at Chapter 10, "Influencing the Opinion Leaders: How to Get High Impact for Low Investment," and Chapter 11, "Getting the Maximum from Product Reviews: A Practical Guide for Creating a Reviews Campaign.")

Adopt a Can-Do Attitude

The final and immensely important piece of advice these developers offer is to approach the U.S. market with a positive attitude and open mind. Penetrating a market as large as the United States can seem daunting, especially to smaller developers. However, if you do your homework, learn the differences between doing business in the United States and your home country, adapt to these differences and then adopt a can-do attitude, breaking into the United States will be more feasible.

Blyth Software's Michael Minor says it well: "Depending on your mentality, you can look at the differences as major obstacles—or instead view them as challenges and opportunities."

ꜱ

CHAPTER THIRTY-FIVE

How to Approach a Global Product Launch

By Laura Elmore and Bob Michelet, Regis McKenna, Inc.

Laura Elmore is a principal and Bob Michelet is a partner of Regis McKenna, Inc., a Palo Alto, California, firm that specializes in marketing and communication services for high-technology companies.

AT Apple and some development companies, successful international product launches have always been a critical element in getting market acceptance for products from the start. Many high technology companies, including Apple, obtain 40 percent or more of their revenues internationally. Although a perfect model for a global product launch does not exist due to numerous variables, the most successful efforts share certain traits that can be used as a working model.

A helpful analogy for such a model is the concept of the "rugby" approach to product development, as described in an article by Hirotaka Takeuchi and Ikujiro Nonaka in the January/February 1986 issue of *Harvard Business Review*. Although the model was specifically applied to product development, the basic idea can also be applied to the global product launch. Depending on a developer's resources and size, it will require some modification—but it's a good starting point.

In the article, Takeuchi and Nonaka outlined the superiority of a rugby approach versus a "relay race" approach: "The traditional sequential or 'relay race' approach...may conflict with the goals of maximum speed and flexibility. In contrast, a holistic or 'rugby' approach in which a team tries to go the distance as a unit, passing the ball back and forth, may better serve today's competitive requirements. Under the rugby approach, the product development process emerges from the constant interaction of a hand-picked, multidisciplinary team whose members work together from start to finish." When you apply this model to the global launch of a product, international considerations become well integrated at the early stages of the planning process because the process begins with an international team. It is important to point out that this model assumes that a new product will be available in the key geographic markets within 60 to 90 days of domestic availability, therefore making a simultaneous product announcement a credible proposition.

On the other hand, the relay race approach to global product launches is reflected in structures in which a corporate team takes responsibility for the launch activity and passes duties to field operations, which include local subsidiaries and distributors/republishers. This is typically done with little or no advance involvement from the international people closest to the local markets. International considerations become an accessory to corporate strategies, instead of a well-integrated part of such strategies.

The relay race approach thereby results in lost sales opportunities, particularly for U.S.-based companies, because it does not take into consideration that news of the product from the United States quickly "spills" into other countries via news wires, international editions, foreign affiliates, and U.S.-based foreign correspondents. These articles carry U.S.-centered messages, product positioning, and marketing strategies (including pricing information) that add little to local marketing efforts beyond creating short-term awareness.

Global product introductions made by Apple and some developers, on the other hand, closely mirror the rugby approach. The effort begins with an *international* product launch team which "moves down the field," reporting back to the corporate or central group at different junctures to ensure that international needs are well integrated into the process.

A typical international product launch team consists of a central, core group that includes product, marketing, manufacturing, sales, service, engineering and communication representatives/functions, as well as a communication manager from each of the targeted geographic regions. These individuals often reside in the United States. In small organizations, such as with smaller developers, an international communication manager replaces the regional representatives in the group. In many cases, the team members do not reside in the developer's home country. If they are geographically dispersed, much of the conversation will take place in conference calls, supplemented with quarterly meetings. Ongoing communication with all members of the team is critical.

Each member of the core team is responsible for insuring that counterparts in other countries are represented in the decision-making process and are kept abreast of developments. This team should be formed 9 to 12 months before the product announcement date to allow proper time for planning and implementation.

In the rugby approach, international communication managers are part of the decision-making process and ensure that all marketing efforts address key international needs and opportunities. It's important that the international members of the team be knowledgeable about their respective regions because much of the decision-making occurs during team meetings. Companies often make the mistake of assigning an international project coordinator to play a similar role on the team. Although such an individual may do a good job of dispersing team information to the field, if that person is not senior enough to make an impact on the decision-making process, he or she will not be able to adequately represent the field during decision-making.

GLOBAL BALANCING: PLANNING FOR "SPILLOVER"

Once the entire team is in place, the communication function focuses on formulating the right messages and communicating them to key internal and external audiences. The rugby approach employs "global balancing" techniques, which address the fact that information is transmitted abroad almost simultaneously. Global balancing is based on the principle that a company can influence the spillover of media across foreign borders by working with the source of the information, such as local correspondents for foreign publications, to communicate messages that benefit both the other international markets that are receiving the information as well as the domestic one. Global balancing includes the following steps:

- identifying and assessing the perceptions of opinion leaders who have an impact on sales in target geographic markets

- internationalizing product introduction materials, including press releases, company backgrounders and executive speeches

- formulating an international plan for educating opinion leaders in target geographic markets, including local correspondents for foreign publications

- strengthening and educating the local infrastructures (media, distributors, government representatives, customers, trade officials, channels, market research consultants, and financial analysts) of all target geographic markets to reduce their dependency on news and information generated by the home country

- underscoring the international success of the product within both the infrastructure in the home market and the target countries to validate that the product has been accepted throughout the global marketplace

- evaluating and monitoring ongoing perceptions to proactively identify issues and opportunities.

TAKING THE TEMPERATURE OF TARGET MARKETS

In the relay race approach, once the product introduction team has been put in place, the main thrust is to get the product out the door, with little time spent on assessing the current environment for the product in key geographic markets; market intelligence is a mere afterthought.

In the rugby approach, the team identifies what it does and doesn't know about its target markets. Where information doesn't exist, it's important to conduct a qualitative assessment of the current perceptions relating to the product and company. This information is used to validate or modify product positioning and to formulate key marketing messages.

At Regis McKenna, Inc., we gauge the temperature of each of the target countries through an international audit of key opinion leaders. This audit is known as a "global thermometer check." This activity relies on the 90-10 rule, which states that because 90 percent of any population is influenced by the other 10 percent key opinion leaders, it's important to understand who these opinion leaders are and how they perceive a company, its products, and its competition.

The goal of the global thermometer check is to identify key opinion leaders who will have an impact on the product's success and assess their current perceptions. Although the scope of such a study can vary according to the availability of your resources, the methodology remains the same. A typical global thermometer check consists of these steps.

- The study is closely coordinated with the launch team and local management within the target countries to address corporate and local objectives.

- The study targets countries that are strategically important to the developer. This usually takes from two to six countries (the more the better) into consideration, as well as the home market (if the information isn't already available).

- A questionnaire is developed, usually with 10 to 20 key questions relating to technology, product, company reputation, distribution, pricing and other marketing issues.

- Approximately 10 to 20 key opinion leaders in each country are selected to participate in the study. Depending on the country, these individuals should represent the key infrastructure segments mentioned earlier.

- Depending on the confidentiality of the information, the discussions are conducted in one-on-one meetings or by telephone under non-disclosure agreements, until the public release of the information.

Developers often look to outside consulting firms to conduct these studies because participants are thus more likely to volunteer candid opinions. In sensitive situations, the company's name may not even be mentioned. This is usually the case when a developer wants to assess current perceptions regarding a new technology, but for competitive reasons doesn't want to divulge its name.

The information is analyzed and presented to the product introduction team and other internal departments as an important tool in validating and formulating product introduction messages, both in a general sense and on a market-specific basis. All corporate messages should address the international marketplace, not just domestic opportunities.

INTERNATIONALIZATION VS. LOCALIZATION

Once the messages have been formulated, it's important that they are properly communicated both internally and externally. In the relay race approach, product introduction materials—including press releases, corporate backgrounders, executive speeches, collateral, advertising, sales, and training materials—typically address only the local marketplace. But the rugby approach recognizes that the content of these materials will eventually be communicated in many parts of the world. Therefore, all of the materials are "internationalized." This means that key international messages—along with certain clauses, country examples, case studies and other international information—are incorporated into all documents as appropriate, ensuring that news about the product is received in each country within a strong framework that local operations can build on.

Editor's note: Chapter 36, "Avoiding Cultural Mishaps During Localization," contains an interesting review of various cultural considerations to watch for when internationalizing materials.

However, internationalizing should not be confused with localizing of press materials and other related documents. The latter deals more with customizing a document for a specific country, such as in language translation, which is usually handled by in-country communication managers.

Here are several examples of how to internationalize launch materials.

- To the lead paragraph of a press release or executive speech, add that the product will be rolled out worldwide or that it will be available in the listed geographic markets. This helps reinforce that the company is an international player.

- Incorporate messages and examples that underscore the company's international experience or leadership, including international market share, country-specific successes, or large installations.

- Use quotes or testimonials to reinforce international opportunities for the new product.

- When important marketing strategies—including distribution, product positioning, and pricing strategies—differ from the domestic market, add clauses that clarify these issues.

- Use analogies and examples that an international audience will understand. For example, companies often compare products and technologies with items that are not as common in other markets, such as microwaves and dishwashers. It's important to look for more universal comparisons. In addition, when quantifying a statement in, say, U.S. dollars, remember to clarify in a footnote that the numbers are expressed in U.S. dollars.

- Include information about the company's international operations in the corporate backgrounder. You can include such things as product availability, local pricing, whom to contact in each market area, who the local distributors and dealers are, and so forth.

Internationalizing communication and marketing materials allows a company to set itself apart from the competition, while paving the way for new products in key geographic markets. In-country communication managers will still need to localize materials to meet local objectives, but those messages will then be supported by a broader corporate platform.

EXECUTING A WELL-COORDINATED PLAN

An effective product launch requires understanding how information flows in and out of targeted geographic markets. For example, an estimated 95 percent of the news that appears in Singapore trade publications is sourced from four U.S. publications, according to Singapore editors. Knowing this, the corporate or international communication manager would then make sure to include these four publications in the U.S. launch efforts and should think twice about the kind of messages the company spokesperson delivers to those publications.

In the rugby approach, efforts to influence media coverage should begin at least four to five months prior to the announcement because many monthly publications need information three months prior to a product introduction. Efforts should be coordinated with your company's or distributor's local PR manager in the country. Also, whenever possible, coordinate those efforts with the Apple third-party and public relations representatives in that country to leverage those valuable resources.

Here are several ways that international or corporate communication managers can influence the "spillover" of U.S media coverage to other countries.

- Work with the communication manager in each target market to identify the two or three key publications; then determine how each one generally receives information. For example, many U.S. trade publications have licensing agreements with journals outside the U.S. that often reprint their articles. Many foreign publications subscribe to U.S.-based wire services or have their own correspondents in New York or Silicon Valley. There are more than 1,000 correspondents in the United States who write for foreign publications, including approximately 50 key technology correspondents.

- Contact your locally based sources to encourage their participation in local product introduction activities (if they aren't already involved), and inquire about the international distribution of their articles. Read their publications to see whom they quote and make sure these individuals are briefed as part of the launch activity. (The people who are quoted are usually opinion leaders who were identified earlier.) With the communication managers in each target country, discuss the key international messages they feel are important to communicate to U.S.-based sources.

  Although most U.S.-based correspondents feel their charter is to cover U.S. events, they often can be convinced to include a sentence or paragraph noting the differences in product positioning, pricing, distribution and availability between key geographic markets. If journalists are writing for regional or national publications, such as *Asia Computer Weekly* or the *Japan Economic Journal*, they can provide more country-specific information.

- Closely coordinate all communication efforts with a country's local communication managers to ensure the team is working rugby-style. This is especially important when dealing with U.S.-based correspondents.

  Several months prior to the public announcement, the entire international communication team should agree on how to approach the top tier of publications in their respective markets; the home country communication manager is responsible for local international influencers.

OPTIMIZING LOCAL COMMUNICATION EFFORTS

In addition to influencing U.S. media spillover, it's equally important to begin strengthening and educating the entire infrastructure of target countries prior to the formal product announcement. This minimizes the dependency of those infrastructures on U.S. information. For example, you can use international versions of *Macworld* magazine and other similar publications that are distributed worldwide in various languages. The U. S. offices of those publications often have a directory of worldwide offices to contact for more information and other resources that can be helpful. In any case, the critical issue is timing.

Although the practice of educating key opinion leaders (the "infrastructure") in the United States is common, few U.S. companies have approached international markets with the same thinking. Although the infrastructure varies from country to country, it plays a significant role in the success of a product in a given marketplace. Chairman and CEO Regis McKenna has often stated, "A company can never promote its way into a technical market. The infrastructure has to be a participant. If they accept you, then, and only then, can a company be successful." Often, the smaller the market, the greater the influence of infrastructure members.

REINFORCING MARKET ACCEPTANCE

Once a product has been introduced worldwide, it's important to play back international successes to the home market. The relay race approach tends to showcase local acceptance when, in fact, key international markets may have embraced the technology first. By using the rugby approach and leveraging your international successes simultaneously or during the early stages of a rollout, your company benefits by enhancing its competitive posture.

News of international successes will eventually spill back into the international marketplace, enhancing the overall success of the product. As part of this effort, many companies create centralized databases that store international success stories and customer testimonials. This information is used internally by many departments, including each country's communication managers, who use it in their own local public relations efforts. Again, international awareness needs to be boosted on both sides of the ocean in the early stages of the rollout.

It is often said that effective communication with a company's target marketplaces begins with effective internal communication. Nowhere is this truer than in global launches of technology products. The diversity of market environments, customer attitudes, and local business practices demands that companies not only disseminate information to many countries, but also gather information from those countries first.

Reprinted with permission of Regis McKenna, Inc.

CHAPTER THIRTY-SIX

Avoiding Cultural Mishaps During Localization

By Lauri Jones, Intracom, Inc.

Lauri Jones is the former vice president of Intracom, Inc., a firm based in Cambridge, Massachusetts, that helps American companies localize software and develop multilanguage and multicultural marketing programs.

LOCALIZING your product is a critical step in expanding your international sales, but product localization alone isn't enough. The best products will suffer from scant sales if international buyers don't perceive you as a local player, one who respects their language and culture and who effectively wraps that culture around your product. Therefore, you must create marketing materials—ads, press releases, brochures, point-of-purchase aids, and so forth—that are steeped in appropriate language and local culture.

COLLIDING CULTURES

Perception—the way we view the world around us—is a huge component of culture. For example, a survey reported by James A. McCaffrey and Craig R. Hafner in the October 1985 issue of *Training & Development Journal* demonstrates how our cultural background influences how we behave and the choices we make. A hundred Asian men and the same number of American men were asked to put themselves in the following situation: You are on a sinking ship with your mother, your wife, and your only child, and you are the only one who knows how to swim. You can save only one of your loved ones. Which one would you save?

Each one of the Asian men responded that he would save his mother. The rationale: You can always remarry and have more children, but you cannot have another mother. In contrast, 40 percent of the Americans said they would save their wife, and 60 percent said they would save their children.

While some may feel this is an overgeneralization, these results are indicative of differences not just between Americans and Asians or Westerners and Easterners, but also of the contrasts between all cultures. Although technology has provided the world with some degree of common ground, don't be deceived into thinking that we are becoming alike. In *Megatrends 2000*, Naisbitt and

Aburdene observe that "...as our [global] lifestyles grow more similar, there are unmistakable signs of a powerful countertrend: a backlash against uniformity, a desire to assert the uniqueness of one's culture and language, a repudiation of foreign influence." Members of different cultures think and respond differently to similar situations and stimuli.

WHAT TO AVOID

To be successful in the global marketplace, you must make a conscious effort to create marketing materials and campaigns with appropriate cultural images; this will help you avoid some of the difficulties and potential rejection that result from making a cultural *faux pas*. Don't be lulled into thinking that a successful domestic campaign can simply be "translated" for the international marketplace—unless you've planned it from the start for worldwide use. Problems arise when you try to force-fit existing campaigns to a market other than your home territory.

There are several common "high risk" themes and cultural characteristics that can be successful in your domestic marketing, but you should be extremely careful about exporting them to other markets. There are too many to discuss comprehensively here, so I'll give examples of a few hot buttons that should start you thinking about how tricky it is to slide between cultures.

Religion is at the top of the list, and is a particularly risky category. No matter what appears on the surface, each country derives a great deal of cultural identity (and usually pride) from its religion(s). Each country has acceptable uses of and references to religion in marketing and advertising, but it's far too dangerous to apply them to other cultures.

Sports is also a potential ground for cultural collision. Americans love football. The rest of the world, which leans toward soccer, is trying to figure out why! In Mexico, the national sports are bullfighting and soccer. Many Japanese are wild about golf. And in many Middle Eastern countries sports are, shall we say, less than significant as a life-style component. Sports just don't cross borders very well, so I recommend (unless you're the Nike of software) avoiding sports symbolism entirely.

Humor is perhaps the least translatable cultural phenomenon. What may cause one culture to shed tears of laughter may be a profound insult to another.

If you've traveled a lot, you know that sexual innuendo is viewed differently from culture to culture. Europeans and Latin Americans tend to be much more explicit than Americans. Asian and African cultures are usually at the other extreme. For example, putting an illustration of a man and woman together on the bottle of a popular American mouthwash caused it to fail miserably in Thailand. When the image was replaced by one with two females holding hands, the product became a success. Another example: Condom advertisements have been running in Europe for years. In the United States, such ads are still controversial. Whenever possible, avoid sexual reference or implication.

Also, be very careful about putting animals into your ads. Animals mean very different things in different parts of the world, and many peoples see animals as sacred. President John F. Kennedy once experienced a close call when calfskin picture frames were planned as gifts for the Indian Prime Minister. Fortunately, someone in the American embassy stopped the gift-giving before an international incident took place. As you probably know, cows are sacred to some Indians.

There are traditions, superstitions, and beliefs to be aware of in every culture in which you do business. Whatever your opinion of them, they can devastate marketing efforts and exhaust your budget if you use the wrong ones. Numbers are particularly interesting. In the United States, 13 is an unlucky number, although Americans don't avoid it with any great effort. In Japan, however, the number 4 is the same as the symbol for death and is generally taken extremely seriously. For example, when an American company tried to market boxes of four golf balls in Japan, very little product moved off the shelves until the packing count was changed.

A telecommunications company ran an ad in the Middle East showing an executive with his feet on his desk. Showing the soles of one's feet is highly offensive in that part of the world, and the ad was quickly rejected—at no small cost to the advertiser. Some other examples: In France, red roses mean "I want to seduce you." So a bouquet wouldn't be an appropriate prop in an ad. In Japan, white roses symbolize death, as do clocks. In such cases, no amount of translation will help.

Although I can continue ad infinitum with examples of what to avoid, the most important thing is that you be sensitive to cultural issues and review your international marketing materials and try to see them not as Americans, Japanese, French, or members of whatever your culture may be; instead, learn the cultural atmosphere of your target country and try to make your marketing ideas come to life in that context.

THE IMPORTANCE OF LANGUAGE

There is no greater component of culture than language. It is the only way to significantly access another culture. As a company marketing products internationally, you can benefit from this or be hurt by it.

Although the world's population is studying English at an unprecedented rate, there is also a resurgence of pride in native languages. There are many examples of the trend toward linguistic nationalism. Singapore, after 20 years of educating its people in English, is experiencing a major "Speak Mandarin" campaign. In Spain, Catalan, which was outlawed during Francisco Franco's reign, is now spoken (with vigilance) by almost six million people in the Catalonia region. In the Canadian province of Quebec, 85 percent of the people speak French. Laws have been passed there requiring citizens to speak French at work; English-language signs have been banned, and violators may be fined. And in Wales, the nearly extinct Cymric language is making a comeback. In 1983, only 20 percent of the Welsh population spoke it; today millions are studying Cymric.

"But," you may ask, "isn't English the predominant language of trade?" It would be hard to dispute that English has become the common language in world business. But less than 10 percent of the world's population speaks English as its native language—approximately 400 million people in 12 countries. Another 400 million people speak English as a second language. Native English speakers often forget that non-native speakers have a limited vocabulary. Second-language speakers generally have a vocabulary of approximately 2,500 words. So it is important to respect the native language and culture of your markets.

When the Same Language Isn't the Same

French. English. Spanish. Portuguese. Chinese. The list goes on. Ignoring the differences from one "similar language" country to another can damage the best of marketing campaigns. In the Canadian use of French, for example, uppercase letters must have accents. In France, no accents, please—unless you want to appear to be a foreigner. Dutch is the language of the Netherlands. Flemish, a variation of Dutch, is the language of Flanders in Belgium and in the city of Brussels. The two languages are similar yet different enough that the speakers of each take pride in the distinctiveness of their language.

Also, remember that although another country may speak the same basic language as yours (consider, for example, the United States and Great Britain), the cultures may be unique and very different; this requires the same close attention to localizing marketing materials as does localizing between cultures that speak radically different languages.

HOW TO APPROACH LANGUAGE/STYLE

There are several major things to keep in mind when moving between languages. Many things don't translate at all. Furthermore, writing style is a cultural difference that cannot be ignored. When translating a message from one language to another, you need someone who can do more than just translate literally. The French often prefer flowery language. For Germans, just the facts will do, danke schön. The Japanese want lots of graphics (and love cartoons); a good rule of thumb for producing documentation for use in Japan is to make it 50 percent text and 50 percent graphics.

When it comes to idioms, homonyms, and slang, press the delete key when localizing. Expressions that are part of one language and culture can rarely be comprehensibly reproduced in another. English is especially rich with idioms that simply can't cross borders. What is "Greek" to an American is "Chinese" to a Spaniard. (Confused? If you are, then I consider my point made.) The Italians say someone has "his hands in the dough" to express being "with it" or "on target." A literal translation would definitely not "cut the mustard." As an example of why not to use homonyms, forgive me but let's talk about, ah, Windows. Windows isn't windows in any language other than English.

A quick aside while I'm on the subject of language. Not only can incorrectly chosen words kill a good campaign, but graphic materials can either embarrass you or point you out as a foreigner. Simple things such as electrical wall plugs differ around the world. In a photograph, the right plug in the wrong place will show that you're an outsider who isn't paying attention to the local market. In addition, photographs of people can carry too much symbolism. A glossy of someone doing the American hand symbol for OK could spell trouble in Brazil, for example.

Other graphic elements have various connotations in certain countries. For example, triangular shapes in countries such as Taiwan, Hong Kong, and Korea are seen very negatively. Watch out for them in logos and designs.

Language Comes in All Sizes

A-4 (210mm × 297mm, or 8.3 × 11.7 inches) is the standard page size worldwide—except in the United States, where 8.5 × 11 inches is the norm. Brochures, press releases, and ad copy should conform to the local culture. Many a U.S-based company has submitted ads to international magazines only to find that the film didn't fit the publication.

Also, during translation the length of your text will expand or shrink. For example, translating from English to French, Spanish, Portuguese, or Italian can expand text length up to 30 percent. And when designing page layout, consider such things as the length of German words. Likewise, up to three Asian language characters may be required for a single English word.

HOW TO DO SUCCESSFUL TRANSLATION (LOCALIZATION)

In my business, we're careful about what we mean by translation. It's important not just to literally translate but also to totally localize during the translation process. This requires knowing and understanding all the cultural factors mentioned so far, and then some. Knowledge of laws, accounting practices, currency, date formats, and, not least of all, technological understanding must go into the translation.

Using the right people to do the work is critical. Here are five things a successful translator/localizer must be.

- *A native speaker of the target language.* Not just fluent, but native. Even if someone in your company has lived abroad and speaks the target language extremely well, it isn't enough. All it takes is the use of "to" instead of "for" (and those are minor possibilities) to let your readers know that your text wasn't written by a native speaker. The following sign found in a Paris hotel elevator was probably not written by a native English speaker: "Please leave your values at the front desk."

- *A good writer.* Being a native speaker of any language does not qualify a person to write, especially in the field of marketing communications. This is an art that few people possess, so choose your resources accordingly.

- *A full-time professional.* Being up-to-date in technology translation requires a full-time commitment. I constantly see companies contract students, spouses of diplomats, and other very intelligent individuals to be "temporaries" in the language field, when what they really need are professionals. Good translators have access to electronic databases for the latest terminology and work with terminology-management software. They subscribe to numerous periodicals in their field of expertise. Most important, they bring invaluable experience from years of training and delivery of quality documentation. Full-time professionals also travel regularly to their native countries (when living elsewhere). This is extremely important for keeping abreast of cultural and linguistic evolution.

- *Knowledgeable about your company's goals and desired image.* Provide translators with your annual report and all the product information you can. Talk to them or to the company representative you're working with. They need to understand you and your corporate culture.

- *Knowledgeable about the product.* Translators don't have to be product experts, but they do need to have a clear understanding of your field and possess expertise that prepares them to write about your product. Most professional translators specialize in particular industries.

When localizing, never rely on one translator from start to finish, no matter how good the translator. Everyone has bad days, and no one is immune to keyboard errors. I suggest using a team consisting of a primary translator, an editor, and a proofreader. The same professional credentials needed in a translator should also be required of other team members.

Especially in high-tech markets, having appropriate localized technical terminology is critical. A major computer company once divided the translation of a large manual among several groups, without the guidance of an approved glossary. Consolidation of the work revealed five different terms for disk drive. Before translation begins, your team should develop a bilingual glossary of terms. This document will provide their suggested translations for industry-, company-, and product-specific terminology. Before the process begins, have your in-country distributor review this glossary for accuracy and appropriate usage.

Another reason to develop a glossary is to determine what words should not be translated at all. Often, if a product has been developed and named in the United States, the common terminology for the product abroad may be in English. For example, software stays "software" in many Romance language translations.

Decisions about terminology shouldn't exclude your company and product names. Most companies marketing technical products choose to keep their original name rather than translating it. In most cases, this choice works, but it pays to check before making that assumption. One of our translators once recommended a product-name change for France when localizing a software product. The written name was fine, but the French pronunciation of the product name would have been vulgar. (The client agreed to change the name.) Another example: Some years ago, General Motors tried to market its Chevrolet Nova automobile in Latin America, but *no va* means "doesn't go" in Spanish, a very poor name choice for a car in that market.

THE DIFFERENCE CAN BE EXCITING

What makes our world such an exciting place is our differences. It's amazing how much more buy-in you can get from an overseas partner, distributor, or customer when you commit to understanding cultural differences and adapt your marketing and advertising strategies to them.

CHAPTER THIRTY-SEVEN

Setting Up a Subsidiary

HOW TO TRANSITION AWAY FROM A DISTRIBUTOR AND SET UP YOUR OWN OFFICE

By Rod Turner, Symantec Corporation

Rod Turner is a former general manager of the Peter Norton Group of the Symantec Corporation, a Cupertino, California, software company of which he was also executive vice president.

THERE'S no survival manual for setting up a subsidiary in another country, no guidebook that will change the odds of whether you'll swim or sink when you take the plunge. There are so many questions to ask and situations to deal with that the process can be overwhelming. However, there are several key approaches that, if well considered, will reduce the potential pain and setbacks when making the transition from a distributor to a subsidiary.

If you are setting up a subsidiary, up to this point you've most likely been using a distributor. (Usually when starting a venture of some sort, either independently or as part of a large company, you initially aren't big enough to be forming international subsidiaries right away.) However, in very competitive markets, I suggest not hiring a distributor who may be only half committed because of the competitiveness of the market. Instead, hire an employee and have one person on-site who cares 100 percent about protecting and furthering your interests. That person can manage the local distribution channels. If you hire a mediocre distributor and have the attitude of "I'll change it later," it may be a big mistake. Changing horses midstream is difficult and isn't conducive to success. So in these cases, it's often best to start a subsidiary early on, even if it's a very small one.

Chances are, though, you'll be working with a distributor. One of your biggest challenges will be to smoothly transfer the business away from him. Making the transition can be a sensitive and sometimes painful experience for all parties if it's not handled with thorough forethought, planning, and diplomacy. You should handle the transaction delicately and carefully; otherwise the distributor can become antagonistic and "turn off the tap."

HOW TO SMOOTH THE TRANSITION

There are several things you can do to minimize potential problems. When you negotiate a distribution agreement, set the expectation from the start that your partner won't be your partner for life. Let your partner company know that if you're successful together, you may replace it with a subsidiary at some point. (You might not; the distributor may be so successful that you'll continue business as is.) If possible, define a plan for a possible transition in the contract, including terms that spell out exactly what will happen if you terminate your partner to set up a subsidiary rather than because your distributor has failed you. You need your partner on your side while making this transition. And when the time comes, give the distributor appropriate advance notice. Even if your contract doesn't require it, it's good business to do so.

Give the distributor an incentive to continue supporting your product during and after the transition. One option is to define a royalty you'll pay your distributor for a specified period after the transition (for example, five percent for a year and a half) on all sales in that market, because a subsidiary will take exclusive rights away from this partner. The main goal is to arrange something that will make it in that company's interest to cooperate, something along the lines of "In return for providing my company with the specified level of performance, technical support, marketing effort, sales resources, and cooperation, we will give you a specific percentage royalty on all our sales during the following period." Or "We'll give you an advantageous discount of the following amount for the next year—if you deliver." Be specific about what the distributor must do; don't leave it as a general understanding that this partner will be good to you if you're good to it. Often that will work, but when it doesn't, the cost can be devastating.

Make sure that you own outright all translations and localized versions of your products and that there are no cumbersome complications. Also, be sure that you have in hand the source code and everything else needed to produce the translated product. Don't be caught at the last minute without all the disks, or discover that you have version 1.0 instead of version 3.0 of your French product, or find that you're missing a disk because a bug was being fixed and the code was never returned to you. Likewise, make sure that you have an electronic copy of the documentation so that you can reproduce it if necessary. Be forewarned that although you may contractually have all the rights to software, documentation, and the like, it still can be a nightmare to actually get possession of the items and begin manufacturing the product yourself.

Take It One Step at a Time

During the transition, don't start by doing everything at once. Take over the various responsibilities from the distributor one step at a time while also taking an appropriate percentage of the profits. Try to avoid a situation in which you've got all the responsibility for technical support, marketing, and sales while the distributor has only distribution responsibilities—and *gets most of the profit*. Frankly, distribution is a relatively easy function and doesn't warrant a huge profit margin.

One way to do that is to calculate, with the distributor's input and buy-in, what proportion of revenue is profit, cost of goods, technical support, marketing, sales, and translation. Allocate the profit to each of those areas of real costs on a pro-rata or value basis. (You can negotiate the rates with your distributor.) Then take responsibility for one function at a time, along with its calculated "profit loading." For example, say that the cost of maintaining the sales force is 10 percent of revenue. If you've calculated that a quarter of the profit margin should be allocated to this function, then you'll also take a quarter of the profit when you take responsibility for the sales force.

SOME KEY DECISIONS ABOUT THE SUBSIDIARY

Here are a few important questions to ask yourself when opening a subsidiary.

- *In which country should you set up a subsidiary?* There are typically three basic issues to consider: where to base the financial headquarters, where to manufacture, and where to have marketing and product support. One way to decide is to examine these issues from a tax point of view. For example, when doing business in Europe, you may want to manufacture in Ireland because you get certain tax breaks there; you may wish to establish a financial headquarters in Holland for several reasons, including the tax benefits; and you may opt to place marketing and support headquarters in the target country.

  Be aware that geography is an incredible delegator. Being physically separated from your office will give a great deal of autonomy to whomever is in charge there and can easily lead to a loss of control. So put the proper control and feedback procedures in place; make sure you visit the subsidiary often enough to stay in touch with what's really transpiring, and make sure that employees of the subsidiary come to see you often enough. Don't finally make a visit there only to find that your managing director is driving a very expensive car that you didn't think was a part of the employment contract—but actually was.

- *How many people should you hire?* A frequent misperception is that you need to open a subsidiary with 8 to 12 people or with a fixed percentage of the number of people in your home-country operation. However, one person (the right person) can generate great results; this may be the best approach for you.

Nonetheless, when setting up a European operation, I caution against hiring one person to be in charge of all of Europe right away. It's a very big risk; in some cases, the European market may be larger than the U.S. market for your products. One way to put this decision into perspective is to ask yourself: If you were based in Europe, for example, would you be prepared to hire one person in a country as large as the United States, put him or her in complete control of such a huge market, and give that person who is so far away a large degree of autonomy? If you did that, you wouldn't be aware of what was really going on in the subsidiary for a long, long time.

The same caution holds true for setting up business in Europe. A good strategy is to divide it into several regions, each with a managing director. After a while, you'll get to know those people very well, and then you can appoint someone to be the European managing director. It's a very important position, and hiring the wrong person can be a big mistake.

In the case of a U.S.-based company, should you hire locally or send over a tried-and-true American employee? There's no simple answer, but there certainly are some big mistakes you can make by relying solely on Americans in international markets. Americans are not popular in some places and often aren't well educated enough about a foreign culture or its practices. However, if you know someone who is particularly savvy and sensitive enough to the local issues—and who has the know-how to tune in to local people for advice rather than overrunning them with his own opinions—then that person may be a good choice.

- *How do you find job candidates?* Hiring an international employee is not easy the first time around. You don't have to spend a month in the target country to hire a managing director; but if you don't have someone in that country you can rely on yet (an employee, a head-hunting firm), it can take time. You don't have to go to the expense of hiring a top-notch recruitment firm, although it's probably a very good idea.

  Another option is to find a marketing firm or agency you can trust. Typically these are fairly easy to find. They can run local recruitment advertisements and prescreen the resulting candidates. Then by telephone you can determine if the candidates' caliber is approximately right and decide whether to spend time in that country interviewing those people.

- *How should you support the subsidiary properly?* You must support it the way you would support an excellent sales force in your home country. Subsidiary employees need fantastic competitive information (not only for the home country but also specifically for the local market), good training, and proactive information transfer from you.

- *How should tax issues influence your decisions?* Strongly. Not understanding these issues up front can cost you dearly. Some examples of questions to ask: If your subsidiary has contract-signing authority, what is your tax liability in that case versus having contracts signed in the home country? If you incorporate, are you taxable in that country? Never make assumptions about tax issues; hire an expert to help you make the appropriate decisions. The same holds true for understanding a country's governmental, bureaucratic, and trade requirements.

AFTER YOU SET IT UP

Once the subsidiary is functioning, keep it focused. Because international subsidiaries have a lot of autonomy, they tend to want to do things that aren't part of your overall goals or plans. A subsidiary should do marketing, sales, and technical support, and probably drive the translation process. Typically, you don't need to do anything else in an international subsidiary. However, it may want to start developing or acquiring new products or divert too much effort to developing value-added versions of your product. Although in some cases these may indeed be the right things to do, you should at the very least know exactly what is happening before the subsidiary embarks on that path.

The best advice I can give you: Once the subsidiary is up and running, if you avoid the "out of sight, out of mind" mentality that is so easy to slip into—if you continue to give this "distant relative" a high level of constant focused attention, scrutiny, and care—you are more likely to swim than sink after you take the plunge.

INDEX

Copyright, 323
Copyright Protection Fund, 200
Copywriting, 137, 143
Corporate customers, and site
    licensing, 192
Correct Quotes, 268
Coupons, in ads, 139–40
Courier font, 131
Crampton, Ann, 293, 302
Credit card fees, 261
Credit card processing, 258
*Crossing the Chasm: Marketing and
    Selling Technology Products to
    Mainstream Customers,* 15, 21, 31
Cultural mishaps, 337
  contrasts, 337–38
  high risk themes, 338–39
  images, 338
  language, 339–40
  language and style, 340–41
  traditions and superstitions, 339
  translation and localization, 342–43
  translator, 342
Customer
  database, 249–51
  description of, 62–63
  feedback, on-line services, 325
  needs, 246–48
  satisfaction, 220–22
Customer focus, 55–57
  follow me home, 57–58
  future challenge, 59
  reach out and touch them, 57
Customer newsletter, 227
  cost and return, 230–31
  creating the newsletter, 228
  exchanging information, 227–28
  planning, 228–30
  See also: Customer support *and*
      On-line services
Customer support, 217, 226
  company improvement, 222
  customer satisfaction, 220–22

department organization, 225
follow up, 224
operator attitude, 223
support mission, 219–20
support operators, skills, 224–25
teaching customers, 222–23
WordPerfect, 219–20
See also: Customer newsletter *and*
    On-line services
Customer-based fantasy, 75
Customers' view, of competition, 61–63

Data sheets, 141
Database, 66–67
  companies and brands, 113
  customer support calls, 229
  opinion leaders, 84–85
  public relations, 92
  repeat customer, 249–50
  searching, 43–44
  trademarks, 113
  user groups, 284
Dataquest, 44, 80–82
Davis, Jeff, 161
DayMaker, 292, 299, 302
Dealer/distributors, 180–81
Dealers, and antipiracy, 214
Dealers, and consumer demand, 11
Delbourg-Delphis, Marylène, 312, 315,
    318–19, 324
Delphi, 67
Demo '92, 278
Demo software, 178, 254
Demographic information, 43
  recording during survey, 52
Demos
  attract loop, 150
  contest disks, 155–56
  deadly demo traits, 152
  defining audience needs, 153–55
  development time, 156–57
  direct response, 149
  point-of-sale, 149–51